The far right in Europe

Resistance Books

International Institute for Research & Education

Resistance Books and the International Institute for Research and Education would be glad to have readers' opinions of this book and any suggestions you may have for future publications or wider distribution.

Our books are available at special quantity discounts to educational and non-profit organisations, and to bookstores.

Contact Resistance Books at PO Box 62732 London SW2 9GQ, email contact@socialistresistance.org or visit www.resistancebooks.org. Contact the International Institute for Research and Education at Lombokstraat 40, Amsterdam, NL-1094, email iire@iire.org or visit www.iire.org.

Published by Resistance Books and the IIRE, October 2015 as issue 59 of the IIRE Notebooks for Study and Research

Edited by Fred Leplat

Cover design by Maral Jefroudi

Cover photograph: iStock.com/Pascal Le Segretain

Printed in Britain by Lightning Source

ISBN 9780902869752

The far right in Europe

Contents

Preface

Nearly 70 years after the fall of the Nazi regime, the far right and even fascism are again a significant threat in Europe. Across the continent, racist and fascist attacks against migrant and minority communities are a day-to-day reality. In the May 2014 European Parliament elections, organisations representing a range of fascist, racist and anti-migrant perspectives won significant votes in a number of European countries, including the National Front topping the poll in France and explicitly Nazi parties winning seats in countries like Germany and Greece.

In Britain, UKIP (the United Kingdom Independence Party) is a major force in politics. At the European elections in 2014, it topped the poll with 26.6% share of the vote. Despite only winning one parliamentary seat at the 2015 general election, UKIP polled 3.8 million votes or 12.6% of the total, making it the third party behind the Conservative and Labour parties. The rise of the anti-migrant UKIP is pulling the mainstream parties further in the direction of racism and xenophobia as they seek to compete with anti-migrant policies and the rhetoric of racist scapegoating.

The global economic crisis of 2007 has given renewed energy and confidence to racists and fascists, as the left has generally been unable to give hope to the millions affected by the crisis. Some far-right parties such as UKIP, the Danish People's Party and the Party for Freedom in the Netherlands are firmly in the neoliberal free-market camp. But others, from Attaka in Bulgaria to the National Front in France, denounce the evils of globalisation and promote an 'anti-capitalist' capitalism to appeal to those hit by the economic crisis. This 'anti-capitalist' capitalism only offers a nationalist solution: an authoritarian social contract between the millions of dispossessed and their own national bourgeoisie. Despite these differences, the far-right parties are in general 'euro-sceptic', some campaigning for an exit from the European Union. This is based on their deep-seated nationalism, racism and xenophobia, which in many of these parties can be traced back to their historical Nazi or fascist origins.

While these far-right parties try to cleanse their image by ridding themselves of their overt ethnic racism, anti-Semitism, or references to historical fascist origins, they have embraced a new form of racism: Islamophobia. This is one of the consequence of the imperialist wars in Iraq and Afghanistan, justified on one occasion by US President George Bush as a 'clash of civilisation', which has provided the basis to caricature all Muslims as 'radicals' and therefore potential terrorists. This has been developed by people such as Geert Wilders of Party for Freedom who argues that Islam is incompatible with progressive western culture and in fundamental contradiction with the Enlightment, and that it therefore denies equal rights for women and lesbians and gay men. Opposition to migration of people who are Muslims, it is therefore argued by these far-right parties, is not racism but a defence of European progressive values.

The refugees and migrants arriving in Europe in 2015 have further highlighted the racism and xenophobia of the far right. Islamophobic and racist propaganda has characterised all Syrian refugees and others as Islamist terrorists. UKIP's Nigel Farage has warned that those fleeing were probably 'extremists of the Islamic State or other jihadist groups'. This is not much different to what Syrian dictator Assad wrote on twitter: 'Terrorism will not stop there, it will export itself through illegal immigration into Europe'. If the far right does not characterise them as terrorists, it accuses them of threatening the 'Christian' roots of Europe. This is what claimed Hungarian Prime Minister Viktor Orban, while Farage has called for accepting only Christian refugees. Marine Le Pen of the Front National goes further. She calls for 'opposition to all immigration, whether legal or not', and claims that those fleeing Syria are not 'real' refugees like those from Spain and Germany in the 1930s.

The situation we face is grave. There has not been a growth of an anti-austerity left comparable to the growth of the far right. In France, the election of Marine Le Pen as President in 2017 is a possibility, giving her access to draconian powers allowed for under the Constitution, which Mitterrand once described (in 1964, before himself becoming President in 1981) as a 'permanent coup d'état'. With the working class failing to resist austerity and neoliberalism, the ruling class does not need an authoritarian rule of fascist type as in the 1930s. But the dynamic of authoritarian far-right parties coming to power through elections can be independent of the actual needs of the bourgeoisie, who can easily accommodate itself to such an outcome if it occurs.

In the past, the left has rightly focussed on seeking to build united mass mobilisations against far right and fascist organisations. In Britain, examples include:

- The mass demonstrations against Mosley's British Union of Fascists in the 1930s that saw 150,000 demonstrate in Hyde Park in 1934 and many hundreds of thousands mobilise in the East End in 1936 in what has become known as 'The Battle of Cable Street' – these demonstrations were in the teeth of opposition from the leadership of the labour movement.[1]

- The mass demonstrations against the rise of the National Front (NF) in the 1970s, including anti-fascist mobilisations at Red Lion Square in 1974, Lewisham 1977 and Southall 1979; these demonstrations sadly included the deaths at the hands of the police of two anti-fascist demonstrators, Kevin Gately and Blair Peach.

---

[1] See *Defeating the Fascist Threat in the 1930s*, by Dave Rosenberg, www.resistancebooks.org.

- The creation of the Anti Nazi League (ANL) after Lewisham in 1977, which achieved popular success in linking the term 'Nazi' to the NF, contributing to their political demise, and mobilised thousands of young people in carnival and music events (along with the Rock Against Racism movement).[2]

- The mobilisations of thousands particularly by Unite Against Fascism (UAF) in the 2000s against the rise of the neo-fascist BNP and the street hooligan racists of the English Defence League (EDL).

The recent and seemingly relentless rise of the far-right party UKIP alongside the decline of the British National Party and the English Defence League poses challenges of a different kind to that of confronting traditional openly fascist parties. An important recent study[3] of UKIP has shown that it draws mass support from racist ideas and operates in a different way to more traditional fascist parties. The growth of UKIP is moving politics to the right and the three main political parties are competing with it by adopting ever more anti-migrant politics.

The political challenge of confronting UKIP's message calls for an urgent and different type of response to the tradition of confrontational mass anti-fascist mobilisations of the past. There needs to be united action by community groups, trade unions, socialists and migrant communities, but also a political response articulated around principles such as:

- **Internationalism and Global Solidarity.**
  Building movements in a globalised world that connect people in struggle across national boundaries is one of the

---

[2] See *ANL & RAR: Cultures of Resistance*, Piers Mostyn, www.resistancebooks.org.

[3] Robert Ford and Matthew Goodwin, Revolt on the Right: Explaining support for the Radical Right in Britain, Routledge, 2014.

most important ways of combating the spread of racism and fascism. The economic crisis is being used to blame minorities and migrant communities. Fighting racism and fascism is a central aspect in the struggle globally for economic equality, workers' freedom and liberation, and against the man-made ecological crisis that threatens the human race.

- **Mass mobilisation of communities to confront racist and fascist attacks.**
  Where black, Asian and other minority communities are under physical attack from racists and fascists, their self-defence and mobilisation should be supported. No reliance should be placed on the state or on vigilante action. Stronger laws against racist behaviour can give more confidence to communities under attack.

- **Combatting the fascist and racist organisations.**
  The spread of racist and fascist ideas should be combatted vigorously. Explicitly fascist organisations should be denied a platform for the spread of their propaganda and threats, and directly confronted on the street. But racism and xenophobia needs to be combatted politically by challenging the ideology of racism and putting forward an alternative message that migrants and black people are welcome in Britain. This means different tactics in creating a political response to organisations like UKIP, which are quite clearly not fascist, and similar individuals putting forward anti-migrant policies. Such a political response primarily includes campaigning, solidarity and setting out alternative policies, rather than prioritising physical confrontation.

- **Free movement for all, for the opening up of borders and an end to immigration controls.**

Rich people have the right to move freely between countries. Both Labour and Tory/Liberal Coalition governments have made it easier through the immigration laws for wealthy oligarchs from across the globe to settle in Britain, while denying or increasing obstacles for ordinary working people to move, including refugees fleeing wars and persecution. Everybody should be able to move freely and the regime of immigration laws that divide people should be ended. No one is illegal![4]

- **Opposing racism, national chauvinism and xenophobia in all its forms.**
  The ideology of racism, chauvinism and xenophobia needs to be challenged wherever it rears its head – in the national press and media, on the streets and through local and national propaganda. The trade unions and left organisations are critical to this by combating all manifestations of racism in the workplace and in the communities. Central to this is the notion of solidarity between peoples and communities and an end to chauvinist arguments that divide the working class, such as *'British Jobs for British Workers'*.

This survey of the far right by academics and activists covers just seven countries of Europe. There are big gaps in the survey, which will have to be filled at a later stage, in particular Greece[5] but also Russia.

---

[4] For an excellent political case against all immigration controls see: *'Open Borders'*, Teresa Hayter, Pluto Press, 2000.

[5] For more about Golden Dawn in Greece, see *Mapping Ultra-Right Extremism, Xenophobia And Racism Within The Greek State Apparatus*, Dimitris Christopoulos ed., 2014, Rosa Luxemburg Institute, http://rosalux-europa.info/userfiles/file/ RightWing_A4_WEB.pdf, and 'The Night before the Dawn', Piers Mostyn, 2013, *Socialist Resistance*, http://socialistresistance.org/5316/the-night-before-the-dawn-historical-roots-of-greek-fascism.

The survey reveals a disturbing picture of far-right parties, some with a mass base, which have been able to drag the mainstream political parties to the right. This book is intended to be a contribution to understanding the nature of these far-right parties and of the threat we face.

Fred Leplat, September 2015

Introduction

The anti-fascist and anti-capitalist struggles today

Manuel Kellner

Elections for the European Union parliament only give a snapshot of public opinion, and have little effect because the European Union (EU) parliament does not elect a government. Power actually lies with the un-elected Council of the EU that is the Assembly of Heads of State and Governments. But it is important to examine the motivation for how people cast their vote in the recent 2014 EU elections, in particular whether the electorate used the elections as a protest against the governments in each country.

In ten out of the 28-member states, far right, nationalist and right-wing 'populist' parties have achieved significant electoral successes. There is a polarisation, but only a polarisation in which in general benefits the right. Electoral victories for the left, such as for SYRIZA in Greece, Podemos and Izquierda Plural in Spain and the left alliance around the Portuguese Communist Party have been exceptions. In France and Great Britain, with the Front National and the United Kingdom Independence Party (UKIP), far right parties have, in this election, reinforced their position and become much stronger political factors.

Of course, the participation in the 2014 EU elections was very low with an average of about 43%. This is probably a reflection of the fact that people do indeed know that the EU parliament has very few powers. Participation was as low as 13% in Slovakia, and rose to 49% in Sweden (Belgium and Luxembourg are exceptions because in these countries participation in elections is a legal obligation). This low level of participation reflects the low legitimacy of the EU institutions among large parts of the population. But this should not be confused with a politically conscious protest, rather, it results from resignation, lack of knowledge about the importance of the political balance of power in the EU, and lack of interest for political processes beyond the national borders.

The electoral successes of right-wing forces should not be underestimated. It is related to the increasing inability of the traditional left (in general social democracy), which is correctly perceived as part of the existing system, to provide credible answers to the impact of austerity, in particular mass unemployment and increasing existential uncertainty for an increasingly large section of the European population. Thus, more and more people are driven to express their protest by voting for far right parties. They are driven into the arms of nationalism along with the rejection of solidarity with the poor and weak and of any class-struggle approach to the problems in society.

The first political effect of this electoral surge of far right parties is the tendency of the traditional right-wing parties to take up their issues and demands in order to rapidly re-capture their electoral influence. The consequence is that the migrants pay a high price and their situation becomes even worse. But to 'combat' in this manner far right or populist right-wing parties is totally unproductive. It legitimises them and makes them acceptable, and encourages their supporters to believe that it is useful to vote for them as this allows the far right to put into in practice their political programme.

These EU elections revealed a specific weakness of the left. With the exception of Greece and to some extent Spain, Portugal and perhaps Denmark, the left has not been able to strengthen itself by mobilising against and relating politically to the protest against the undemocratic and anti-social character of the EU. The brutality of neoliberal adjustment plans and the great-power ambitions of the EU have largely gone unchallenged. The left, up until now, has not been successful internationally in formulating and popularising a left alternative programme with concrete and transitional demands, in a spirit of solidarity, to respond to the crisis.

As long as this situation remains, the logic of searching for a solution within each nation state will increase the tendency towards welfare chauvinism and reactionary anti-emancipatory radicalisation. This will not only affect the result of elections, the example of the Golden Dawn in Greece shows that real neo-Nazi organisations, ready to utilise brutal terror against the political left, refugees and minorities, which are closely linked with the personnel of the repressive apparatus of the state, can emerge and grow in the given situation.

As for Golden Dawn, there is no doubt that it is a genuine fascist organisation. But how can the far right forces that were so successful in the European elections be characterised? It is important to understand what they are, despite all the differences between countries, in order to better understand how to fight them effectively. The first analogy that comes to mind is that of the historical fascism and Nazism.

A simplistic denunciation of far right parties such as the Front National, UKIP or the Alternative für Deutschland (AfD) as 'fascist' forces does not help and is misleading. It is important to remember what fascism and National Socialism in the 20th century were to carefully bring out the differences and similarities with today's forces of the far right.

First of all, fascism in Italy took power in 1922 after the defeat of a proletarian mass movement for workers-control in 1919-20. This could have led to a socialist revolution if reformist political and trade-union leaders had not succeeded in disorienting and, in the end, demoralising the masses fighting for power. Similarly, when Hitler took power in Germany in 1933, the bourgeois ruling class chose the alternative of Nazi-rule rather than a decisive victory of the working class. At the same time, this ruling class did not see any other solution to their economic problems other than to prepare a new global, or at least continental, war.

The readiness of the bourgeoisie and the ruling class to back the seizure of power by fascist or similar political forces is directly related to their actual fear of losing control and the capitalist mode of production being plunged into an existential crisis of survival. Today, we seem to be far away from these preconditions for the installation of such a regime in the overwhelming majority of the countries of the EU, with the possible exception of Greece. There, the combination of greater and greater radicalisation followed a possible rapid deception of the broad masses following the failure of a left government to find solutions to the crisis in their interest, could lead to an rise of counter-revolutionary despair, and with that to an unexpected growth of a deeply reactionary mass-movement.

There was already a detailed discussion at the IVth Congress of the Communist International on the experience of the fascist movement in Italy. The speeches by Radek and Bordiga, and a series of other contributions, gave important insights: unlike traditional right-wing organisations, fascism was a mass movement that was based on the radicalisation of the impoverished petty bourgeoisie that was in social decline. This movement was a battering ram and was a terrible threat to the physical existence of the labour movement. In contrast to its social base, which it served up with social demagogy, the political class-role of fascism was to defend the power and the interests of capital.

With the subservience of the Communist International to the Stalin faction, the Communist movement lost the ability to analyse fascist movements in Marxist terms and replaced with empty phrases such as the infamous one from Dimitrov, who said that fascism would be 'the open terrorist dictatorship of the most reactionary, most chauvinistic, the most imperialist elements of finance capital'. Certainly the fascist and the Nazi regimes became 'bureaucratised' to a certain degree after their seizure of power and abandoned most of the pseudo-'socialist' content of their demagogy, yet, unlike classical dictatorships, they still retained real mass-support. They would not have otherwise been able to organise an army of block wardens, informers and spies against the repeated outbreaks of protest and resistance in factories and working class residential areas.

Trotsky and other 'dissident' communist revolutionaries and theorists continued the differentiated analysis of fascist movements and regimes interrupted by Stalinism, and developed answers to the question of how to combat these reactionary mass movements effectively. They first fought against the refusal of the Stalinists to develop a united front approach to Social Democracy in order to make possible broad mass-actions against the Nazis, and after that, they denounced their resignation from the class struggle in order to forge or to stimulate alliances with the 'anti-fascist' or 'anti-monopolistic' forces of the bourgeoisie.

A similarity with historical fascism and Nazism to today's right-wing forces is their social demagogy. The wider the electoral base of such a party, the more it can lead to inconsistencies in its rhetoric and its policies. This is demonstrated quite clearly by the Front National in France.

The Front National has to pick up the prejudices and the interests of their classic middle-class base. In addition to xenophobic and racist slogans, they must therefore argue that entrepreneurs pay too much in taxes, that small bosses are disadvantaged, and that unions obtain too high wages and good working conditions for their members through strikes and labour disputes.

On the other hand, the Front National wins over an increasing number of voters and supporters from the working class. To extend its electoral base, the party must therefore also articulate demands that are in the fundamental interests of these workers, for example, for higher wages and better working conditions.

The Front National privileges periodically the one or the other kind of rhetoric, and tries to hide that both do not really fit together. The strategy of Marine Le Pen, as opposed that her father when he was still president of the party, is to present the Front National as a 'serious' political force. She therefore does not allow Holocaust denial, praise for Hitler, or slogans that openly fascist or reminiscent of those of the Nazi by leaders and spoke-persons of her party.

This strategy has been a success. Marine Le Pen is often present in the major media in giving interviews and making statements. The aim of her strategy is to get the Front National to form a government, and thereby, perhaps, being in power. This is however, can only be possible, if the Front National is electorally even more successful than it is today and is able to find allies in the ranks of traditional bourgeois right-wing forces.

This not reassuring, and on the contrary, it is very worrying. One must remember that Hitler became Chancellor after the parliamentary elections of January 1933, and only then did he build up the Nazi dictatorship using all the possibilities of the structures of the state and its repressive organs. The rise of the Nazis was carried out with a mixture of extra-parliamentary mobilisations and violence alongside the legal participation in parliamentary elections in which they became, in just a few years, the strongest political force.

The most alarming development would be that the rise of a party of the far right like the Front National is combined with the rise of strong organisations ready to fight and to attack refugees, migrants, gays and lesbians, and left wing and trade union activists, meetings, bookshops and their offices. Such a development could come gradually, and to some extent, we are witnessing such a phenomenon in different European countries.

An atmosphere of violence and civil war in the Ukraine has led to the emergence of right-wing, semi-fascist and fascist forces on both sides. At the same time, the forces of the radical left, let alone those of revolutionary-Marxism, are very weak, and there is no party representing and articulating the interests of the working class, the wage earners, the poor and the oppressed in society. Unless this changes, it is very probable that further radicalisations will tend to re-enforce even more the extreme right-wing forces.

In Great Britain, UKIP, a party to the right of the traditional Conservative Party, came first in the 2014 European elections with a spectacular 27.49% of the votes cast, ahead of Labour with 25.4% and the Conservatives on 23.93%.

UKIP articulates a strong rejection of the EU and its institutions. Traditionally, there is a powerful tendency in Great Britain against the EU, probably linked to the 'glorious' colonialist past of the British Empire. A growing section of the population does not believe that established political parties are unable to resist the politics of the EU, which are largely influenced by Germany and its Merkel-government and that the answer is to simply walk out of the EU.

But there is also an erosion of the political credibility of the established parties in general. They all stand for the same pro-austerity policies. The leader of UKIP, Nigel Farage, claims to speak up for the interests of the 'little people' and of the underdogs, who are the victims of the banks and the speculators of the financial capital. In addition, he also easily exploits the fears of many wage earners about migration and its downwards pressure on wages and working conditions in general. Farage gives the impression of being the 'nice guy' with whom you can have a beer in the pub, and say nasty things about politicians and foreigners. The success of UKIP has led to a broader acceptation of xenophobia and racism in the public political discourse.

Just like in France with the Front National, the media in Great Britain has willingly opened the space for UKIP demagogy and allowed to articulate its positions publicly. And like in other countries, both the Conservatives and the Labour Party have radicalised their positions by adopting more restrictive policies against migrants and refugees in an attempt to marginalise UKIP.

UKIP got only one Member of Parliament elected at the 2015 general election because of the undemocratic character of the first-past the post electoral system. But it is biting at the heels of the Conservative and Labour Parties, as it came second in 125 constituencies. It is undoubtedly gaining support, it has the backing of rich sponsors, and threatens to influence even more British politics, not only on the EU question with a referendum to be held by the end of 2017, as some leading Conservative politicians start to discuss possible alliances with UKIP.

It is difficult to imagine how to stop the rise of UKIP in Britain, or similar forces elsewhere in Europe, without new successes in building a political alternative to the left of the traditional 'social democratic' parties such as the Labour Party or the Socialist Party in France. Indeed, the rise of SYRIZA in Greece, which won the general election in January 2015 and formed an anti-austerity left government challenging the Troika, has been able, for time being, to stem the rise of the neo-fascist Golden Dawn. That party had gained 7% of the vote to the Greek general election in 2012, 9.4% at the 2014 EU parliamentary election, and just 6.3% at the last general election. With its 17 members of the Hellenic parliament, it is certainly still a dangerous threat that cannot be ignored. But the popularity of SYRIZA, confirmed by its victory in the July 2015 referendum against further austerity from the Troika, has prevented the polarisation in society from favouring the far and extreme right. Of course, as mentioned previously, if the hope placed in the SYRIZA government to meet the needs of the people of Greece is deceived, then the despair that follows could favour reactionary forces, including Golden Dawn.

In Germany, the Alternative für Deutschland (AfD) which was established in 2013, is certainly not as openly on the far right as, for example the Front National or UKIP. The AfD has been successful not only in the EU elections, but also in local elections. In the 2014 EU parliament elections, it came fifth with 7.1% of the vote and won seven members of the EU parliament. It is now represented in the regional parliaments of Saxony (with 9.7% of the vote), Thuringia (10.6%), Brandenburg (12.2%), Hamburg (6.1%) and Bremen (5.5%). The AfD now also achieves a 7% score in the opinion polls at the federal level.

The AfD opposes the EU making financial savings to maintain the euro. The spokesman of the party, Bernd Lucke, a radical free-market neoliberal Professor of Economics, wrote when announcing the founding of the new party:

> The AfD will demand the dissolution of the euro in favour of national currencies or smaller currency unions. It will argue for an end to the multi-billion dollar bailouts and against a European transfer union. It will work for streamlining and reducing the bureaucracy of the European Union by transferring back the powers to the national level.

The AfD opposition to the euro springs from a nationalist stance against the population of the economically weaker countries of the EU. Bernd Lucke has spoken out for further cuts in the social welfare benefits and against excessive wage increases. Lucke has also voiced his support for the PEGIDA demonstrations against Islamism in late 2014, based mostly in Dresden. Hans-Olaf Henkel, the other prominent leader of the AfD and a former President of the Federation of German Industries, continues to represent corporate capitalist interests against those of workers and the unemployed.

Big business and employers organisations did not back the AfD until now because they supported the EU policy of Angela Merkel and her grand coalition of Christian Democratic Union and social democratic SPD party. But family entrepreneur associations and many small bosses now do back the AfD. The AfD represents not only the higher earning sections of the middle class, but also a specific faction of capital, a part of the business community.

In the 2014 European parliamentary elections, the AfD called for more democracy (for example referendums in an allusion to the referendums in Switzerland) and spoke out against increased immigration. But all democratic-sounding rhetoric of AfD cover-up an anti-democratic ideology. The propaganda of the AfD states that entrepreneurs are under-represented in political institutions and have, by large, too little influence in politics.

The campaign of the AfD against 'benefit tourism' is not very different from the statements during the election campaign by the Bavarian Christian ultra-conservatives of the CSU. After the European elections, the Merkel government drafted a law restricting immigration from EU countries of people presumed wanting to 'abuse the social welfare-network of Germany'. Of course, there are confirmed 'right-wing populists' in the AfD, and naturally right-wing extremists and neo-Nazis of all kinds feel encouraged by the electoral break-through of the AfD. But the idols of the AfD are neoliberal icons such as von Hayek, cherished some time ago by Margaret Thatcher, Ronald Reagan and Augusto Pinochet. The AfD expresses the process of de-civilisation of a part of the bourgeoisie, mobilising at the same time the fears and social prejudices of petty-bourgeois individuals and others who are losing confidence in the future and in the political establishment, while at the same time attracting sections of what is remaining from the workers-movement.

Alarmingly, the AfD took many votes in the 2014 regional elections in the eastern part of Germany from Die Linke (the Left Party), and not only from the classic bourgeois parties and the small parties of the far right. So the Left Party is being punished because it has adapted itself too much to pro-capitalist policies, for example by being in coalition in regional governments (such as Thuringia) with the social democratic SPD. It is more and more perceived as being a part of the 'establishment' by broad sections of the masses, and is no longer able to appear as a political expression of protest against the policies of the ruling class and as a protagonist of a systemic alternative with demands capable of mobilising workers and youth for solutions against the interests of capital.

The rise the far right today in Europe is without precedent since the 1930s. Its ideas contaminate the classical bourgeois parties and also a part of the social-liberal 'social democratic parties'. There are many varieties of far right political forces, some are more or less integrated, or on the way to being integrated, in the bourgeois parliamentary institutions and to being accepted as 'normal' political forces by media and establishment. Some are still more or less perceived as outsiders and unacceptable extremists because they are openly anti-Semitic or refer openly to Nazi-tradition, in which case they are often identified by bourgeois commentators as being the counterpart to 'left wing anti-capitalist extremism'. But there are also points in common: principally nationalism, racism, xenophobia, homophobia, islamophobia, anti-communism and authoritarianism.

The rise of these far right forces is linked to the deepening of the systemic and structural crisis of capitalism since 2008, but not in a mechanical fashion. Indeed, in the Spanish state or in Portugal, whose populations have been prominent victims of the devastations caused by EU structural adjustment plans and neoliberal austerity policies, the far right remained marginal. In Greece, where millions have been thrown into misery, an openly neo-Nazi party like Golden Dawn has arisen, but the forces of the political left, in particular SYRIZA, have become much more popular than them, at least until now. On the other hand, in Switzerland and Austria, countries that have hardly been affected by the crisis, have strongly established right-wing parties such as the SVP and the FPÖ.

This kind of phenomenon is not new. An economistic explanation would be misleading. In Germany, for example, racism and even violent assaults on refugees, is stronger in some areas with few migrants and refugees compared to other areas with a greater population of migrants and refugees. In France, the vote for the Front National was particularly high in rural areas with hardly any 'foreigners' living there. The racism against Roma is widespread in countries where they are only a very small minority. Anti-Semitism, even when it not confused with a critical attitude towards Israel and Zionism and solidarity with the Palestinians, remains deeply implanted in the mind of many Germans, even though there are only about 100,000 Jews living in Germany today. The readiness to take up racist attitudes is linked to the need to find excuses for the crimes of one's own nation and governments.

Major right-wing parties like the Lega Nord in Italy, or the Vlaams Belang and the Nieuw Vlaamse Alliantie in the Flemish part of Belgium are successful not because of misery and distress in the population, but on the contrary because of welfare-chauvinism, that is the feeling that you are part of a privileged region or layer in society of your country and that you want to defend your privileges against others (the outsider, the stranger, the foreigner, the migrant). The worsening of the global economic crisis reinforces the propagation of such feelings, especially if there is no uprising of mass-actions for emancipatory solutions and the growth of clearly anti-capitalist movements and political parties.

This welfare-chauvinism is also characteristic of the AfD in Germany, in this case working at the European or even planetary level: 'we don't want to pay for the Greeks; we need an economy stronger than that of the Chinese, etc.'. In former colonial countries such as France or England, the memory of the 'glorious past' and the nostalgia that 'our' country has by large not the same influence and power as it did in this past may be one of the ingredients of right-wing resentments.

The classic Marxist approach to right-wing extremism, as explained above, contains the idea that the objective function of fascism is to crush the workers movement in order to prevent a socialist revolution. But the workers movement today has been on the defensive for decades and the socialist-revolutionary forces are weak, representing tiny minorities in the working class and in the populations as a whole. It could be possible to deduce from this that there is no real danger because the rule of the bourgeoisie is in no way challenged, and it will therefore not help install a dictatorship which would, even if it defends the general interests of capital, be analogous to the fascisms of the 20th century. The result of such a dictatorship would mean the political expropriation of the bourgeoisie, while a parliamentary system allows the broad participation and direct influence of bourgeois currents in the political decision-making process.

But it is not useful to comfort one-self with such historical analogies. For example parties of the far right can win elections and come to government even if only a minority of the bourgeoisie backs them. Even in the case of Hitler and the German Nazi-party, the majority of the bourgeoisie started to back them only after Hitler and the Nazis took over the government. Reactionary aggressive mass-movements can emerge and grow even in situations where their main potential enemy, the workers movement and the political left, are very weak. This weakness even tends to encourage aggressive reactionary forces. And the bourgeoisie is probably flexible enough to adapt itself to new situations and to exploit them for its own class-interests, even if its rule is not in seriously put in danger to by the class-struggle from below and strong anti-capitalist movements.

The danger embodied by the rise of far right forces should in no way be underestimated. The way to respond to this danger and to fight these right-wing forces is a very important subject of reflection and discussion on the political left, in the trade-unions and in the emancipatory social movements.

It is certainly important to incorporate the experiences and the theoretical achievements of the past into this reflection and discussion. But real history does not simply repeat what happened decades ago under conditions in many aspects different to the actual conditions today. It is important to combine the theoretical knowledge accumulated by critical Marxism (and by other critical and emancipatory approaches to social reality) of analyses of the experiences of the past with efforts to understand what is new today.

One point of debate is whether legal action should be taken against right-wing forces, or perhaps at least against openly fascist forces. The normal Marxist response to this is 'no'. Normally all laws or measures of repression against 'extremism' practiced by a bourgeois, even a democratic one, state also leads to repression against leftist forces. And often, the far right organisations are symbiotically linked with the repressive apparatus of the state. Moreover, legal action against fascists or Nazis tends to substitute for mass-action and self-organisation from below and by this, indirectly, weakens the potentially only real deadly enemy of extreme right movements and organisations.

But maybe this refusal to use legal action against the extreme right should not be applied in a dogmatic manner. If victims of right-wing aggression are too weak to defend themselves, or too isolated to mobilise enough people to defend them, then they would be badly advised not to appeal to the police and not to take legal action against their aggressors.

In Germany, Article 139 of the Grundgesetz (the German constitution) stipulates the following: 'Die zur, Befreiung des deutschen Volkes vom Nationalsozialismus und Militarismus erlassenen Rechtsvorschriften werden von den Bestimmungen dieses Grundgesetzes nicht berührt' (The legislation adopted for the liberation of the German people from National Socialism and Militarism is not affected by the provisions of this Basic Law). What does that mean? It means that the legislation adopted by the allies of the anti-Hitler-coalition ruling Germany after its liberation from the Nazi-dictatorship in 1945, is intended to prevent any re-birth of a Nazi-like chauvinistic, racist, anti-democratic and war-driving movement in Germany. It is not surprising that bourgeois ideologues believe this article 139 to be 'obsolete'.

It could be politically productive to promote the development of a movement in Germany demanding the application of this explicitly anti-Nazi constitutional law against organisations and movements in continuity with historical Nazism. This is really not the same as a legislation directed in general against 'extremism'. And if such a movement would link such a demand with the readiness to implement the article 139 by its own actions, and not to substitute their own actions with legal constitutional procedures, it could indeed be a good and useful thing. There is no consensus about this approach either in the anti-fascist movements or in revolutionary-Marxist circles in Germany. We should be clear that it is absolutely not possible to get rid by legal action a reactionary political force that is based on millions of voters and with support on a mass-scale. In these cases, the only hope is the mobilisation of even broader masses.

An important part of the revolutionary Marxist tradition regarding the struggle against fascism and right-wing forces is to combine the largest possible common action in the spirit of the united front, which would include all parties and organisations of the workers movement (even if they promote bourgeois politics such as social democracy), with the rejection of 'people's front', that is cooperation with genuinely bourgeois parties or forces. Trotsky is sometimes quoted as saying that even 'the shadow of the bourgeoisie' should not be included in the united front.

The idea behind this is that bourgeois forces would in every case defend the 'sanctity' of the private property of the means of production, and therefore break the dynamic of a proletarian anti-fascist mass movement which, if successful, would go further and put in question this private property and bourgeois rule. For Trotsky and the political current associated with his name, there was no 'Chinese wall' between a successful mass movement against fascism and the anti-capitalist struggle. It seems not to be useful to apply this idea in a dogmatic manner. Indeed, why should we exclude bourgeois forces from a common action to mobilise, for example, against a public Nazi, fascist or right-wing demonstration? There were cases in Germany, when not only all tiny groups of the radical left, Die Linke, trade-unions and social movements, but also the local SPD and local genuinely bourgeois parties called for such actions. In these cases, it would be unfortunate to hear Marxist activists explaining publicly why a 'people's front' is bad and that the bourgeois forces should be excluded. Even if it is the forces of the left, and not the bourgeois ones, that are responsible for the mobilising effort, at the same time their readiness to join officially such an appeal to action makes mobilisation much easier. This was indeed the case in Cologne where there was a mass mobilisation against an international islamophobic far right 'conference'. The broad appeal made possible the mass mobilisation of people from schools, factories, universities and the popular residential areas. Each case should be evaluated concretely in order to apply the tactics that are the most appropriate to ensure the largest possible mass-action.

But the following question arises: is the distinction between genuinely bourgeois parties and others the same as it was in the 1930s or even the 1970s? This is in not certain. First of all, neither New Labour (in Britain) nor the SPD (in Germany) are the same. Can such parties still be characterised as 'bourgeois workers parties', part of the workers movement, even if their politics are pro-capitalist? In the era of social-liberal social democracy, there is not a clear difference, in the eyes of the broad masses, between social democratic parties and conservative or liberal parties. Social democracy has lost many of its traditionally proletarian roots, even if it maintains, like in Germany and some other countries, a more or less close relationship with at least the leaders of the trade-union movement.

In formulating theses on the rise of right-wing forces in Europe and how to fight them, Michael Löwy concludes with the following remark:

It is sometimes possible to unite with the ghost of 'republicanism', but any organised anti-fascist movement will only be effective and credible if it is driven by forces situated outside of the dominant neoliberal consensus. This means a struggle that cannot be limited within the borders of a single country, but must be organised at the level of Europe as a whole. The struggle against racism, as well as solidarity with its victims, is one among the essential components of this resistance.

The reminds me of a discussion in Athens with comrades of DEA, a revolutionary-Marxist organisation in solidarity with the Fourth International working inside SYRIZA and its left wing. They explained to me, why they argue against including the social democratic PASOK as a party in fronts for joint actions against the neo-Nazis from Golden Dawn. New Democracy and PASOK have been totally discredited after many years of austerity against the working class and the poor and of servile attitude towards the Troïka (EU, IMF and European Central Bank). If a left party include PASOK in joint initiatives for action, they would in turn become discredited in the eyes of the masses.

We should not forget that the neoliberal policies have produced deep frustrations in a big part of the population and it has radicalised many people against the politics of the establishment. There is a race to capture this radicalisation by both the forces of the radical left and those of the extreme right, in order to influence the content of political conclusions drawn by those that have been radicalised either in the direction of emancipatory aspirations or towards reactionary despair. If they are identified with the political forces responsible for the neoliberal austerity policies, the radical left can only lose this race.

Michael Löwy also draws another very important conclusion. Even if they are nationalists, extreme right-wing forces cooperate at the European and the international level. To mobilise nationalist feelings is part of their demagogy, but it does not prevent them from co-operating, even if they encounter some difficulties and contradictions in doing so. Internationalism is at the heart of emancipatory socialist convictions and politics. It is therefore crucial to organise a broad European-wide anti-fascist movement capable of organising real mass-mobilisations across the borders of countries.

It is within this framework that, as Löwy stresses, the defence of the victims of racist discrimination and aggression is a very important issue. I would add that it is necessary to organise common international working class action around demands such as for the defence of wages and working conditions, better social legislation and the reduction of the working week without loss of earnings. It is the only way to fight the existing and increasing competition between different layers of wage earners that is encouraged by employers who use impact of migration to drive down the condition of the working class.

Furthermore, a sober and non-hysterical approach should be developed by the revolutionary left to ensure the security and safety of migrants, refugees, social movements, left wing organisations and trade-unions that are under threat by the rise of far right and extreme right. This should be done without any anti-emancipatory romanticisation of violence, and the necessity of self-defence and mutual support against far right aggressions should be patiently argued for. In Greece, in Hungary and in the Ukraine, this is evidently an actual necessity today. In other countries, it will be the same sooner or later.

The discussion is not closed, but open. Many problems need to be resolved. A combination of local initiatives, mobilisations on a regional, national and international level, the building of broad unity of action, a European-wide anti-fascist and anti-racist movement, the education in the necessity of self-defence and mutual help, the promotion of international common action of wage-earners to defend their class-interests against capital, and the building of broad clearly anti-capitalist organisations and parties, are all tasks that are linked to the battle against the far right, the extreme right, the neo-fascist and neo-Nazi forces.

In conclusion, I want to underline the necessity of building a revolutionary international, not only to co-ordinate international actions, but also to develop a common international reflection on strategies for linking the anti-fascist and the anti-capitalist struggle for universal emancipation, for a society without exploitation, oppression, and alienation, and which does not destroy the natural resources essential for us to survive.

Ten theses on the
far right in Europe*

Michael Löwy

I.

The European elections confirmed a tendency that has been apparent for some years across most of the continent: the spectacular rise of the far right. This is a phenomenon without precedent since the 1930s. In many countries this movement obtained between 10 and 20 percent of the vote; today in three countries (France, United Kingdom, Denmark) is has already reached 25 to 30 percent. Moreover, its influence is greater than its own electorate: its ideas contaminate also the 'classical' right and even part of the social-neoliberal left. The French case is the most serious, with the Front National's breakthrough exceeding even the most pessimistic predictions. As the website *Mediapart* wrote in a recent editorial, 'it's five minutes to midnight'.

II.

This far right is very diverse, a variety ranging from openly neo-Nazi parties like 'Golden Dawn' in Greece to bourgeois forces who are perfectly well integrated into the institutional political game, such as

* Resistance Books is grateful to Verso Books for allowing us to re-publish this text. It was originaly published in August 2014 on the Verso website at http://www.versobooks.com/blogs/1683-ten-theses-on-the-far-right-in-europe-by-michael-lowy.

Switzerland's UDC. What they have in common is their chauvinist nationalism, xenophobia, racism, hatred of immigrants – particularly 'non-Europeans' – and Roma (the continent's oldest people), Islamophobia and anti-communism. To that we could add, in many cases, anti-semitism, homophobia, misogyny, authoritarianism, disdain for democracy and Europhobia. On other questions – for example their stances for or against neoliberalism or secularism – this movement is more divided.

III.

It would be mistaken to believe that fascism and anti-fascism are phenomena belonging to the past. Of course, today we do not see mass fascist parties comparable to the NSDAP in the Germany of the 1930s, but already in that period fascism was not limited to this model only: Spanish Francoism and Portuguese Salazarism were very different from the Italian and German models. A significant part of today's European far right has a directly fascist and/or neo-Nazi framework: this being the case for Greece's 'Golden Dawn', Hungary's Jobbik and the Ukrainian parties Svoboda and Right Sector; but also, in a different way, France's Front National, Austria's FPÖ, and Belgium's Vlaams Belang, among others, whose founding leaders had close links with historical fascism and the forces that collaborated with the Third Reich. In other countries – such as the Netherlands, Switzerland, the UK and Denmark – the far-right parties do not have fascist origins but do share in their racism, xenophobia and Islamophobia. One of the arguments used to show that the far right has changed and no longer has much to do with fascism is its acceptance of parliamentary democracy and the electoral route to power. Though we might remember that a certain Adolf Hitler made it to the German Chancellery by a legal vote in the Reichstag, and that Marshal Pétain was elected Head of State by the French Parliament. If the Front National made it to power by electoral means – a hypothesis that can sadly no longer be dismissed – what would remain of democracy in France?

IV.

The economic crisis that has riven Europe since 2008 has almost everywhere (with the exception of Greece) favoured the far right more than the radical left. The two forces are totally out of proportion, contrary to the European situation of the 1930s where in many countries the anti-fascist left rose in parallel to fascism. The current far right has without doubt profited from the crisis, though this does not explain everything: in Spain and Portugal, two of the countries hit hardest by the crisis, the far right remains only marginal. And in Greece, though 'Golden Dawn' has enjoyed exponential growth, it has very much been left in the wake of Syriza, the Coalition of the Radical Left. In Switzerland and Austria, two countries largely spared by the crisis, the racist far right often gets above 20 percent support. Thus we should avoid the economistic explanations often advanced by the left.

V.

Historical factors have without doubt played some role: a long anti-semitic tradition widespread in certain countries; the persistence of those currents who collaborated during the Second World War; and the colonial culture that impregnates attitudes and behaviours long after decolonisation – not only in the former empires, but in almost all European countries. All these factors are at work in France and contribute to explaining the success of Le Pen's party.

VI.

The concept of 'populism' employed by certain political scientists, the media and even part of the left, is wholly inadequate to explaining this phenomenon, serving only to sow confusion. If in the Latin America of the 1930s to '60s the term populism corresponded to something quite specific – Vargas-ism, Peronism, etc. – its European usage from the 1990s onward is ever more vague and imprecise. Populism is defined as 'a political position that takes the side of the people against the elites', which goes for almost any political party or movement. When applied to the parties of the far right, this pseudo-concept leads – whether deliberately or not – to legitimising them, making them more acceptable, or even appealing – who isn't for the people against the elites? – while carefully avoiding the troubling terms racism, xenophobia, fascism, and far right. 'Populism' is also used in a deliberately mystifying fashion by neoliberal ideologues in order to make an amalgam between the far right and the radical left, characterised as 'right-wing populism' and 'left-wing populism', since they are both opposed to neoliberal policies, 'Europe', etc.

VII.

The left as a whole, with only a few exceptions, has severely underestimated this danger. It did not see the brown wave coming, and thus did not see the need to take the initiative of an anti-fascist mobilisation. For certain currents of the left, seeing the far right as nothing more than a side-effect of the crisis and of unemployment, it is these causes that must be attacked and not the fascist phenomenon itself. Such typically economistic reasoning has disarmed the left in the face of the far right's racist, xenophobic and nationalist ideological offensive.

VIII.

No social group is immune to the brown plague. The ideas of the far right, in particular racism, have contaminated a significant part of not only the petty bourgeoisie and the unemployed, but also the working class and young people. This is particularly striking in the French case. These ideas have no relation to the reality of migration: the vote for the Front National, for example, was particularly high in certain rural areas that have never seen a single immigrant. And Roma immigrants, recently the object of a hysterical racist campaign that made some impression – with the generous participation of the 'socialist' Interior Minister of the time, Mr. Manuel Valls – number less than twenty thousand across the whole of France.

IX.

Another 'classic' left-wing analysis of fascism is that which explains it essentially as an instrument of big capital to crush the revolution and the workers' movement. Since today the workers' movement is very much weakened and the revolutionary threat non-existent, big capital has no interest in supporting far-right movements and thus the risk of a brown offensive is non-existent. This is, once again, an economistic reading that does not take account of the autonomy of any political phenomenon – electors can, indeed, choose a party that does not have the big bourgeoisie's backing – and one that seems to ignore the fact that big capital can accommodate to all sorts of political regimes without too much soul-searching.

X.

There is no magic recipe for fighting the far right. We must be inspired – with a proper critical distance – by the anti-fascist traditions of the past, but we must also know how to innovate in order to respond to the new forms of this phenomenon. We must know how to combine local initiatives with solidly organised and structured unitary socio-political and cultural movements, at both the national and continental levels. It is sometimes possible to unite with the ghost of 'republicanism', but any organised anti-fascist movement will only be effective and credible if it is driven by forces situated outside of the dominant neoliberal consensus. This means a struggle that cannot be limited within the borders of a single country, but must be organised at the level of Europe as a whole. The struggle against racism, as well as solidarity with its victims, is one among the essential components of this resistance.

UKIP and the politics of ultra-Thatcherism

Phil Hearse

The 2015 general election in Britain confirmed the definitive arrival of the United Kingdom Independence Party (UKIP) as a major force in British politics. Despite only winning one parliamentary seat the party polled 3.8 million votes or 12.6% of the total, making it the third party in terms of popular mandate behind the Conservative and Labour parties. This had a major impact on the overall outcome, but the vagaries of the British electoral first-past-the post system meant that the party held on to just one of its two seats, that of Douglas Carswell in the Essex seaside resort of Clacton. UKIP leader Nigel Farage failed to win in the Kent town of South Thanet after the Conservatives poured in huge resources to keep him out.

From a formal point of view the reward in terms of seats for UKIP is spectacularly undemocratic. The first-past-the-post system rewards parties whose votes are highly concentrated. For example the Scottish National Party (SNP) won 56 seats with 1,454,436 votes, well under half of UKIP's much more spread out votes. From the viewpoint of electoral representation, UKIP just failed to hit a 'tipping point' that would have ensured dozens of MPs.

The apparent failure of the party to make a decisive breakthrough at parliamentary level led to sustained infighting among the UKIP leadership, which revealed some of its fault lines. Some leaders from Conservative party backgrounds were shocked when in a pre-election TV debate Farage claimed that foreigners coming to Britain for HIV treatment were costing the health service huge sums. He went on to claim that 60% of the 7,000 people diagnosed with HIV every year in the UK were born abroad. Economics spokesperson Patrick Flynn was ousted when he suggested that Nigel Farage appeared 'snarling, thin-skinned and aggressive'. Deputy 'chairman' (sic) Suzanne Evans was purged when she suggested that Farage was 'divisive' and should not be made the leader of the 'out' camp in the upcoming referendum of the UK's membership of the European Union.

Doubtless these divisions represent frustration at the electoral outcome. But UKIP's huge vote was a major factor in the Conservative victory. In dozens of constituencies in the Midlands and North of England, UKIP came second to the Conservatives, taking most votes from Labour, enabling the Conservatives to win. As the 'elections etc' website pointed out: 'The rise of UKIP that was expected to disproportionately hurt the Tories, but in fact (it) seems to (have) undermined the Labour performance more.'[1]

Handing victory to the Conservatives while winning just one seat themselves was a bitter disappointment to UKIP, but in reality the party was faithfully fulfilling its role – to be a cutting edge of the process of pushing British politics to the right, deepening the neoliberal counter-revolution started by Margaret Thatcher. Of course UKIP has its own party ambitions, and winning just one seat was not part of them. After the election result was announced, Farage attacked right-wing papers such as the Daily Mail that had appeared sympathetic to UKIP, but viciously turned against it in the last weeks of campaigning when it seemed that UKIP might be badly damaging the outcome of the poll for the Conservatives.

In the process of pushing UK politics to the right, sections of the Conservative Party itself are a decisive component, but UKIP acts as a

---

[1] http://electionsetc.com/2015/05/08/how-did-the-tories-win-a-majority.

permanent external pressure, linking up with right-wing Tory MPs and the vitriolic right-wing press in ruthlessly use of racism and xenophobia. UKIP has been able to establish a base among working class former Labour voters using populist racist themes in a way that would have been impossible for the Conservatives. Thus the comments by Nigel Farage on HIV tourists were precisely designed to appeal to UKIP's racist base, with open disdain for 'respectable' public opinion. People outraged by Farage's remarks were never going to vote for UKIP anyway.

The success of UKIP under Farage's leadership has been to extend the party's base into the working class, winning over former Labour voters – especially older male voters. UKIP's profile as 'the Conservative Party in exile' has been overcome and its popular base extended way beyond the ageing middle class former Conservatives who were its former electoral mainstay.

The roots of UKIP's rise

UKIP, a right-wing authoritarian pro-capitalist party, has succeeded where its fascist competitors like the British National Party (BNP) and the 'storm in the streets' English Defence League (EDL) failed. The trick was to present thinly-disguised racism in respectable garb, which the fascist organisations could never do given the role of the Second World War and Nazism in the country's collective memory.

Such a spectacular turnaround in the political order represents the coming together of a number of social and political processes, including the long-term decline of the main political parties – Labour, the Conservatives and the apparent terminally declining Liberal Democrats - and deep changes wrought in Britain's social order by decades of neoliberalism which intersect with the changing structure of the working class and ethnic profile of the country. It is impossible to explain UKIP without referring to major sociological changes that underpin the decline of traditional working class, 'Labourist', social democratic consciousness.

In the latter part of 2014, UKIP gained its first two Members of Parliament, both defectors from the Conservative Party who had resigned their parliamentary seats and stood again for election under the UKIP banner. Both Douglas Carswell in Clacton and Mark Reckless in Rochester were re-elected with huge majorities in constituencies on Britain's south east coast. Both these towns reflect some of the deep social changes – the destruction of traditional jobs and a white working class mired in long-term poverty – upon which UKIP depends for significant proportion of its votes.

Long term poverty, especially for older male workers, is now decades old in some towns in the North and Midlands, where traditional industries like mining and steel production were destroyed in the 1980s and 1990s. Around Manchester, in South Yorkshire, the North East, Liverpool, London, the West Midlands and in some South West town like Southampton, so-called 'sink estates' have grown up where the majority of workers are unemployed, drug crime and domestic violence are endemic, poor health is widespread and hopelessness is universal. If people do have jobs they tend to be temporary and low paid, or on 'zero hours' contracts. In some of these areas during the 2000-2008 period, the British National Party built a base. Most of that has now gone over to UKIP, and support for Labour in these areas has significantly declined.

Stoke-on-Trent in the Potteries is a classic case of Labour decline and the rise of UKIP. Control of the city council has been taken over by a group of Independents, which complicates UKIP's intervention. In the 2015 council elections, while not winning a single seat because of the Independent intervention, UKIP beat the Tories, or Labour or both in every ward where they stood. It's a bet that in the medium term the Independents will disappear as a group and that UKIP will be ready to challenge the control of the council.

In the Stoke-on-Trent South constituency parliamentary election held the same day, UKIP got more than 8,000 votes, compared with 15,000 for Labour and 12,000 for the Tories. The Greens got just over 1,000 votes and the Trade Union and Socialist Coalition2 just 329.

In the former steel town Rotherham, in the heartland of what was previously jokingly known as 'the socialist republic of South Yorkshire', Labour came first with 19,800 votes, but UKIP came second with 11,400. In the local council elections Labour won 17 seats and UKIP won four seats. But no other party won a seat and in all of Labour's 17 gains, UKIP came second.

In the general election UKIP won more than 20% and sometimes 30% of the vote in Labour strongholds such as Hartlepool, Heywood and Middleton, Barking, Dagenham and Rainham, Houghton and Sunderland South, and West Bromwich East.

If we analyse the top 20 seats where UKIP came second, most of them are not rural or middle class areas:

UKIP's top 20 second places, by percentage of vote

Constituency	% vote	votes
Boston and Skegness	33.8	14,645
Thanet South	32.4	16,026
Heywood and Middleton	32.2	15,627
Castlepoint	31.2	14,178
Rochester and Strood	30.5	16,009
Rotherham	30.2	11,413
Dagenham and Rainham	29.8	12,850
Rother Valley	28.1	13,204
Hartlepool	28.0	11,052
Basildon South and Thurrock East	26.5	12,097
Thanet North	25.7	12,097

---

[2] TUSC (the Trade Union and Socialist Coalition) is an electoral coalition that includes the Socialist Party and the Socialist Workers Party.

Constituency	% vote	votes
Hornchurch and Upminster	25.3	13,977
West Bromwich West	25.2	8,836
Wentworth and Dearne	24.9	10,733
Sittingbourne and Sheppey	24.8	12,257
Doncaster Central	24.1	9,747
Bolton South East	23.6	9,627
Barnsley East	23.5	9045
Cambridgeshire North East	23.5	11,605
Norfolk South West	23.3	11,654

However there is a counterpoint to the 'Labour votes going to UKIP' narrative. Writing on the Dream Deferred website, Martin Smith and Tash Shifrin tend to minimise the extent to which Labour voters turned to UKIP and point out that in some places where UKIP did well, the Labour votes actually went up. But:

> But it is UKIP that has benefited most from the suicide of the Lib Dems, whose collapse following their coalition with the Tories would otherwise have been much more enjoyable.
>
> UKIP is now the repository for the votes of the 'working class Tories' who have always existed even in Labour heartlands, and the populist party is the new home for many of the voters disaffected by both the two main parties, who previously opted for the Lib Dems.
>
> Labour's disaster – and its shame – is that after five years of Conservative-led austerity government it has done so little to grab the Lib Dems' votes for itself or to pull away voters from the Tories.
>
> And - key to its appeal in a climate of austerity – UKIP is a racist party, building on scapegoating of immigrants and Islamophobia just as far right racist populist parties and outright fascists have done across Europe.

Through the election campaign Farage ratcheted up his racist rhetoric, culminating in claims that EU moves to address the migrant boat crisis in the Mediterranean 'could lead to half a million Islamic extremists coming to our countries and posing a direct threat to our civilisation.'

It should not be forgotten either that the fascist British National Party – now collapsed – had its electoral base in Yorkshire and Lancashire. The English Defence League's fascist and racist street thugs focused on these areas in their turn. These are areas where Farage now trumpets UKIP's successes as the new challenger to Labour.

There is no doubt that UKIP has scooped up the votes of those who backed the BNP at the last election – this has given it a useful base of 5% or so on which to build in a number of constituencies.[3]

Whether it was mainly through Labour voters going directly over to UKIP, or through UKIP winning over Lib Dem voters and working class Tories, it was Labour's failure to create an anti-austerity, anti-neoliberal, pro-working class crusade that left UKIP claiming to be the anti-establishment and even sometimes the anti-big business party.

By any standards UKIP's forward surge represents an extraordinary turnaround in national politics with its third place in the general election following the May 2014 European elections in which UKIP won 27.5% of the vote, and the local municipal elections in England the same month where UKIP won 163 seats (up from 161), with about 17% of the national vote.

The prospects for the two main parties in Westminster are being rewritten with rise of UKIP coming simultaneously with the rise of the Scottish National Party. The SNP gained 56 out of the 59 seats from

---

[3] http://www.dreamdeferred.org.uk/2015/05/election-analysis-ukips-rise-with-full-listing-of-second-places.

Scotland in the Westminster Parliament at the 2015 general election. This follows the 45% vote for Scottish independence in the September 2014 referendum (a vote with a significant left wing character in the urban centres). What is being played out is the result of 30 years of neoliberalism, Conservative Party 'Thatcherism' followed by Labour Party 'Blairism' that has sapped support from both Tories and Labour, putting the two-party system in question.

Why now?

Why has this right-wing surge happened now? Millions of voters are disillusioned and cynical (to put it mildly) about the main Westminster parties. This is especially the case seven years after the 2008 financial crash, which has deepened poverty among millions of working class people and after the parliamentary expenses scandal which had peaked in 2009. In this scandal dozens of MPs were shown to have submitted false expenses claims to parliament, sometimes amounting to tens of thousands of pounds. Mass cynicism with mainstream politicians has only been confirmed by MPs awarding themselves a 10% pay increase in 2015 while most people in the public and private sectors will get this year 1%, 2% - or nothing.

The scope of working class poverty and immiseration in Britain, while nothing like Greek or Portuguese levels, is often not appreciated outside the country. Since 2008, and especially since the 2010 general election, it has amounted to a conscious attempt to pay down the government financial deficit by driving sections of the working class into permanent poverty of a type not seen since the 1930s. Some of the effects of this are:

- Sharp reductions in unemployment and welfare payments.

- The rise of zero hours work contracts that mean the workers concerned must be permanently available for work, while no work at all is guaranteed. Most jobs that have been created since 2008 are zero hours or part-time jobs.

- A vicious 'sanctions' regime against the unemployed that forces them to accept pitifully paid part time work, or work for no wages but only their unemployment benefit. Claimants can be sanctioned and thrown out of benefits for a host of misdemeanours including for example turning up half an hour late for an interview at a job centre. Job Centre workers are pressured to find ways to sanction claimants and stop their benefits.

- A huge rise in the price of houses and rents, taking 50% of the income of millions of workers, especially in London. This combines with wage freezes and continued hikes in utility bills to force millions into utter poverty. Forty per cent of the employed workforce is reckoned to be one electricity or gas bill away from financial ruin.

- A consequent sharp increase in homelessness and people reliant on food banks set up by voluntary organisations and charities.

The main opposition Labour Party, under the 'Blairism Lite' leadership of Ed Miliband and disastrous shadow chancellor (finance minister) Ed Balls, showed itself utterly incapable of presenting an attractive and inspiring alternative which promised anything significant to working class people, or provided a narrative that explained the economic crisis and pointed the way out in the interests of working people. Labour's shadow economy minister Ed Balls criticised the austerity measures of the Conservative-Liberal Democrat Coalition as being a little too harsh, while insisting Labour in power would carry out its own austerity measures and stick ruthlessly to deficit reduction targets.

As Guardian journalist Seumas Milne explained about Ed Miliband's performance at the 2014 Labour conference:

> Sure, there were plenty of commitments welcome to most people across Britain, from a boost to the minimum wage and restoring the 50% top tax rate to scrapping the bedroom tax and clamping down on zero-hours contracts.... But there was little evidence of the determination to break with the past seen in his earlier Labour conferences, when Miliband denounced predatory capitalism and promised an energy price freeze and compulsory purchase of unused developers' land banks. Instead, Ed Balls' pledges of undying austerity and 1990s-style New Labour policy fixes set the tone. Eight months before the general election, the 'shrink the offer' merchants are back in the ascendant.[4]

The 'shrink the offer' basically means Labour saying, 'OK to an £8 an hour national minimum wage, but we give absolutely no pledges on government spending because we don't know what the tax take will be' – i.e. we can't promise anything very much.

But why exactly has Labour's abject failure benefitted UKIP in such a spectacular way?

There are three factors that are important here: 1) the social changes as a result of neoliberalism and austerity; 2) the sharp turn in UKIP's policies and target audience in 2010-11; and 3) the turmoil inside the Conservative Party. Let's look at these one by one.

Since the Thatcherite era of the 1980s there has been a prolonged collapse of 'traditional' manufacturing industries – and of course mining – with very uneven geographical effects. Especially in

---

[4] 'Austerity has failed, and it isn't only Labour's core voters who want change', Seumas Milne, the Guardian, 24 September 2014, http://www.theguardian.com /commentisfree/2014/sep/24/austerity-labour-core-voters-ed-miliband.

the north and north east of England, Scotland and the Midlands, there are whole towns that have never recovered from the economic collapse of the early and mid 1980s. Long-term unemployment has only partially been alleviated by part-time and zero hours jobs in call centres and warehouses. Young people have moved away, but many middle aged and older men have not worked for years. In these white working class communities in urban centres, sometimes referred to as 'sink estates', resentment against the political class and a more nebulous 'middle class, London-based elite' is massive.

Surveys show a major surge in UKIP support among older white working class voters, especially men, who cleave to 'traditional' values, including xenophobic nationalism, hostility to gay marriage and sexual 'deviants', contempt for what are seen as 'middle class' issues like human rights and multiculturalism, and of course outright hostility to immigrants, seen as being privileged and 'taking our jobs'.

Paradoxically, among UKIP voters support for social democratic welfarism – for example the National Health Service and greater economic equality – is high. This contradiction reflects the fact that these poorer sections of the white working class think New Labour under Tony Blair and Gordon Brown did nothing for them. The absence of a significant alternative to the left of Labour opened up these often formerly Labour areas to a right-wing popular discourse.

In the 2010-11 period UKIP carried out a major renovation of its tactics to target the poor white working class, and to try to consolidate a dual base – among middle class Conservatives in the south of England and poorer sections of the working class in the urban centres. The party was at first built around the single issue of British membership of the European Union and mainly attracted dissident, middle-class, Conservatives. This led to the popular belief that UKIP – almost exclusively led by former Tories – was an 'external faction' of the Conservative Party.

The UKIP leadership spotted a potential opening among white working class voters as a consequence of the strong vote in some white working class areas in the European elections of 2009. To gather that vote they decided to de-emphasise the European issue and put the immigration - 'Britain is overcrowded' - to the forefront. In doing so UKIP was able to 'steal' the small but significant base being built up in the European elections and municipal elections by the fascist British National Party (BNP), which elected 33 local councillors in the 2006 municipal elections and two MEPs in the 2009 European elections. Shocking though the vote for the BNP was, it was always hamstrung by the fact that the least hint of fascism is political death in Britain, given the role that the historical memory of the Second World War plays in national consciousness and official nationalist iconography. Once UKIP obviously emerged as a major player in British politics, the BNP vote mainly switched to UKIP, something which Nigel Farage himself acknowledges.

The process of swivelling UKIP's propaganda and gaining a new base is explained by Robert Ford and Matthew Goodwin in the following way:

> Some (UKIP activists around Farage) saw disenchanted working class voters as offering UKIP an opportunity to expand beyond their traditional base of Eurosceptic Tories in the South, and bringing in working class Conservatives who thought Cameron had betrayed their core ideals, and blue collar Labour voters who felt marginalised by the two main parties' shift to the centre and acceptance of mass migration.
>
> The strategy of supplementing Euroscepticism with appeals on immigration and attacks on the established political class had become increasingly evident in campaigns between 2011 and 2013. During this period the context had become as favourable as UKIP had ever known, and their support in the opinion polls had tripled from 3% in 2010 to over 10% at the end of 2013. There were now numerous opportunities to present a socially conservative, Eurosceptic,

anti-immigrant message: an on-going Eurozone crisis; an ailing national economy; in early 2012 the delayed deportation of radical Muslim cleric Abu Qatada, from Britain following a ruling by the European Court of Human Rights; in early 2013, frequent revolts by Conservative backbenchers against their leadership over gay marriage and plans for an EU referendum; and through much of that period growing public concern over immigration from Bulgarian and Romania, unstoppable under EU rule. UKIP had never had it so good.[5]

UKIP could not have made the advances it has without mass disaffection inside the parliamentary Conservative Party. It was able to win two MPs in 2014 because Douglas Carswell and Mark Reckless who were sitting Conservative MPs had resigned and stood again under the UKIP banner. UKIP's breakthrough has to be seen as part of a wider process in British politics, and not just due to the actions of Farage and UKIP, although they are the cutting edge of this process. UKIP has become a realistic challenger for Westminster seats, even having the apparent possibility of holding the balance of power at the 2015 general election. This was the culmination of a prolonged campaign waged by the Tory right-wing, key sections of the media like the Mail and the Telegraph, former Tories in smaller right-wing parties and right-wing TV commentators to make another decisive shift in British politics to the right. It seems now that the ultra-Thatcherites have in fact been victorious in the Conservative Party as far as main key policy planks are concerned.

Not content with the anti-working class reforms of the Thatcher-era such as privatisation, the anti-union laws and selling off social housing, the ultra-Thatcherites want to deepen the counter-revolution of the Thatcher years by further weakening the forces of the labour movement and social progress, dismantling the welfare state and

---

5   Robert Ford and Matthew Goodwin, *Revolt on the Right*, Routledge 2013

victimising immigrants. While UKIP was in the vanguard of pushing this ultra-right-wing agenda forward, it seems as if it has now won inside the Conservative Party and is now the backbone of the government's legislative agenda.

Ultra-Thatcherism

The imposition of a deepened ultra-Thatcherite order aims to makes a more definitive break with the post-war settlement, wrecking the welfare state as well as the mixed economy, which has now virtually gone. The Conservative government is on course to usher in a more authoritarian Britain, with many more people in prison, and nationalism and xenophobia rampant, Britain possibly outside the EU, the health service and social services slashed to ribbons, trade unions being further crushed, and civil liberties and human rights in the garbage bin.

This type of social order is not – in the main – in the objective interests of big business or the capitalist class as a whole. In fact the profits crisis of Tesco – Britain's largest supermarket chain - shows that prolonged deflationary austerity is not in the interests of significant sections of the bourgeoisie, although ironically companies like Tesco, that operate on the basis of minimum wage labour are helping to sustain the deflation and the reduction of working class income that is wrecking their business. It is *not* in the interests of British manufacturing or finance capital to be outside the EU. But the issue of Europe is central for the Tory ultras because British nationalism and British exceptionalism is key to its ideology. This is a view of Britain as exceptionally cultured, democratic, enlightened etc – and definitely a world leader - is based on the long history of the British Empire, something that of course today does not exist.

But politics is not a 'rational interest' game in which the interests of the capitalist class are simply ranged against those of the working class. Things would be much simpler if this were the case. Politics is traversed by irrational and self-contradictory elements. Right-wing Tory irrationalism reaches right into the heart of the cabinet because it is right in the heart of the Conservative Party more generally.

How did this ultra-right-wing trend in the Conservative party start? Of course there have always been hard right, extreme reactionary trends in the Tory party, and Margaret Thatcher mobilised them superbly. The truth is that the mainly petit bourgeois Conservative rank and file have historically been to the right of the leadership, or at least mainly were in the 1945-75 post-war boom period. The brand of racism championed by the late Tory MP Enoch Powell in the 1960s and 1970s was anathema to the Conservative leadership, but Powell was the darling of the rank and file. The election of Thatcher as Tory leader in 1975 was masterminded by MP Robert Moss, (a former member of the security service) and a likeminded cabal of right-wing ultras, and widely applauded by the Tory ranks.

The new Tory parliamentary levy from the 2005, 2010 and 2015 elections are the sons and daughters of Thatcher, steeled in neoliberalism and the nationalistic patriotism that is the ideological cornerstone of their party, and utterly hostile to the EU and especially the European Court of Human Rights and the Human Rights Convention. The one nation Toryism of Harold MacMillan and 'Rab' Butler in the 1950s, and even of Edward Heath in the 1970s, has been buried by successive waves of Thatcherism and now ultra-Thatcherism.

Before the general election it seemed that sections of the Tory hard right were quite prepared to seriously damage or even split the party. As Conservative journalist Matthew Parris put it:

> UKIP and the Tory irreconcilables are perfectly relaxed about the possibility that Mr Cameron could lose the next election; they do not want the EU referendum that would follow his victory. They want the present Tory leadership to stumble and

fall, and, from the internal battle that would follow, they see the emergence of a new kind of party led by a new kind of leader from the anti-European right.[6]

Right-wing pundit Ian Martin went further:

> Although there have been frequent crises in its affairs, for a remarkably long period it has been widely accepted that conservative-minded Britons cluster around the Conservatives. The party itself having been shaped by the splits and breakaways of the 19th century, its members and leaders came to understand that being a broad coalition of interests gave it enormous electoral clout. Suddenly, a significant chunk of conservative opinion is rejecting this historically successful approach. It is nothing like a majority, but it is a large proportion and it is starting to feel as though the split may be irrevocable.[7]

After the election, with a clear Tory majority, these scenarios have for the moment receded, as the Conservative party itself imposes an even harsher pro-austerity, anti-welfare, anti-trade union and anti-immigrant agenda.

There are however significant strains even inside the hardest of the hard right Tory neoliberals. This is evident in the new levy of ultra-Thatcherites who came into the Commons in 2012 who, unlike UKIP and the traditional Tory right, are socially liberal.

Five of them, Kwasi Kwarteng, Priti Patel, Dominic Raab, Chris Skidmore and Elizabeth Truss, have published a book *Britannia*

---

[6] *The Times*, 30 April 2014.

[7] *The Telegraph*, 20 May 2013.

Unchained: Global Lessons for Growth and Prosperity,[8] which is dripping with vicious right-wing class hatred and a demand to finally end the post-war political settlement which gave workers a welfare state and employment rights. Among its propositions is the idea that: 'The British are among the worst idlers in the world. We work among the lowest hours, we retire early and our productivity is poor. Whereas Indian children aspire to be doctors or businessmen, the British are more interested in football and pop music'.

The Guardian interviewed Dominic Raab, whose key argument was for employment law to be radically altered to enable workers to be more easily sacked, thus imposing a much harsher work regime on workers already suffering from stagnant pay, zero hours contracts and harshly restrictive trade union laws.[9] The British, in fact, are among those who work the longest hours in Europe.

A fake people's crusade

In the run-up to the 2014 European elections, UKIP leader Nigel Farage claimed to be leading a 'people's crusade' against the 'establishment', over immigration, and was prepared to attack 'big business'. But this is a fake and demagogic 'crusade'. In order to deepen and consolidate his party's base outside its long-term petty bourgeois base into sections of the working class itself, it has required some nifty political footwork, disguising the right-wing, pro-business agenda of the party. For example, Nigel Farage repeats that he is 'quite clear' that UKIP's manifesto for the 2015 general election included a state-funded National Health Service, free at the point of need. But Farage has been filmed at an internal UKIP meeting explaining that probably Britain can't afford the NHS, and will have to move over to an

---

[8] *Britannia Unchained: Global Lessons for Growth and Prosperity*, Kwasi Kwarteng, Priti Patel, Dominic Raab, Chris Skidmore and Elizabeth Truss Palgrave/McMillan 2012.

[9] http://www.theguardian.com/profile/dominic-raab.

American-style insurance-based scheme. Farage says that's just a discussion for the future, but it will certainly become active policy in a UKIP or Tory-UKIP government.

Like the US Tea Party movement, the trick is to get tens of thousands of working class and middle class people to campaign for a series of policies that are against their interests. Like lots of right-wing populist parties, UKIP's policies can be a moveable feast, dependent on the whims of the leadership. But established UKIP doctrine promises a raft of measures to undermine the welfare state and the National Health Service, double the number of prison places, and double defence spending and which include:

- A regressive 'flat tax' income tax in which all incomes are taxed at the same rate.

- A reduction of public spending to 1997 levels with the loss of two million national and local government jobs, to be (allegedly) compensated for by the creation of a million new manufacturing jobs.

- Doubling the number of prison places to around 170,000 through building many new prisons

- A five-year freeze on immigration for permanent settlement followed by a 50,000 annual cap. Work permits to be time-limited and overstaying made a crime. No amnesty for illegal immigrants: all returned to home country.

- A five-year minimum wait to obtain British citizenship with no rights to benefits and all asylum seekers to be held in secure units.

- Ending to the active promotion of the doctrine of multiculturalism in schools and other public bodies.

- Deporting dangerous imams, terror suspects and wanted criminals more easily by scrapping the Human Rights Act.

- Scraping the 'politically correct' Crown Prosecution Service and return to local police prosecutions.

- Doubling the defence equipment budget to £8bn, increasing defence spending by 40%, doubling the size of the Territorial Army and increasing total armed forces numbers by 25%, buying three new aircraft carriers and 50 more Typhoon fighter jets, and arming four new submarines with US nuclear missiles.

- Privatising key health services including hospitals and GP surgeries to companies and charities. Creating voucher system to allow people to opt out of NHS system entirely.

- Scrapping key unemployment benefits and invalidity benefits. Paying child benefit for the first three children only. No benefits for anyone who has not lived in the UK for five years.

- Supporting coal-fired power and oppose wind farms and spending £3.5bn on nuclear power plants to provide 50% of energy. Stopping funding UN's climate change panel. Banning schools from showing Al Gore's film, *An Inconvenient Truth*.

- And allowing smoking rooms in pubs.

This demagogic trick of playing on people's hostility to corrupt mainstream politics and claiming to side with the day-to-day concerns of ordinary people, is typical of the new breed of right-wing wing 'populist' parties in Europe like the Front National in France and the Freedom Party in Austria. It is a trick with some nasty historical precedents in pre-war Germany and Italy. In each case closer analysis reveals that these parties ultimately defend the interests of the middle class and big business.

The social basis of UKIP

Robert Ford and Matthew Goodwin have produced an interesting graphical account[10] of the social basis of UKIP support, compared with other parties. Unfortunately this is confused a little by their class categories, especially their catch-all 'professional/managerial class' which includes teachers, CEOs of big corporations, doctors, and social workers, i.e. people from different social classes, but it still provides fascinating insights.

Social class	UKIP	CONSER-VATIVE	LABOUR	LIB DEMS	GREENS
Professional/ Middle Class	30	44	36	43	39
Non-manual working Class	27	28	29	29	27
Manual working Class	42	28	35	27	33
Education: left school at...					
16 years	55	36	40	31	21
17 or 18	21	24	20	19	18
19 or older	24	40	40	50	60
Under 35	12	24	28	32	37
35-54	31	41	38	33	35
55 plus	57	39	34	35	38

Each number shows the proportion of supporters of the relevant party, not the proportion of the electorate who support each party. Table adapted from Revolt on the Right by Robert Ford and Matthew Goodwin

This table does not show the gender and ethnic distribution of support. UKIP has the most male supporters at 57%. The Greens has

---

[10] Robert Ford and Matthew Goodwin, *Revolt on the Right*, Routledge 2013.

the most female supporters, with 56% female as opposed to 44% male, while all the other parties have a slight majority of their supporters being female. Support for UKIP among non-white people was negligible, a not very surprising statistic.

What this table mainly shows is that UKIP has by far the oldest group of supporters, the highest proportion of manual workers, the least educated and the most male group of supporters. By contrast the Greens and the Lib Dems had the most educated and the highest proportion of younger supporters. These figures are no cause for smug contempt from political opponents of UKIP. What they show is that a section of the white manual working class that used to vote Labour now supports UKIP. The racist reactionary right now occupies terrain that was once occupied by the social democratic left. This is a major defeat for all forces fighting for social progress and against racism. Terrain that is lost in this way is very difficult to win back.

Nigel Farage has succeeded in carrying out an operation which has some very unfortunate historical precedents. He and the group around him have maintained their base in the reactionary petty bourgeoisie while at the same time extending it into sections of the poorest and 'left behind' working class. UKIP has succeeded in focusing hostility against 'the political establishment', university-educated professionals, and sometimes even 'big business' - but not of course against austerity or capitalism as such. But UKIP must expand its social base into younger sections of the population or it will simply die out over time.

The Scottish exception

In Scotland the political situation is completely different, because of the national question and the huge majority that rejects the Conservative Party, Thatcherism and neoliberalism. For two decades, Scotland has been a 'no go' zone for Conservatism. After the 2015 election, only one of the 59 Scottish MPs in the British Parliament is a

Conservative – an extraordinary result for the main party of government.

The main Scottish conurbation – the Strathclyde region around Glasgow – has been traditionally radical since the days of 'Red Clydeside' before and after the First World War. For decades it returned mainly Labour MPs with huge majorities. Now all that has changed with the rise of the Scottish National Party (SNP), accelerated by Scottish hostility to the right-wing leadership of the Labour Party in Britain. In the 'devolved' Scottish Parliament, that has a wide range of local powers, the majority party is the SNP and the first minister is the leader of the SNP, until recently Alex Salmond but now Nicola Sturgeon. Labour leads the opposition.

There is simply no room and no ideological sympathy for UKIP in Scotland, which is largely seen as an 'English' party with ultra-Thatcherite views. The party that represent revolt against the establishment in Westminster, and to a limited extent a defence of the welfare state, is the SNP. At the election UKIP won just 47,000 votes in the whole of Scotland, about 1.5% of the total.

The role of the media

Given that the rise of UKIP is universally seen as part of the crisis at the centre of British politics, the question is exactly why did the radicalisation go mainly to the right and not the left? There are several related factors, and of course the record and role of Labour Party and the ideological collapse of British social democracy are part of the answer. A connected part of the same process is the decline in the organisational weight and political clout of the trade unions, which are hobbled from taking effective action by the anti-union laws and in general, politically tail-ending the Labour Party leadership. Labour leader Ed Miliband can get away with saying he will not support strikes or give the unions any promises about what Labour would do in office, because most trade union leaders have no political vision outside the framework of the Miliband leadership itself.

The decline of the organised labour movement of course is a major factor, but the role of television and the newspapers in Britain is often underestimated or even dismissed by socialists in the UK. 'Of course the media is reactionary, it always has been, what do you expect?' is a typical response. But this gravely underestimates the specific role and character of the British media.

The press is overwhelmingly right-wing, and generally rabidly so. The Daily Express, owned by former porn mogul Paul Desmond, is viciously racist and attacks Cameron from the right. Desmond has himself donated £300,000 to UKIP's election fighting fund. The two most widely read papers, The Sun and Daily Mail, are both right-wing Tory papers that have given acres of publicity to Nigel Farage and UKIP. Only the Daily Mirror of the popular 'tabloid' press backs Labour and Miliband. Of the serious 'broadsheet press', the Times is, like the Sun, owned by Rupert Murdoch and backs the Tories, and the huge circulation Daily Telegraph is virtually the house journal of the Conservative right-wing.

UKIP has received millions of pounds worth of free publicity from this right-wing press. By contrast there is in practice a near-total ban on publicising activities of the left, labour movement, the Greens and the peace movement – however large and significant those activities are. For example in July 2014 there were three national demonstrations protesting the Israeli attack on Gaza, each of which was more than 50,000 and two of which were probably over 100,000. These were just ignored by most newspapers, and even downplayed by the left-liberal Guardian, which is extremely circumspect about reporting events involving the far left.

But apart from that, the most widely read papers - the Sun and the Mail, and the Telegraph among the broadsheets – keep up a barrage of right-wing neoliberal propaganda that is frequently racist, sexist, homophobic and always trenchantly hostile to immigrants, the trade unions and the left. A key technique is known as 'monstering': the papers will target someone and throw huge amounts of dirt at that person for days – making them out to be 'monsters', idiots, incompetents or evil. This has been done in the past to George Galloway and Wikileaks founder Julian Assange. Currently it is being done to radical comedian/actor Russell Brand, whose calls for 'revolution' has excited a lot of interest. It is also routinely being done to Labour leader Ed Miliband, portrayed as socially inept, stupid looking and in the pay of 'left wing' unions.

The columnists of the Daily Mail and Express are the functional equivalent of the United States radio and television 'shock jocks', that is people who rant extraordinarily violent tirades against the left, multiculturalism, the unions, immigrants, lesbians and gays or 'political correctness'.

It can of course be pointed out that the circulation of the daily press is in secular decline and is not the main source of news for most people. However older people are more likely to read newspapers and to vote. Newspapers get to a lot of the political right's target audience. Moreover, newspapers own some of the most visited news websites. For example the Daily Mail's website is the most visited English language newspaper website in the world. Visitors are brought there especially by its notorious front-page celebrity gossip column, the core of which content revolves around female celebrities and what they are wearing (or what they're not wearing). This tactic stands in some contrast to the mainly socially reactionary character of the comment of its columnists: a cynical ploy to maximise its political audience and advertising revenue.

In addition, whatever their exact circulation, newspapers play an important role in setting the terms of public debate and news. Key TV news programmes, especially the late night BBC flagship Newsnight, but also Sky News and the BBC news channel, have spots to highlight what's in tomorrow's papers, and frequently have newspaper columnists on their shows.

Of course the main source of news is television. The BBC was savagely attacked by the Blair government for its coverage of the 2003 Iraq war and because the corporation has frequently been attacked by Conservatives for alleged left-wing bias, and crucially it has been threatened by Conservatives with the withdrawal of its license fee and role as public service broadcaster. As a consequence, the BBC news coverage sticks within the framework of the main political parties, and the same is true of ITN, with the exception of the Channel 4 news. Sky TV news (Sky is also owned by the Murdoch empire) is basically Conservative Party news. Panellists brought in to discuss the news are overwhelmingly right-wing and reactionary. In other words, although television news is never allowed to be as rabid as the newspaper columnists, it sticks to a mainly right-wing agenda. In 2014 UKIP leader Nigel Farage was a semi-permanent occupant of television studios. Invitations to Green Party leader Natalie Bennett – which throughout the last Parliament had one MP, Carline Lucas, to UKIP's nil – were very infrequent. And the socialist left is never invited, if not unofficially banned.

In this situation UKIP is cutting with the grain of much media commentary, especially about race and migration, but also about austerity and the economy, while the left and the Greens are cutting against that grain. In this situation building a right-wing alternative is much easier than building a left alternative.

The crux of the matter: racism and xenophobia

In the June 2015 Danish general, the Social Democratic leader Helle Thorning-Schmidt and the government parties were defeated by a centre-right alliance, following a strong showing of the populist right-wing Danish People's Party (DPP). One of the notable things about the election campaign was the similarity in the anti-immigrant rhetoric of the three main parties. This resulted in the most consistent anti-immigrant force, the DPP, being the main beneficiary. Electoral outcomes all over Europe (though not for the moment in Greece and Spain) are being fashioned by the strength of xenophobic anti-immigrant parties. This of course reflects a dominant political discourse that is relayed daily by the mass media and official politics. It feeds off the right-wing interpretation of key events in Europe and world-wide, namely the Mediterranean boat people immigrant humanitarian crisis and of course the linked discourses on Islam and terrorism – most particularly the rise of the so-called Islamic State (ISIS).

As Catherine Thorleifsson points out:

> Populism is threatening to become the new normality in Europe. In response to growing economic and social crises, the radical, far right and populist social movements are experiencing a remarkable surge in support. Across different European contexts, citizens cast their votes for parties with xenophobic roots, rhetoric and policies. This is evident in countries like Greece, France, Hungary, the UK and Sweden, where the radical right forms the spearhead of larger renationalisation processes directed at forces seen as threatening their 'national culture and values.[11]

Fighting back against this reactionary tide is made much more difficult by the abject failure of social-democratic leadership everywhere to confront and repudiate this form of racism. We have moved out of the era in Europe when 'centre-left' parties alternated with 'centre-right' and where significant electoral showings by right-wing populist parties were a rarity. The old form of politics corresponded with the post-war Keynesian welfare state settlement.

---

[11] Europe's thriving xenophobia', Catherine Thorleifsson (https://www.open democracy.net/can-europe-make-it/cathrine-thorleifsson/europe's-thriving-xenophobia.)

The rise of the reactionary right in the last 20 years is the punishment dished out to the left and the workers movement for its inability to prevent economic and social defeats for the working class.

But racism and xenophobia are not just a discourse from nowhere, a 'useful' invention of the right-wing media, plucked out of thin air. Obviously racism and xenophobia are deeply rooted in the history of imperialism and the slave trade. There are deep wells of this poisonous reactionary ideology inside all classes in society, including the working class. Some optimists, especially in the UK, argue that old forms of racism are being defeated by multiculturalism. Sunny Hundal, writing in the Guardian, argues:

The former Tory chairman Lord Ashcroft did a representative survey of British ethnic minority voters last week, and found that 90% think we have become a multicultural country, and a similar proportion say this is a good thing. A broader national survey found that 90% of all Britons also agreed Britain had become a multicultural country, and 70% were in favour of this development.

Just to reiterate: 70% of all Britons think becoming a multicultural country was a good thing for the UK. This is an extraordinary figure, one that certain parts of the country will always hate to accept, and has social and political implications for our country. The poll found that only group where a majority (57%) were opposed to multiculturalism was UKIP voters.

Multiculturalism has become shorthand for a multiracial and multi-ethnic Britain at ease with its modern identity. Right-wing criticisms are therefore seen merely as an attack on modern Britain. The Conservative party's swift condemnation of Tory councillor John Cherry after his remarks on ethnic minority children is another example. It's time right wingers accepted that the apocalyptic future imagined by Enoch Powell, Margaret Thatcher and the Daily Mail never materialised. The British public has seen through the fear mongering and shrugged it aside.[12]

This has a strong element of truth to it of course, especially as regards to young people. But it ignores the contradictions in popular multicultural and anti-racist consciousness. It is quite possible to be for equality, to oppose racism in everyday life, but also to be hostile to further migration and to believe the wilder fantasies of the mass media about Muslim communities. Subjective anti-racist feelings cannot provide a barrier unless the racist anti-immigrant discourse is replaced in popular consciousness with an alternative narrative about the nature of the economic and social crisis through which Europe is passing.

The Labour leadership and the left

Many commentators have picked up on the fact that UKIP has appealed to a section of mainly older, and mainly poor white, working class voters disillusioned with Labour. Racism is widespread in this part of the community as it is in older sections of society as a whole. But in general the tactic of appealing to this constituency on the basis of racism has been enabled by the pathetic inability of Ed Miliband's 'Blairism Lite' to connect with the dispossessed white working class on crucial economic and social issues.

This is not exactly rocket science. If Miliband had just promised a national minimum wage at £10 an hour (not exactly luxury), the banning of zero hour contracts, inflation level pay increases for public sector wages, enforcement of this minimum wage for all workers including immigrant workers, a major programme of house building and a massive expansion of social housing at affordable rents, a wealth

---

[12] 'Multiculturalism has won the day. Let's move on', Sunny Hundal, *The Guardian*, 22 April 2013, http://www.theguardian.com/commentisfree/2013/apr/22/multiculturalism-won-uk-move-on.

tax, significant increases in pensions and welfare benefits for single parents and a national child care system – with just this small basket of proposals a major left crusade against the Tories and UKIP could have been started. This is absolutely not enough and is way below the demands of the militant left, but even this could have swung huge numbers behind the prospect of a Labour government.

Ed Miliband's failure was compounded by his grovelling to the reactionary right over 'tightening' the Labour Party's immigration policy.[13] The debacle of Ed Miliband and the other Labour leaders is just a consequence of the failure of the party leadership to break from the fundamentals of Blairite neoliberalism and propose a significant alternative to the Tories and UKIP.

But the failure of the 'left' is wider. Why is there no left wing analogue of UKIP? Why no left wing formation that can rival the pull of the hard right? Part of the reason is objective. As explained above, while UKIP and the right will always get onto the TV and in the papers, it is always going to be more difficult for the left, who are bitterly opposed by the mass media and traditional politicians. In Britain there is something a virtual boycott of left-of-Labour organisations and radical campaigns on television and in the press.

But an even bigger reason for the absence of a left equivalent to UKIP lies in the failures of the left-of-Labour forces themselves. The Morning Star and its patron, the Communist Party of Britain, has stood umbilically tied to Labour, immobile and incapable of change.

Since the 1970s and the early 1980s the so-called revolutionary left in Britain has numerically declined and been beset by numerous splits and crises. Since the year 2000, there have been several attempts to build a broad political formation to the left of Labour, but they have all failed, mainly due to the blind factionalism of the two major left of Labour groupings, the Socialist Workers Party and the Socialist Party.

---

[13] The Labour Party's election pledge no. 4 was 'Controls on Immigration'. It was so proud of this pledge that it produced a red mug for sale from its on-line shop.

Widespread radicalism and opposition to the reactionary right means absolutely nothing if it is not articulated by a mass party project. It will go nowhere unless and until all the campaigns, demonstrations, coalitions and conferences get focused on building a unified Left Party.

Bulgaria: the rise of Ataka

The rhetoric of Volen Siderov and the rise of Ataka

Martin Marinos and Georgi Medarov

Introduction

At the end of 2013, Bulgaria drew the attention of the international media because of the situation of Syrian asylum seekers. The refugees faced not only dire living conditions in squalid buildings across Bulgaria, but they also witnessed a wave of grassroots demonstrations and border blockades protesting at their presence in the country. Even worse than this was a spate of racist violence that resulted in a series of brutal neo-Nazi attacks against refugees and ethnic minorities. Human rights organisations, including Amnesty International, called on the Bulgarian authorities to act quickly to curb the spiralling violence. All of a sudden, everyone in Bulgaria seemed to recognise the existence of forms of extreme racism, xenophobia and neo-fascism. The mainstream demonisation of the Syrian refugees, coupled with the almost daily physical attacks against them, challenged the widely accepted myth of the 'traditional Bulgarian tolerance' that, among other things, 'saved' the Bulgarian Jews during World War II.

In World War II, Bulgaria had joined the Axis as its ruling classes saw this as an opportunity for realising their nationalist claims for territorial expansion. After the Axis invaded Yugoslavia and

Greece, Bulgaria was allowed to occupy parts of what is now Republic of Macedonia and Northern Greece. Although the fascist character of the Bulgarian authoritarian regime in the 1930s and throughout the war had been exaggerated during the post-1945 period, there were strong pro-Nazi tendencies both within the government and in society in general, such as the paramilitary Union of Bulgarian National Legions (UBNL). The Legions did not object in principle to the collaboration of the Bulgarian government with the Nazis. However, they saw Bulgaria's actions neither as sufficiently pro-German nor sufficiently anti-Semitic, despite the fact that the government had passed anti-Semitic legislation prior to joining the Axis and later participated in the deportation, and hence in the extermination, of most of the Jewish population in the occupied territories. However, deportation was delayed in the so-called 'old territories' (Bulgaria proper) and the Jewish population there was 'saved'. This happened because of a strong resistance from both the elite and from the opposition at a grassroots level in the form of anti-fascist actions.

The anti-fascist movement was led by the communists, under the leadership of Georgi Dimitrov, and included left-wing agrarians, anarchists, but also some rightist military colonels. Without delving into the details of that history, what is key to remember is the fact that the complexities of this period demonstrate the unsustainability of simplistic questions such as 'did the Bulgarians save the Jews or not?', or 'was the Bulgarian government fascist or not?', or 'was the resistance against deportation a product of a tolerant civil society or not?'. Unfortunately, these types of questions are dominant in framing the current debates. However, this history was the result of complex struggles between movements, factions, positions and ideas all of which were in the end socio-political in nature rather than being the outcomes of imaginary innate characteristics of the Bulgarian nation as a whole.

At the end of 2013, the blatant racism against Syrians trying to escape a bloodbath once again made the self-congratulatory and anachronistic claims of 'Bulgarian tolerance' sound hollow. The positive outcome of this realisation was the emergence of a more sober and substantial debate on the high levels of racism in the Bulgarian society. Perhaps, this heightened sense of the dangers of far-right discourse and violence precipitated a strong opposition against an annual neo-fascist march, called the 'Lukov March'. Every year since February 2003, far-right groups from Bulgaria but also from abroad, including from Croatia, Belgium, Romania and Germany, gather in the capital of Bulgaria, Sofia, to commemorate Hristo Lukov - the fascist lieutenant general who founded the Union of Bulgarian National Legions and who was assassinated in 1943 by communist anti-fascist resistance fighters. Conservatives, liberals and centre-left parties, as well as human rights NGOs, activists and radical leftists have spoken out against this neo-fascist march. In 2014, this pressure, coupled with the ugly television images of an attack on a mosque in Bulgaria's second largest city only a few days prior to 'Lukov March', persuaded the authorities for the first time in eleven years, to impose certain restrictions on the organisers. Despite this, the far-right sympathisers of Lukov gathered. They were few and they were not allowed to light torches or march along their usual route. In 2015, similar restrictions were imposed, particularly after pressure by the US and the Russian embassies.

Despite this more acute sense of the high levels of racism in Bulgaria, mainstream political forces continued to rely heavily on the popular cliché about the 'traditional Bulgarian tolerance'. However, this myth obscures the fact that racism is nothing new in Bulgaria. On the contrary, it has been lurking for years with the far-right surfacing at many levels. Violent attacks by neo-Nazi groups have taken place against ethnic (mostly Roma) minorities, LGBT people, foreigners and leftists throughout the post-1989 period. Unfortunately, the authorities and the media rarely mention these attacks. Furthermore, far-right parties participated in various ruling coalitions since 1989. What is more alarming is that practically all the major parties and many political commentators have accepted certain extreme right-wing arguments. For instance, during the series of far-right attacks against refugees at the end of 2013, many in the government and the opposition condemned the violence; but also branded asylum seekers as a 'threat', a 'security risk', as 'terrorists', 'diseased', 'illegals', a 'burden to the welfare system', and as 'illegal economic migrants'. Some even called them 'cannibals'. Thus the neo-Nazi vigilante groups simply stepped into an already existing widespread institutional and media racism.

It is important to note that the critique of the dominant idea of 'the traditional Bulgarian tolerance' should not be replaced with its opposite, that is to assume that Bulgarians are somehow 'inherently' racist. Racism is socially constructed out of existing political relations and social inequalities. Thus it can be challenged only through direct actions and concrete policies rather than through the reliance on empty liberal slogans about 'respecting the Other' or the denunciation of 'discrimination'.

The example of the Syrian refugees is only one instance that demonstrates how far-right rhetoric can become mainstreamed and normalised within societies. In Bulgaria, along with the deepening of social inequalities, rising unemployment and insecurity that followed the collapse of socialism in 1989, extreme nationalist rhetoric also proliferated often cutting across the political spectrum. The real questions are what is it that makes it appealing, how did it become mainstreamed and was there an opening or a moment that precipitated its emergence and success? This chapter focuses on Ataka ('Attack' in English), the first far-right party to enter the Bulgarian parliament in its own right, and more specifically the discourse of its leader, Volen Siderov.

As a prolific writer, journalist and a television host, Siderov has been a major figure in the articulation of the far-right agenda after the socialist period. While he has been playing with far-right language and themes since the 1990s, his political project Ataka became mainstream in 2005. The party has since remained a major element in the Bulgarian parliament, governance and political life. Hence Siderov's rhetoric and the success of Ataka require special attention. Before engaging with the specificities of Siderov's appeal, it is necessary to place him and Ataka within the broader context of Bulgarian nationalism after 1989.

Bulgarian Nationalism

In Bulgaria, the first post-socialist far-right movement was formed in the early 1990s. It was comprised of the nationalist wing of the Bulgarian Communist Party (BCP). In 1989, after a power struggle inside the BCP, the transition to neoliberal capitalism began in earnest. The BCP renamed itself the Bulgarian Socialist Party (BSP) and began a transformation. Part of this process was the return of the right to Bulgarian Muslims to have their original names, which were forcefully changed to Slavic sounding ones in the 1980s. However, this alienated some of the BSP officials who felt marginalised. In particular, these party members felt that nationalist and racist policies should be maintained as part of the programme of BSP and opposed the restoration of Muslims' original names.

After the 1950s, Bulgarian socialism began to rehabilitate itself, although in doing so it adopted key elements of pre-socialist nationalism. On the one hand, this happened by reasserting pre-socialist irredentist claims towards Macedonia, although in a softer manner. This fitted well with the tensions between the Soviet Union and Yugoslavia, a conflict in which Bulgaria had adopted a pro-Soviet stance. On the other hand, this shift also affected the Turkish and Muslim minorities. Once again this reflected the international conjuncture and Bulgaria's position towards Turkey, which sided with the West in the Cold War. The latter process led to the abandonment of the earlier promotion of minority languages, culture and rights and culminated in the forced change of names of all Bulgarian ethnic and religious minorities, (including Muslims, Roma, Pomaks and Turks) to Bulgarian names. Ultimately, this so-called 'Revival Process' led to the expulsion of approximately 300,000 Bulgarian Muslims to Turkey in 1989 in what came to be referred to as the 'Great Excursion'.

The entanglement between communist ideology and nationalism is a multifaceted phenomenon that is beyond the scope of this study. Scholars usually focus on the 'exhaustion' of the earlier more 'revolutionary' ideology during Stalinism (before 1956) to claim that nationalism came as a source of legitimacy after the ideological crisis of the post-1956 de-Stalinisation. However, others have shown that it is a much more gradual shift whereas nationalism was the 'unexpected but inevitable by-product of decades-long policies of mass mobilisation in relatively closed and isolated national states'.[1] Moreover, in Bulgaria, extreme right-wing intellectuals and high-standing military officials, such as, Kimon Georgiev, not only joined the communists, but also occupied key governmental positions.[2] Inspired by Italian fascist corporatism, in 1923 Georgiev participated in the military coup against the democratically elected radical left agrarian government. The coup was followed by a brutal repression against the left. Georgiev participated in another military coup in 1934 after which he shortly served as a Prime Minister.

Some would argue that nationalism could be understood as a consequence of the process of building socialism in one country. Nationalism was instrumental both for criticising 'socialism' in Bulgaria, as well as for its legitimisation, and sometimes for both at the same time. For instance, the Communist Party engaged in nationalist rhetoric at the time of the huge state-led celebrations of the so-called '1300 years of Bulgarian statehood' at the end of the 1970s and the

---

[1] Marinov, Tchavdar and Alexander Vezenkov, 'Communism and Nationalism in the Balkans: Marriage of Convenience or Mutual Attraction?' p. 480 in ed. Daskalov, Roumen, Mishkova, Diana, *Entangled Histories of the Balkans: Vol 2: Transfers of Political Ideologies and Institutions* (London: Brill, 2014).

[2] Marinov and Vezenkov, 481.

early 1980s. At the same time, some 'liberal' dissident intellectuals used nationalist rhetoric against the Communist Party and the Soviet Union by accusing them of not being 'European'. They even compared the Soviet system to the Ottoman Empire on the grounds that they both were 'multi-ethnic' and 'Asian'.[3]

After November 10, 1989, when Todor Zhivkov was replaced after thirty-three years at the helm of the Bulgarian state, the marginalised nationalist hardliners did not approve of the change in policy that allowed the use of Bulgarian Muslim names and, in general, of the sympathetic policies towards Bulgaria's minorities.[4]

They tried to instigate ethnic tensions by staging racist marches and organised attacks. Thus they attempted to regain power during the rapid regime change that was taking place in the early 1990s. Subsequently, the Bulgarian Socialist Party (BSP), that is the reformed communists, managed to re-integrate the disillusioned extreme nationalists in its ranks by granting them powerful positions within the party. In this way, the extreme right was pacified and they softened their rhetoric.

A prominent figure in the nationalist movement within the BSP was Georgi Parvanov. Not only did he join the ranks of BSP, but he also managed to earn a powerful position and was elected twice as the President of Bulgaria (2001 and 2006) as a candidate for the BSP. His successful political career tamed his earlier extremism, and he turned into a rather moderate nationalist. Nevertheless, in 2007 he was instrumental in fuelling the nationalist hysteria against the historians Martina Baleva and Ulf Brunnbauer who were scheduled to present academic papers at a scientific conference. Their topic was on the

---

[3] For more information on the debates about the socialist regime's national politics see Maria Todorova, *Bones of Contention: The Living Archive of Vasil Levski and the Making of Bulgaria's National Hero* (Budapest: CEU Press, 2009).

[4] On the 10 November 1989, Zhivkov was 'retired' in an internal coup within the Communist Party. Most Bulgarians refer to this process as the 'changes' and view it as the end of socialism in Bulgaria.

social construction of the popular memory of Ottoman repressions that followed the quelling of the uprising of April 1876. However, Baleva and Brunnbauer were accused of denying the repressions. This was despite the fact that they never did this, but rather explored the historical transformation of the representation of the Ottoman violence. Parvanov, who was President at the time, used his position and his training as a historian, and along with other conservative nationalist intellectuals, waged a media war that alleged that Baleva and Brunnbauer were 'hired' by 'the West' to 'falsify' history. This scandal culminated with the banning of the conference. There were also violent threats in the media against the scholars and even the burnings of books by a few extreme nationalists.

In 2013 Georgi Parvanov distanced himself from the BSP. However, the BSP has been in a formal coalition with a fringe anti-Semitic and extreme nationalist party called 'New Dawn'. At the end of 2012 and at the beginning of 2013, the BSP cooperated with other far-right organisations during a campaign in support of the construction of a new nuclear power plant in Bulgaria. Moreover, in 2013 the BSP headed a minority government formed with the support of Ataka, the largest far-right party in Parliament. Ataka managed to get 23 MPs (out of 240) elected and their support was needed to form a minority government composed of the BSP and the Movement for Rights and Freedoms (DPS) a liberal party supported by large parts of the Turkish minority. This enabled the exclusion of the centre-right GERB (this literally translates as 'coat of arms', but it is also an abbreviation of Citizens for European Development of Bulgaria) that had won a majority of the votes and 97 of its members became MPs. After it backed a government that included the so-called 'Turkish' party DPS, Ataka's electoral support fell dramatically and in the European Parliament elections in 2014 they were unable to get even one MEP elected.

The history of the BCP, and subsequently of the BSP, demonstrates that many commentators are correct to focus on the 'communist' origins of the Bulgarian far-right. However, the rest of this chapter argues that one should not underestimate the role of anti-communists in mainstreaming the far-right. In fact, far-right ideologies and nationalist trends were a major part of the anti-communist intellectuals' ideology. For example, in the 1980s Iliya Minev headed one of the major anti-communist human rights groups. Minev spent decades in prison and was harshly persecuted under Zhivkov. However, his persecution does not mean that he was a liberal democrat. Between 1941 and 1944 he was active in the pro-Nazi paramilitary movement called the Union of the Bulgarian National Legions and he never ceased to describe himself as a nationalist. After 1989, liberal activists revered him as a victim of communism and a model human rights activist, despite the fact that in the 1990s he wrote articles that denied the Holocaust, spread anti-Semitic conspiracy theories, rejected liberal democracy and praised Nazi Germany. But Minev is not the only point of intersection between the anti-communist movement and the far-right.

During the 1990s, the anti-communists were united in a big coalition called the Union of Democratic Forces (UDF). It was comprised not only of social democrats and liberals, but also included a small extreme right-wing party called the Democratic Forum (DF). The DF was not strong either in terms of electoral support or membership, but it was influential within the UDF. For instance, when the UDF was able to form a government alone for the first and only time in 1997, it was a DF member (Muravey Radev) who was appointed the Minister of Finance. Furthermore, it was Radev who signed the agreement with the IMF that imposed a currency board, austerity measures and structural adjustment. The DF claimed to be the continuation of the pro-Nazi Union of the Bulgarian National Legions, although they denied that the Legions were ever anti-Semitic and fascist. In 2001, the UDF collapsed into a number of smaller parties and the DF became marginal. However, it continued to be instrumental in the rehabilitation of Bulgarian Nazis through, among other things, its support of the annual 'Lukov March'. In the previous parliamentary elections of 2013, the DF campaigned in coalition with Democrats for a Strong Bulgaria (DSB). DSB was formed in 2013 as a conservative party that now heads a new right-wing and anti-communist coalition called the Reform Bloc (RB). Although the DF did not enter the RB, the DSB never expressed remorse for their involvement with the far-right. Some RB activists have claimed that Ataka is not 'authentically' nationalist because it is allegedly pro-Russian and that 'real' nationalists should be anti-Russian. Moreover, some RB activists have often expressed concerns about the fact that 'too many' Bulgarian Roma are voting in elections. This is coupled with extremist rhetoric about 'clashes of civilisation' between the 'tolerant West' and the 'oriental Asian empire', along with conspiracy theories about 'foreign spies' and 'communists in disguise' secretly pulling strings from behind the curtain.

Ataka, and Volen Siderov's own example, is even more telling of this often ignored side of the rise of the far-right in Eastern Europe. The 2009-2013 government, which was led by the centre-right GERB, enjoyed the support of Ataka. Furthermore, GERB did nothing about the fact that Ataka organised an attack against the mosque in Sofia during Friday prayers in May 2011. This should come as no surprise since Boyko Borisov, the leader of GERB, once argued that the only problem with the so-called 'Revival Process' (the above-mentioned forced renaming of Bulgarian Muslims during late socialism) was that it was not executed 'properly' In addition, GERB's extreme anti-communism also contributes to their conservative historical revisionism regarding Bulgaria's role during World War II. This is particularly clear in their positions regarding Macedonia's demands that Bulgaria should recognise the atrocities during its occupation of the region in World War II. Thus GERB could be viewed as a continuation of the 1990s anti-communist rhetoric, which advocated a very similar understanding of Bulgarian history. They deny the role of the anti-fascist resistance because, they maintain, there was no hint of fascism in Bulgaria during that period.

These examples illustrate that the explanation of how the far-right in Bulgaria gained a mainstream status will be incomplete if one ignores the anti-communist discourse of centre-right and liberal ideologues and parties. But in order to fully understand the formation of the far-right, it is necessary to look more carefully into its most visible form, Ataka and its leader Volen Siderov. Siderov took his first political steps as a dissident, anti-communist and a member of the UDF. Since 2005, Ataka had not only supported both centre-left and centre-right parties, but it generally sets the agenda for the far-right in Bulgaria.

Ataka

Until 2005, Bulgaria remained somewhat of an exception in the region because it lacked a 'consolidated racist extremist movement or aggressive nationalist leader'.[5] However, after the parliamentary elections of 2005, Ataka changed this situation. It needs to be noted that Ataka's 'unexpected' success came precisely at the moment when the national elites had firmly established a stable neoliberal consensus. The two-party model of the 1990s had collapsed after 2001 and practically all parties adopted technocratic ideologies, presenting themselves as 'neutral experts' supporting EU Accession, NATO membership, the establishment of US military bases, active support for the wars in Iraq and Afghanistan, in addition to economic liberalisation. Founded only six weeks prior to the elections, Ataka stunned many commentators after it won 9% of the vote. At that point, many thought that this far-right party was an ephemeral phenomenon. But in 2006, its leader, Volen Siderov reached the run-

---

[5] Cas Mudde 'Introduction' in *Racist Extremism in Central and Eastern Europe*, ed. Cas Mudde (New York: Routledge, 2006), 2.

off for the presidency with Georgi Parvanov and won 24% of the vote. In 2007, the year Bulgaria entered the European Union, Ataka obtained 14% of the vote in the country's first election for the European Parliament. The party continued to consolidate itself and in the national parliamentary elections of 2009 it gained over 9%. Wrecked by internal scandals and falling approval ratings, few expected Ataka to enter parliament for a third consecutive time. But in 2013, riding the tide of massive protests against the high prices of electricity, Ataka once again proved resilient and managed to get over 7% of the vote.

Throughout its nine years of existence, Ataka has not only created a solid niche of support and a platform for its discourse, but it has also played an important role in governance. As previously stated, this included participation in informal coalition with two governments in a row. It is usually assumed that Ataka appealed solely to the so-called 'losers of the transition', namely social groups that were marginalised due to the negative effects of economic liberalisation. This assumption was sometimes paired with the assertion that Ataka is 'anti-capitalist' or 'left-wing'. However, this is highly exaggerated. For example, in the 2005 elections there was hardly any support for Ataka in small towns (which were hit the hardest in the 1990s) and most of their votes came from regional cities.[6] These successes, along with the fact that until 2014, Ataka remained the only far-right party to enter in its own right into the Bulgarian Parliament since 1989, calls for a special attention to its discourse.

Since 2005, Ataka has experienced a series of deep crises resulting in numerous withdrawals of MPs from its parliamentary group, as well as new additions to its core. The party also navigated through shifting alliances and complex relationships with different

---

[6] See Nadege Ragaru 'Prepletenite Vremena na Nastoyashteto', (Sofia: KiH, 2009) pp. 311-312.

political parties and protest movements. Hence, it has had to adjust its political actions and rhetoric to the unstable postsocialist political landscape. For these reasons, it is not an easy task to summarise its political identity during its tumultuous decade-long existence. However, what is crystal clear about Ataka is the fact that it is a political party almost entirely dependent and based on its leader, Volen Siderov.

Almost every issue of Ataka's newspaper (also called 'Ataka') includes a photograph and a statement by Siderov. Across Bulgaria, billboards advertising Ataka's television network, 'Alfa', feature a large portrait of Siderov. To put it concisely: Siderov is the face and the voice of Ataka and he acknowledges this. As he says, everybody knows 'very well that I am the main engine of this idea and political formation'.[7] In his latest book, *Foundations of Bulgarianism*, he speaks to the country's youth and asks them to 'follow my experience, my example, which I provide you with in my battle for Bulgaria…use what I have created, to join me […]'.[8] Siderov, runs the party as his own property, at one point appointing his wife as the editor-in-chief of the party's newspaper, his father-in-law as a coordinator of the party, his stepson, an undergraduate student in his third year, as Ataka's MP in the European Parliament (the 22-year-old Dimitar Stoyanov, became the youngest MP to ever enter the Parliament) and placed a number of his cousins as regional coordinators.[9] His most loyal colleagues also understand the importance of Siderov to the party.   Dessislav

---

[7] Volen Siderov, *Moiata Bitka za Bylgaria* [My Battle for Bulgaria] (Sofia: Boomerang, 2007), 20.

[8] Volen Siderov, *Osnovi na Bylgarizma* [Foundations of Bulgarianism] (Sofia: PP ATAKA, 2011), 98.

[9] This clan-like structure came to an abrupt and acrimonious end in 2011, after it became public that Siderov has an affair with Denitsa Gadzheva, the leader of Ataka's youth structure and a girlfriend of his stepson and MEP, Dimitar Stoyanov. At this point, Kapka, Siderov's wife divorced him and left the newspaper. So did his father-in-law and Stoyanov.

Chukolov, Siderov's right-hand man, named his son Volen in honour of Siderov.

This reveals that if one wants to understand Ataka's discourse, there is no better place to begin than Siderov's rhetoric. In fact, Siderov has a point in chastising commentators and scholars who described Ataka's entry into parliament as a 'surprise' and an 'unexpected event'. He claims that:

> The truth is that 300,000 Bulgarians voted for an idea that I have developed for years through hundreds of articles, books, and almost 700 television shows on the Skat television network. Neither did I come out of the woods yesterday nor did I fly in here with a UFO. For the last ten years I have not stopped writing and talking about the need of nationalism here, of the need to trigger the immune system of the Bulgarians. Well, in the tenth year the effort bore fruit.[10]

The rest of this chapter takes this claim seriously and traces the emergence and development of Ataka's ideology through an examination of Siderov's five books, three of which were published a few years before Ataka's appearance on the political stage.

Two of the books consist of collection of articles and speeches. One of them, *Bulgarophobia*, compiles a selection of articles published by Siderov between 1998 and 2002 when he was deputy editor of the Bulgarian newspaper *Monitor*. The other collection, *My Battle for Bulgaria*, includes a selection of articles and speeches published and delivered by Siderov between 2005 and 2007 as a leader of Ataka. *The Boomerang of Evil* (2002) and its sequel *The Power of the Mammon: Who Robs Us and How?* (2004) are Siderov's first and most popular and controversial books. The fifth and most recent book, *Foundations of Bulgarianism*, was published in 2011. Through the analysis of these

---

[10] Siderov, *Moiata Bitka*, 20.

works this chapter focuses on the intellectual foundations of Siderov's thought that has fed the discourse of Ataka during the last decade. The analysis shows that although occasionally Ataka and Siderov tend to engage in a discourse that resembles leftist arguments, the intellectual roots and development of the movement and its leader belong to the far-right of the political spectrum.

As mentioned above, much of the research analysing the rise of nationalism in Eastern Europe after 1989 focused on the transformation of former communist ideologues into nationalists. Siderov regards himself as an anti-communist 'rebel' who was 'persecuted, but never subdued'.[11] In the biographical note on the cover of his books he writes that

> [...] He participated in the dissident anti-communist movement before 10th November 1989 and in the creation of the political opposition to the Communist Party, the Union of Democratic Forces (UDF), as well as the free press. One of the few who has never been connected with the Bulgarian Communist Party and the secret services of the communist regime.

Before 1989, he belonged to Iliya Minev's 'human rights' organisation called the Independent Association for Defence of Human Rights (IADHR) (see above). Siderov praises Minev as the 'Bulgarian Nelson Mandela', and claims that he was 'a true dissident, unlike the pseudo-dissident careerists who rushed to join political parties or were simply opportunistic converts from communism to liberalism'.[12]

Siderov's anti-communist activities were rewarded in 1990 when he became the first editor-in-chief of the first liberal newspaper *Demokratsia*, a mouthpiece of the UDF. During these years, Siderov

---

[11] Siderov, *Moiata Bitka*, 212.

[12] Siderov, *Bylgarofobia*, 121.

advanced neoliberal, anti-communist and pro-Western rhetoric, which were the trademarks of the UDF. The anti-communism of *Demokratsia* led it to engage in extreme right-wing historical revisionism. It actively denied Bulgaria's flirtation with fascism in the late 1930s and ignored the occupation of parts of Yugoslavia and Northern Greece where the Bulgarian forces actively participated in the persecution of the Jewish population. After Siderov left *Demokratsia*, he remained a prolific journalist and among other things, he continued to work as a deputy editor at *Monitor*, a daily newspaper. Throughout the 1990s Siderov's rhetoric became much more nationalistic, anti-Semitic, conspiratorial and anti-Western. He himself declares that he 'evolved' and is 'not ashamed' to admit that to people who ask him how could he change from being a dissident and an editor of *Demokratsia* to being a nationalist.[13] But the 'evolution' in Siderov's thought is not consistent. His ardent anti-leftist rhetoric remains in place, but it is now buttressed by conservative, anti-Enlightenment, Orthodox Christian views and anti-Jewish conspiracy theories.

Siderov against the left

Siderov claims that 'the inclination to the left is an inclination towards death'.[14] His condemnation of Marx ranges from criticisms of his thought to *ad hominem* attacks that present him as a drunk who 'dedicated poems to Satan' and at one time impregnated his servant.[15] For Siderov, Marxism is a Jewish worldview. In fact, he often speaks of 'Judeo-Marxist' or 'Judeo-Bolshevik' thought and represents it as a plot by Jews and Freemasons to destroy Orthodox Christianity. Thus in his most controversial and most read two-hundred page long book, *The*

---

[13] Siderov, *Osnovi*, 3.

[14] Volen Siderov, *Bumerangyt na Zloto* [The Boomerang of Evil] (Sofia: Boomerang, 2003), 95.

[15] Sideov. *Bumerangyt*, 56 and 84.

Boomerang of Evil, he dedicates thirty pages to a list of names of the major participants in the October Revolution along with their ethnic origins, the vast majority of whom he brands as 'Jews'. He argues that 'the Bolshevik revolution in Russia toppled the last monarchy in Europe that was dangerous for Talmudism, the Romanov's'.[16] Furthermore, he still sees danger in Marxism today because it continues to be 'enriched' by 'neo-Marxist Jews' such as Erich Fromm and Herbert Marcuse who under the slogan of 'leftist' ideas keep alive 'the bacteria of nihilism, of the destructive anti-Christian force, called socialism, communism and nihilism'.[17] In his nationalist worldview, Marxism remains a major enemy for Siderov because 'the thesis about the death of the nations is Marxist'.[18]

In addition, Siderov attacks economic policies associated with the left. According to him, the idea of equality is one of the biggest flaws in Western thought:

> Omitting the simple fact that people are born with different talents and skills, the social engineers from antiquity to the present examine only the issue of redistribution of wealth without taking into account the individual.[19]

Similarly, Siderov is not in favour of full employment, free healthcare and education because they translate into 'abysmally low wages'.[20] With regards to the contemporary situation in Bulgaria, he expresses views that could only be uttered by a person with strong neoliberal views. For instance, in *Bulgarophobia* he includes a piece published in 2001

---

[16] Volen Siderov, *Vlastta na Mamomna: Koi I Kak ni Ograbva* [The Power of the Mammon: Who Robs Us and How] (Sofia: Boomerang, 2004), 156.

[17] Siderov, *Bumerangyt*, 95.

[18] Siderov, *Bylgarofobia*, 132.

[19] Siderov, *Bumerangyt*, 48.

[20] Siderov, *Bumerangyt*, 93.

in which he criticises the focus of political commentators on the left and argues that instead they should be concerned with the 'health of the right', because the right will take care of Bulgarian business. He also condemns all parties for their concern with 'small' and 'medium' businesses and claims that 'big business' is what will bring high incomes. He admits that 'it is true that during the last years we saw 'big businessmen' who were simply Mafiosi', but asks whether 'because of drunk drivers we should halt the entire street traffic?'[21]

When Siderov established Ataka and entered parliament in 2005, few people paid attention to his anti-communist background, as well as to the anti-leftist, anti-Marxist and economically right-wing threads in his discourse. Instead many analysts focused on the social and anti-IMF slogans peppered throughout Ataka's discourse. According to the Dutch scholar of the far-right, Cas Mudde, 'the Bulgarian Ataka presents its preferred economic model as 'social capitalism'.[22] In Bulgarian political discourse most commentators also believed that Ataka is economically 'ultra-leftist'.[23] But this interpretation of Ataka's emergence is not necessarily a misunderstanding on the part of commentators and analysts. Ataka did engage, and continues to engage, in a rhetoric that could also be found in the discourse of many leftist parties.

Siderov's flirtation with the left

Rhetorical criticism of liberal capitalism can be found in Siderov's books. He maintains that the IMF and the World Bank rob people across the globe. To support this, he quotes people such as Joseph

---

[21] Siderov, *Bylgarofobia*, 262.

[22] Cas Mudde, *Populist Radical Right Parties in Europe* (Cambridge: Cambridge University Press, 2007), 122.

[23] Antonii Todorov, 'Prezidentskite Izbori v Bylgaria prez 2006 Godina' [The 2006 Presidential Elections in Bulgaria], Politicheski Izsledvania 1 (2007): 81.

Stiglitz, Noam Chomsky, Greg Palast, and John Pilger. Furthermore, Siderov makes arguments that are nothing short of bold, when as early as 1998, he criticised Western-style capitalism, NATO and the European Union. Such criticisms were rare at that time.

In 1998, Siderov argued that the constant talk about corruption is a smokescreen that prevents discussion of the most important problem for Bulgaria – the low wages. According to him, the purpose of the low wages is to create 'a reservoir of manual labourers for the wealthy West'[24] and that 'political commentators repeat: corruption is the major problem of Bulgaria, everything else is fine. This is equal to claiming that everything is fine with a disabled person except that the bolts of his wheelchair should be tightened after which he will be a self-sufficient human being.'[25] In addition, Siderov reminds his readers that corruption exists not only in Bulgaria, but also in the United States as revealed by the Enron scandal.

As early as 2000, Siderov declared 'the end of the transition and the beginning of class warfare'. And that 'the real time has come for the unions and the writers from Zola's tradition.'[26] He criticises media and politicians for avoiding terms such as 'capitalism', 'wage worker' and 'labour value'.[27] He also criticises the EU and claims that it does not want 'a wealthy Bulgaria but only seeks its cheap labour'[28] His criticism of the EU continues and in his 2011 book he argues that Bulgaria's five years in the EU has led to 'nothing good' but only to requests to 'tighten the belts'.[29]

Siderov also attacks privatisation, while also criticising the omnipresent discussion of the need for revealing all ex-secret agents.

---

[24] Siderov, *Bylgarofobia*, 11.

[25] Siderov, *Bylgarofobia*, 11.

[26] Siderov, *Bylgarofobia*, 163.

[27] Siderov, *Bylgarofobia*, 163.

[28] Siderov, *Bylgarofobia*, 403.

[29] Siderov, *Osnovi*, 98.

He argues that the secret files with the names of the collaborators of the communist era State Security apparatus are a 'children's song' in comparison to the files of the unlawful privatisation deals that have emptied the treasury during the privatisation process.[30]

This type of discourse continued after Siderov's entry in parliament. In his first speech there, he declared that with the election of Ataka, the Bulgarian nation declared that it 'no longer wants to be placed under the experiments of the IMF and the world usurer's oligarchy.'[31] He also attacks Bulgaria's participation in the 'dirty, unlawful war in Iraq' while 'it has no money for medicines and computers in the schools.'[32] This type of critical statement that resembles leftist rhetoric remains a part of Ataka's discourse to this day.

However, it would be erroneous to conclude, as many commentators did, that this section of its discourse turns Ataka into an economically 'leftist' movement (see above). But, this also does not mean that Ataka is purely a right-wing party advocating free market and neoliberal values. Instead a careful analysis of its rhetoric reveals that the left and right divide is something that it criticises while it advances nationalism, a factor that it sees as the 'immune system of the nation'.

Siderov's nationalism as a global alternative

Siderov explains that 'after 1989 from the thesis of 'communism' and the antithesis 'capitalism' was born a new synthesis - globalisation, a new world order.'[33] He maintains that, the 'communist East' and the 'capitalist West' were led into a clash that gave birth to a New World

---

[30] Siderov, *Bylgarofobia*, 253 and 433.

[31] Siderov, *Moiata Bitka*, 5.

[32] Siderov, *Moiata Bitka*, 5.

[33] Siderov, *Bumerangyt*, 212.

Order based on anti-nationalism and anti-Christianity and which laid the foundations of a super state - 'the empire of the Antichrist'.[34] To fight this 'New World Order' one does not need to be on the right or the left. He writes that 'it is clear that the right and the left are a chewing gum for dupes - for seven million Bulgarians, who under a foreign scenario must split into two teams that fight against each other, until they drop dead'.[35] Needless to say, his attack of the New World Order includes a strong anti-Western sentiment. This demonstrates Siderov's transformation from a pro-Western anti-communist to a nationalist who sees the West as an oppressor. He explains this change of heart with his disappointment of the double standards and lack of concern of the West.

'When the Berlin wall fell in 1989, we the dissidents against the communist regime in Bulgaria, thought that all the requirements of the human rights convention would be implemented'.[36]

However, gradually Siderov understood that the 'capitalist globalist system [...] is just as unfair and oppressive as the communist one, but through more perfidious means'.[37]

Siderov's transformation could not be explained solely based on his criticism of contemporary developments (i.e., 'the Iraq war,' 'Western double-standards'). Neither could it be explained simply as an attack on uneven capitalist development. His criticism is more 'complex' and goes all the way back to antiquity. Within Siderov's Christian Orthodox, anti-Enlightenment worldview, the problems of the West start with Plato. He claims that in The Republic, Plato lays the foundation for the centralised state without private property and the family, military discipline, forced labour and other 'unnatural' acts against the 'God given' order which was later embraced by the

---

[34] Siderov, *Vlastta*, 77.

[35] Siderov, *Bylgarofobia*, 7.

[36] Siderov, *Moiata Bitka*, 67.

[37] Siderov, *Osnovi*, 4.

communists.[38] Siderov traces the revival of Platonism during the Renaissance when 'to quote Aristotle' was just as prestigious as it is today for 'a Bulgarian snob to throw a citation of Baudrillard or Derrida.'[39] According to him, neo-Platonism revives atheist, pagan and materialist thought. Thus Siderov asks whether capitalist western democracies and communist totalitarian regimes are not 'twins', and he quotes long passages of Plato's The Republic to prove their common origin.'[40]

The anti-Christian strain of thought of the ancients continues to be a problem for Siderov even today. According to him, the EU constitution is 'based on the values of ancient Greece and Rome and the philosophical anti-Christian currents of the Enlightenment, while it fails to mention even a word about the Christian roots of Europe and the European civilisation.'[41] From its inception in ancient Greece to today, Siderov views the West as imbued with materialist, anti-Christian and anti-spiritual thought. The Enlightenment is the supreme example of the triumph of these values. Furthermore, the Enlightenment is precisely the ideal base for 'Marxists and Bolsheviks' but also for 'capitalists': 'The anti-Christian fury of Voltaire was declared a brilliant ideal for 'communists' and 'capitalists' in a dubious synchrony.'[42]

For Siderov, the Enlightenment and the Renaissance borrow from the ancients the idea of humanism, which regards the human as 'one's own master,' independent of, and therefore in opposition to God. For him communists also read 'bourgeois' thinkers such as Montesquieu and Rousseau because their 'struggle against God' connects them (Rousseau and Montesquieu) with the left. Thus the

---

[38] Siderov, *Bumerangyt*, 48-49.

[39] Siderov, *Vlastta*, 80.

[40] Siderov, *Bumerangyt*, 61.

41 Siderov, *Vlastta*, 352.

[42] Siderov, *Bumerangyt*, 57.

Enlightenment 'elevates godlessness to 'scientific' proportions and paves the ground for the emergence of contemporary communism'.[43] For this reason, he argues that the Middle Ages are wrongly labelled as 'dark' and 'reactionary'. In fact they were a time of 'flourishing of Christian morality in a healthy synchrony with secular rule'.[44] However, Jean-Jacques Rousseau destroyed this synchrony and separated secular and spiritual power, while Descartes and Kant made things worse when they defined man as 'rational and nothing else'.[45]

It is not surprising that Siderov condemns the French Revolution, which he describes as 'the first communist putsch' and argues that until 1789, 'France was the richest country in Europe'.[46] He also claims that 'Louis XVI did not allow even one shot against the lumpens who wanted to lynch him', but in contrast the revolutionaries engaged in tremendous violence.[47] To support his position, Siderov relies heavily on Edmund Burke, a philosopher widely popular among reactionaries around the globe. 'Slaughters, torture, gallows! These are your human rights! [...] I never dreamt of witnessing such misfortunes'.[48] In fact, Burke is one of the most approvingly cited scholars by Siderov. Nietzsche is also cited frequently (with great disapproval) because this 'sick mind' was instrumental in the struggle against God and for this reason was 'equally appreciated' by communists and Nazis.[49]

---

[43] Siderov, *Bumerangyt*, 64.

[44] Siderov, *Vlastta*, 56.

[45] Siderov, *Vlastta*, 90 and 93.

[46] Siderov, *Bumerangyt*, 63.

[47] Siderov, *Bumerangyt*, 63.

[48] Siderov, *Bumerangyt*, 69. It must be noted that Siderov lacks citations in his book that links his myriad of quotes to concrete works. Instead he has a list of works cited at the end of his book, but one can only wonder where in the book they were used (if they were at all).

[49] Siderov, *Vlastta*, 97.

With this criticism, Siderov intends to show that unlike the spiritual Orthodox East, the West is based on materialism, godlessness and violence. Thus he seeks to undermine the cult towards Western values and commodities in postsocialist Eastern Europe. This criticism often results in conclusions bearing a strange resemblance to postcolonial and anti-colonial positions. This is not surprising because attacks on globalisation and (neo)colonialism are not always progressive as the far-right constantly exploits legitimate concerns about the (lack of) popular sovereignty and national dignity. Thus Siderov reminds the reader that some of the first capitalists in England earned their millions through the slave trade and notes that many of the founding fathers of the United States were slave owners.[50] However, as already stated, such attacks on uneven capitalist development, despite their odd similarity with a world-system analysis, are included in a broader framework of extreme right-wing orthodox fundamentalism and nationalism, with a simplified critique of neoliberal globalisation, understood only as inequality between nations and regions stemming from unequal international trade and financialisation. In other words, if social critique is reduced only to inequalities between nations it opens a space for appropriation by the far-right that uses the anti-globalisation rhetoric inside a conservative framework, ignoring class inequalities and conflicts.

This anti-Western sentiment is coupled with an attempt to undermine the anti-populist discourse in Bulgaria that tends to represent the common people as 'backward' and Bulgaria as inherently inferior to the West. For example, in 2001 after the UDF lost the elections, a chorus of liberal intellectuals blamed the loss on the 'retrograde nature' of the Bulgarian people. Siderov quotes a commentator who after the UDF's electoral defeat asked 'what else do you expect from this bumpkin nation?' In fact, he claims that nationalism is precisely the antidote to this liberal rhetoric because it

---

[50] Siderov, *Vlastta*, 212 and 213.

calls for respect for 'the most desperate individual from your nation, the one who is poorly dressed and without teeth'.[51] The anti-populist, snobbish rhetoric is not only akin to postsocialism, but it has historical precedents. For example, Siderov calls for Bulgarians to prove wrong the 19th century Bulgarian poet and politician Petko Slaveykov who famously stated that 'we are not a people, but carrion'.[52] He attacks this type of liberal discourse and argues that 'a poison has been inserted in the nation's organism' through the idea that 'the Bulgarian person in comparison to the 'great' Westerner is simply a nonentity'.[53] Siderov calls on Bulgarians to abandon this disparaging discourse that puts Bulgarians as inferior to the people in the West.

Siderov's nationalism: beyond left and right?

How can one interpret Siderov's often contradictory rhetoric that made him the most successful radical right politician in Bulgaria's post-socialist history? On the whole, with its anti-Semitic, anti-Enlightenment and Christian fundamentalist components, his language resembles that of other reactionaries across the globe. But at the same time how do we interpret his criticisms of the IMF and the World Bank, his anti-colonial rhetoric as well as his occasional reliance on authors such as Noam Chomsky? The answer is contained in the fact that Siderov views nationalism as a new force that opposes globalisation. Furthermore, he argues that nationalism is the only defence system against neoliberalism because both the traditional left and the liberal right have already fully embraced globalisation. Ataka was born at a moment of retreat of the mainstream left and the consolidation of a consensus supportive of neoliberal capitalism. Siderov and Ataka understood this well and took advantage of the

---

[51] Siderov, *Osnovi*, 93.

[52] Siderov, *Bylgarofobia*, 22.

[53] Siderov, *Osnovi*, 18.

political homogenisation. Siderov mocks the left in Bulgaria for 'being to the right of Thatcher' while he ridicules his former colleagues in the UDF for being so deferential to the West that they would 'support a nuclear explosion in the middle of Bulgaria if only Washington requests it.'[54] In other words, Siderov notices an exhaustion and ideological crisis both on the left and the right. While the Bulgarian Socialist Party moved to the right embracing neoliberal governance, the liberal right remained entangled in uncritical praise of Western-style neoliberal capitalism, despite the fact that more and more people began to notice its contradictions. Thus Siderov calls for criticism not only of Moscow, but also of Washington and Brussels and for discussions not only about the KGB but also about the CIA.

Throughout these discussions, Siderov's nationalism is portrayed as the genuine alternative to globalisation. He claims that the trap of contemporary global capitalism is the division between 'left' and 'right', 'just as the trap of global communism was class theory pitting groups of people from the same nation against each other.'[55] Instead, according to Siderov, class struggle can easily be avoided because 'the employer' and 'the wage worker' as well as the 'different layers can work and coexist in harmony, if there is national consensus from top to bottom.'[56] Such statements signal that his alleged 'anti-capitalism' is rather of a corporatist type that tries to replace inter-class conflict with collaboration. But for this to happen, nationalism needs awakening. This is why he often refers to nationalism as 'an immune system' that needs triggering. Siderov sees himself as a catalyst of this awakening or triggering. As early as 1998, seven years before he established Ataka, he saw an opportunity to push this narrative. He witnessed the emerging disillusionment after the euphoria in the early 1990s and most importantly he noticed a petrification of the hegemonic liberal

---

[54] Siderov, *Bylgarofobia*, 26 and 411.

[55] Siderov, *Osnovi*, 93.

[56] Siderov, *Moiata Bitka*, 287.

discourse. Its clichés about the threat from Russia, the communist state security apparatus, the constant discussion of the secret files and purification, and the relentless defence of the free market began to form another 'langue de bois'.[57] Siderov felt the emerging sterility of this discourse and promptly attacked it in his writing. Thus for him, the post-socialist repetition *ad nauseam* of the phrase 'open society' is equivalent to the trope 'classless society' during state socialism.[58] Similarly, throughout his writings he claims that many Bulgarians find the hollow phrase 'functioning market economy' just as meaningless as the slogan 'developed socialist society' from the previous era.[59] Because of this stultification of liberal discourse and the ideological exhaustion of the division between the traditional left and right, Siderov declares that 'the new times call for nationalism'.[60] In terms of the international situation, Siderov sees nationalism as something that will help Bulgaria outlive the European Union just as it helped it outlive 'the barbarian Turkish Empire' and the 'totalitarian Soviet Empire'.[61]

But should we take Siderov at his word that nationalism is beyond left and right? Should we think of it as some sort of an amalgamation between the two (*i.e.*, welfare state combined with racism and xenophobia)? In this sense, Ataka's discourse bears affinities with corporatist attacks of historical fascism on liberal capitalism which aimed at establishing a society in which 'everyone would know their place'. A class society without class struggle.

---

[57] 'Langue de bois' became widely used in reference to bureaucratic language in general but in particular the phrase implied Soviet and Eastern European dull language employed by bland and aging communist apparatchiks remote from everyday reality.

[58] Siderov, *Bylgarofobia*, 9.

[59] See for instance, *Bylgarofobia*, 407 and 438.

[60] Siderov, *Bylgarofobia*, 281.

[61] Siderov, *Moiata Bitka*, 256.

After all, he does not shy away from identifying himself and his political party Ataka with the extreme right of the political spectrum. In a direct quote in an article written as early as 1999, he states that the 'right-wing nationalist movements in Europe' are the only ones that 'resist total globalisation'.[62] Once Ataka gained prominence he claimed that the party 'became part of the European nationalist space and legitimised itself as a European party'.[63] He follows the rise of the far-right in France and Austria and praises Jorg Haider and Jean-Marie Le Pen. Furthermore, he states that in Bulgaria whoever is scared from Le Pen is a person who 'had not come out of his communist-internationalist diapers in which we were wrapped for decades'.[64] With this identification with the far-right in Western Europe, Siderov reveals a vision of the EU that is not 'Eurosceptic' in the way liberal commentators mean it. Instead he claims that Ataka will work for the 'transformation of the EU from a pyramidal totalitarian structure into a democratic community of equal trade and cultural partners in Europe of nations and homelands, as de Gaulle wished'.[65] Needless to say this reliance on de Gaulle and the desire to build a common European community directly contradicts Siderov's occasional anti-colonial statements.

Siderov's anti-globalisation statements need to be placed in a larger context. Once one has read his work, it is easy to conclude that his criticism of the world's 'usurer oligarchy', which includes the IMF and the World Bank, does not stem from a left-wing position. Instead, Siderov is after an enemy who allegedly pulls the strings from behind the curtains; specifically, by this he means the Jews and 'their secret societies'. Siderov's anti-Semitism brings him to admire Holocaust deniers such as his 'colleague and personal friend' Jürgen Graf, Paul

---

[62] Siderov, *Bylgarofobia*, 75.

[63] Siderov, *Moiata Bitka*, 331.

[64] Sderov, *Bylgarofobia*, 381.

[65] Siderov, *Moiata Bitka*, 261.

Rassinier, Robert Faurisson and others.[66] His racism, Islamophobia and anti-Semitism derails his occasional accurate criticisms of world politics. This happens in very overt ways. For example, after quoting Chomsky on imperialism in *The Boomerang of Evil*, Siderov finds it necessary to inform the reader that although Chomsky is a 'Jew' and an 'anarchist' in many of his texts he speaks the truth about the double standards of the US.[67]

The racist side of his argument often overwhelms his discourse. Could there be a leftist party in Bulgaria that ignores the plight of the Roma population - the poorest and the most oppressed, minority in Bulgaria? Despite Ataka's lip service to welfare provision, the Roma and ethnic Turkish minorities (a total of more than 15% of the population) are completely excluded from receiving assistance. For instance, Ataka's leader opposes monetary assistance to families who have a second child, 'because this money goes to those who give birth without thinking, these are mainly the Gypsy families.'[68] His Islamophobia, which is very pronounced, works in similar ways. He maintains that 'the Turks' are 'ignorant, stupid and idle' people who 'have no science of their own and have made no contribution to physics, mathematics and chemistry. Not to mention, art and literature.'[69] Such anti-welfare rhetoric reminds us that fascism and liberalism were never simply in an antagonistic relationship and that the boundaries had always been porous.[70] In fact this became crystal clear after the national parliamentary elections in 2014 when even pro-EU mainstream politicians adopted racist language to legitimise

---

[66] Siderov, *Bumerangyt*, 10 and 168.

[67] Siderov, *Bumerangyt*, 199.

[68] Siderov, *Moiata Bitka*, 294.

[69] Siderov, *Bylgarofobia*, 99.

[70] See Ishay Landa, The Apprentice's Sorcerer: Liberal Tradition and Fascism. London: Haymarket, 2012.

austerity measures by presenting anti-welfare policies as directed against ethnic minorities.[71]

Siderov's legacy

After the 2014 European elections many mainstream commentators in Bulgaria seemed satisfied that no 'Eurosceptic' party managed to get seats in the European Parliament. Ataka lost its two MEPs with only 3% of the vote due to electoral dissatisfaction with its support of two governments in a row, including the DPS in 2013.

However, at present Ataka is challenged mainly from the right, largely on the grounds that it is not 'authentic' and nationalist enough. Even nominally liberal politicians and activists tend to attack Ataka as supposedly serving foreign (Russian) interests. That is to say, such challenges are not coming as an external, new discourse, but from within the very discourse Ataka and Siderov spent so many years creating. Newer far-right parties, that are now growing in influence, such as Bulgaria Without Censorship (BWC) or more importantly The National Front for the Salvation of Bulgaria (NFSB), which split from Ataka, are challenging Siderov's party explicitly from a far-right nationalist perspective. During the European Parliament elections at the end of May, the BWC got 10% of the vote and two of its candidates were elected to the European Parliament. The NFSB did not get a seat in the European Parliament but received 3% of the vote.

The results obtained by the BWC were the 'big surprise' in the 2014 elections. Nikolay Barekov, a mainstream journalist who was among the most vocal public supporters of GERB and its leader Boyko Borisov, only recently established the BWC. When GERB won the elections in 2009, Barekov excitedly pleaded in his personal blog for

---

[71] Tsoneva, J. ,'Bulgaria's Creeping Apartheid, Part I: Mobilizing Racism to Shrink the Social State' In *LeftEast*, 2015 http://www.criticatac.ro/lefteast/bulgarias-creeping-apartheid-ii-liberal-dehumanization.

Borisov to become 'a Bulgarian Pinochet' in order to 'save Bulgaria'. However, in early 2013, just when GERB's government was about to collapse in the midst of anti-austerity protests, Barekov felt disillusioned with Borisov and radically changed his allegiances, later establishing 'Bulgaria Without Censorship'.

BWC was initially a TV show hosted by Barekov. It consisted of big public debates held in squares of dozens of cities around Bulgaria during which all kinds of dispossessed and marginalised groups were invited to share their truly heart-breaking stories of misfortune and suffering. Angel Slavchev who began his political career as an activist for a small radical left party called the Bulgarian Left joined Barekov. Although he used to call himself 'Che' while he was still a member of the Bulgarian Left, Slavchev always claimed that left/right distinctions are a thing of the past and that now is the time for a true national unity against 'foreign threats'. Barekov follows a similar line, arguing for a 'capitalism with a human face' and for 'wild capitalism to only exist in the history textbooks'. However, at the same time, he openly calls for support for big business. Neshka Robeva, an ex-gymnast who worked as the choreographer of a series of grandiose nationalist-volkish dance spectacles, is one of Barekov's supporters. At one point she claimed that what she enjoyed the most about the BWC is the fact that it is 'not a political, but an artistic project'. What could be a more literal reminder of Walter Benjamin's famous claim that fascism gives to the 'masses not their rights, but instead a chance to express themselves'. Surely fascism is too strong of a qualification, but the BWC already adopted extreme right-wing positions against Syrian asylum seekers and entered into a coalition with one far right party.

One of the new MEPs elected on a BWC ticket is Angel Dzhambazki. He has been a member of a far-right party called IMRO – Bulgarian National Movement. However, Dzhambazki has also been a mainstream politician. For instance, he served as a city councillor in Sofia elected with the support of GERB. He actively participated in far-right mobilisations against the annual gay pride marches, as well as in organising the neo-Nazi 'Lukov March' and other similar events. He also collaborated with violent neo-Nazi groups such as 'National Resistance' - a violent group inspired by the *Autonome Nationalisten* in Germany. All this makes him the most right-wing MEP that Bulgaria has had until now.

In the national parliamentary elections in the end of 2014, the National Front for the Salvation of Bulgaria (NFSB), formed a coalition called The Patriotic Front (PF) together with IMRO and got over 7% of the votes. PF entered the new ruling coalition together with mainstream centre-right and liberal parties such as GERB and the Reform Bloc. Daniel Smilov, an influential Bulgarian liberal political scientist, called this new coalition 'the most ideologically pure' possible, omitting the fact that NFSB called for interning Bulgarian Roma in concentration camps in their program. Nevertheless Smilov might have been right as even mainstream pro-EU politicians from the new government have used extreme racist language. For example the healthcare minister Petar Moskov said that the Roma are 'animals' and announced his plans to limit their access to emergency healthcare.

In the midst of the racist hysteria at the end of 2013, another extreme and openly neo-Nazi party called the Nationalist Party of Bulgaria was formed. The ex-Ataka activist Simeon Kostadinov leads it. It also ran in the European Elections, but their results were an utter failure, with only 0.1 % or about 2,600 votes.

Another new party was formed before the 2014 elections, this time as a split from the BSP and led by Georgi Parvanov. It is called the ABV - standing for the first three letters of the Cyrillic alphabet, as well as an abbreviation for 'Alternative for the Bulgarian Revival'. The ABV did not succeed in getting an MEP elected but nevertheless they got 4% of the vote. The ABV cannot be dubbed far-right, but it surely has a nationalist appeal. They were more successful during the national parliamentary elections at the end of 2014 and also entered the new ruling coalition.

Thus one can conclude that Ataka was instrumental in mainstreaming the extreme right discourse. But paradoxically, Ataka's very success is its greatest failure as the mainstreaming of extreme right rhetoric made it more difficult for Siderov to maintain monopoly over it. Its dominant position within the far-right is now being challenged on many levels. There are many disillusioned voters who claim that Ataka is not nationalist enough and they search for alternatives that ironically operate within the discursive space constructed by Ataka itself. Furthermore, major parties feel threatened by the far-right and have adopted many of their positions. The mass media have been complicit with these developments, further entrenching the role of the far-right in contemporary Bulgaria and securing its position in mainstream politics.

By tracing the far-right discourse of Siderov's party, we have shown that Ataka managed to give a voice to the discontent with the new postsocialist inequalities, and with the general social and cultural decline after the collapse of socialism. But, although occasionally mimicking leftist rhetoric, Ataka has articulated these new anxieties within a xenophobic and racist framework that extols Christian Orthodoxy and 'Bulgarianess' while it attacks the left, the West, and in general the Enlightenment and its Renaissance and Greco-Roman roots. This discourse has led to a complex web of affinities with the extreme right-wing and neoliberalism's own anti-left assault, which scapegoats the weakest sections of the population.

Right-wing populism and the Danish People's Party

Tobias Alm

When talking about right-wing populism in European countries, Netherlands, Austria, Switzerland and Italy are often mentioned, but Denmark is rarely referred to, and if so, only as an afterthought. This is strange, given that since 1995 there has been a right-wing populist party, the Danish People's Party - DPP (*Dansk Folkeparti,* DF), which has had crucial influence during the ten years from 2001 when the party supported the Conservative-Liberal governmental coalition, and which was the third largest party in Denmark for almost a decade.

Danish right-wing populism is not a mayfly. Discrimination, xenophobia, and harsh regulations for the asylum seekers have become an accepted and integral part of the political scene and the public discussion. This is a shift from the late 1980s as the society underwent a displacement of interests and needs.

Socio-cultural or value-driven political themes like violence, crime, child abuse, and migration have become more important during that period while socio-economic questions regarding tax and labour policies became less important. Migration has been linked to many of these socio-cultural themes during the last decades. This has meant that refugees and immigrants in general have become the scapegoat for several social problems, including violence and theft. The Danish People's Party has managed to use this shift in society to its advantage.

Right-wing populism and xenophobia

The right-wing populism as a phenomena arose in the 1970s. The lawyer Mogens Glistrup founded a new party, the Progress Party (*Fremskridtspartie*), in 1972 as a protest against bureaucracy in public administration and high taxes in order to promote a liberal fiscal policy.

The following year, the Progress Party made a great impact on the political scene when they gained 15.4 % of the votes in what is called the 'earthquake elections' of 1973, and became the second biggest party. Party culture was characterised by internal chaos and unstructured and provocative attitudes. Despite this, or maybe because of this, the Progress Party had important electoral support until the late 1970s. During that time and until the early 1980s, the party was very popular amongst members of anti-communist and far right groups. The 1980s saw the beginning of the party's decline. Through a spectacular gimmick, Mogens Glistrup tried to turn the tide: in an attempt to expose the inadequacies of the tax policy he turned himself in for tax evasion. The court system reacted with no sense of humour and imprisoned him. The then unknown Pia Kjærsgaard became the new party chairperson, but this did not help the party as it went into a free fall in the next elections in 1983, gaining only 3.8 % of the vote.

After his release, Mogens Glistrup started a campaign against immigration, in particular Muslim immigration, in particular against a new, less restrictive, immigration law adopted in 1983. He managed to connect the theme of immigration with social issues, and succeeded thereby in associating negative images with the refugees and migrants. Glistrup gained a degree of support for his anti-Muslim approach and continued this throughout the 19080s and 1990s. The Progress Party's new role, as a xenophobic party, became the cornerstone in the later success of the Danish People Party.

The second cornerstone was laid in 1987 when the Danish Association (*Den Danske Forening*, DDF) was established. It was led by the priest Søren Krarup and supported by a group of unorganised newspaper columnists and xenophobic groups from the extra-parliamentary far right.

The main policy of the DDF was opposition to immigration, especially of Muslim. It made a great effort to promote this by connecting the fight of the resistance movement against the Nazi occupation in Denmark during the Second World War to their ideological fight against immigration today. The DDF claimed that Denmark was under a grave threat at that time and it is also today. Resistance against immigration is necessary today, just like resistance against the occupation of the country by the Germans. The ideologues in DDF created an image of defending the country from immigration and especially immigration from Muslim regions. Islam was put on the same footing as Nazism, thereby justifying anti-Muslim racism. The DDF is indeed a major key in explaining why Denmark was moved rightwards.

Several central members of DDF later became Members of Parliament for the Danish People's Party. Ever since the foundation of the DDF, it has seen itself as the intelligentsia of the extra parliamentary fundamentalist right. The DDF developed an ideology, argumentation and a strategy that the Danish People's Party, along with other right-wing groups have either adapted, copied or at the least been inspired by.

From chaos to established party

Pia Kjærsgaard and other former members of the Progress Party founded the Danish People's Party in October 1995 after political disagreements inside the party. Some of the most able members of the DDF also joined the new Danish People's Party. The Progress Party never regained its popularity, and the media and politicians did not give the new Danish People's Party many chances. They were wrong.

The presentation of the new party's policies became much more professional. The founders of the new DPP put aside the chaos and scandals that were part of the Progress Party. Problems were now handled inside the party and not outside in the public domain. Immigration and integration were at the core of the party's policy, and the strategy was to make a constant connection between these issues and socio-cultural questions such as crime and violence. This connection offered a coherent global view to the voters.

Another contributing factor for the success of the Danish People's Party was its political rhetoric. Political terms and academic language were avoided from the beginning in a successful attempt to demonstrate that politicians from the Danish People's Party spoke in a language that everybody could understand. Ultimately, an aggressive media strategy exposed the image of a professional party. The Danish People's Party was from a very early on always present in the public sphere. The content its message was often of secondary importance, whereas the primary message was clear: 'The Danish People's Party has an opinion and is it there for you'. That message was understood.

People joined the Danish People's Party because it was communicating in a professional way the same message that was expressed by the DDF and the Progress Party. Social Democracy was not capable of preventing the success of the Danish People's Party and lost many members to the new right-wing party as it took over some of the traditional social democratic key issues. Already in 1998, the Danish People's Party gained 7.8 % of the votes. Many elderly people moved to the right when the social democrat Poul Nyrup Rasmussen, as Prime Minister between 1993 and 2001, broke his central election pledge and reduced the rights to retirement pensions.

In 2001, the Danish People's Party reached a milestone and became a fully recognised and established party, gaining 12 % in the general elections and becoming the third largest party. In order to succeed with his announced 'system change', the new Prime Minister Anders Fogh Rasmussen (leader of the Liberal Party, *Venstre*) and his Liberal-Conservative coalition government had to depend on the Danish People's Party to get a parliamentary majority. The Danish People's Party was very happy to be in this position. Firstly because it got a lot influence on policies with the threat of putting the government in a minority, and secondly, it managed to present itself as an anti-elitist party giving the powerful a hard time and being the true representative of the Danes. The Danish People's Party used this beneficial position to its limits. For instance, they managed to push through massive restrictions on immigration legislation every eight month on an average during the ten years it supported the coalition government.

The Liberal Party and the Conservatives gladly accepted the threats of the Danish People's Party and continued taking into account its reaction when drafting new laws, in particular immigration legislation affecting people from countries outside the EU, especially non-Western countries, who wanted to settle in Denmark. By the end of 2010, the law had been tightened to the point where it became almost impossible for people of non-Western origin to gain residence permits.

After ten years of massive hostility against Muslims, opinion polls showed that voters had become tired of the constant debate about Islam and Muslims. These themes no longer had the same appeal to the voters. The Danish People's Party noticed this change in public opinion and reacted right away, now directing its focus towards the supposed Eastern European gangs that came illegally to Denmark to work, steal or beg.

This became very clear when the coalition parties forced the Danish People's Party to a compromise on retirement regulations, which was one of the party's favourite themes. Just before the negotiations, Pia Kjærsgaard, the leader of the Danish People's Party, said that there could be no compromise on this topic. However, the party could not stick to this promise, and it became a threat to the credibility of the party. The Danish People's Party tried to deflect the attention from this political mistake by creating a media stunt: it demanded the reintroduction of the border control to stop the 'thousands of Eastern European gangs'.

The reintroduction of border controls created a stir in Europe and was only a feeble attempt to keep the supposed Eastern European gangs out of the country. The main purpose was damage control and to raise its profile as a hardline party on immigration. The focus was shifted from Islam to Eastern European gangs, in a hope to score points on the party's usual topics. The tactic did not work and the party experienced its first-ever electoral downturn in its history, thus helping the centre-left parties to take over the government at the 2010 general election. The electoral setback for the DPP was only 1% and the party still obtained 12 % of the vote in these elections, which were held shortly after the assassinations by Breivik in Norway. This demonstrates that the Danish People's Party has a strong and faithful electoral base.

The main themes of the Danish People's Party

The main theme running through the DDP's programme is a comprehensive anti-immigration stance and, in the end, a policy of completely excluding certain ethnic or religious minorities from integration into the Danish society. This agenda is reflected in the constant flow of regulations of asylum and immigration laws for which the party has been the main architect.

The racist focus is not limited to these two themes. It keeps continuously re-emerging in debates that are not directly addressing immigration and integration. The Danish People Party wants to present itself as the heir of the struggle for women's liberation of the 1970s and as defending gender equality. However, one may search in vain in their political programme for an independent policy in this area. The Danish People's Party believes that equality has already been achieved in Denmark. Therefore, the struggle for equality is not defined by progressive feminist positions but only as restrictions against people who do not support equality.

'After 100 years of women's struggle, we as Danes see the equality of women as a matter of course. But not everyone agrees with us on this,' we are told in the film *Equality* on the website of the Danish People's Party's. Taking into account the focus on immigration by the party, it is obvious who is being addressed by this remark, namely immigrants from non-Western and Southern European countries, who it is believed do not accept these progressive values. But it is especially people with a Muslim origin that are being attacked. Their culture and religion is being presented as being backwards, hostile to women and marked by violence and immorality.

Everyone is lumped together. The Danish People's Party's so-called struggle for equality has included the demand to ban burkas and the description of all Muslim men as paedophiles, rapists and criminals. Muslims are being presented as repressed victims, without an opinion of their own. Jesper Langballe, a member of the Danish People's Party in Parliament, wrote in an article in the daily *Berlingske Tidende* on 22 January 2010, that the anti-Muslim author Lars Hedegaar 'should not have said that Muslim fathers are raping their daughters, when the truth is that they are satisfied with killing their daughters (the so-called crimes of honour) and accepting of the sexual violence of the uncles'.

The Danish People's Party's opinion regarding homosexuals repeats this pattern. Policies in this area are only used to differentiate themselves from those they claim to be the 'suppressors'.

Almost all of the argumentation by the Danish People's Party is founded in exclusion, discrimination and national preference. There is no exception when it comes to the struggle for freedom of speech, which has been presented as if it were threatened by 'immigration', 'anti-racism', 'human rights' and 'political correctness'. Oppressive elements in the cultures of immigrants are emphasised, and the corrupt elite, the established parties and the political left are attacked as 'traitors'.

Søren Krarup made this clear in the daily *Jyllands-Posten* on 21 October 2000: 'I regard the Danish People's Party as a resistance movement, in which I can serve my national military service against the national betrayal committed by our members of Parliament. They accept thousands of refugees and immigrants each year at the same time that immigrant gangs destroy and terrorise the Danes and by doing this, they are breaking up the nation'.

The Danish People's Party regards itself as the representative of the true popular voice and a counterpart to the traitors. An immutable picture is being constructed with a 'We' and a 'You'. The 'You' stands for immigration and integration, which is a threat to Denmark. The 'We' is the Danish People's Party and its followers, defending 'Danishness', as defined by them. There is only contempt for the traitors who are placed with the 'You'.

Policies regarding the European Union and protection of the environment follow the same pattern The Danish People's Party is an unconditional opponent of the EU and rejects all kind of interference in national affairs of Denmark.

The frequent international disclosures of infringements of the international standards of asylum rights are completely ignored, as they are seen as irrelevant and an inappropriate interference in national affairs. According to the Danish People's Party, the Danes are becoming a threatened minority inside the EU. These examples show that a significant part the political agenda of the Danish People's Party is based on discrimination, exclusion and nationalism.

The left and the Danish People's Party

The politicisation of the socio-cultural questions has created big problems for the left in Parliament. The discussion of these themes was not confronted with convincing counter arguments or with alternative proposals. The field was left wide open for the right, and a permanent fear of losing voters led to concessions to the right. The result was that the positions of the left, especially that of Social Democracy, was almost invisible. The consequence was a left that was frightened, almost without its own positions, and pushed by the smear campaign of the right.

The xenophobic propaganda was barely being addressed politically. On the contrary, the rhetoric and the demands coming from the right were often adapted by Social Democrats (*Socialdemokraterne*) in a softer version.[1] This led to a break with former Social Democratic ideals, and an opportunistic political line that made it more difficult to distinguish between the parties.

Disillusioned Social Democratic core voters shifted to the Danish People's Party, as it was seen as the new party for workers and elderly people. These two groups felt that the traditional labour parties, Social Democrats and the Socialist People's Party (*Socialistisk Folkeparti)* had left them in the lurch.[2] The Socialist People's Party has carried out a revision similar to that of the Social Democrats in recent years, but in a much faster and calculated rendition. Both parties have even used themes such as gender equality and homosexual rights to direct a 'cultural criticism' towards immigrants, especially Muslims.

A crucial realignment between the left and the Danish People's Party occurred in 2012 in order to reach a compromise on a transport policy, the Social Democrats led government, supported by the Red Green Alliance (*Enhedslisten – De Rød-Grønne*) invited the Danish

---

[1] The Social Democrats (*Socialdemokraterne)* is the traditional social democratic party of Denmark. It was established in 1871 and is a member of the Party of European Socialist in the EU Parliament, along with the Labour Party.

[2] The Socialist People's Party (*Socialistisk Folkeparti,* SF) was established in 1959 by former members the Communist Party of Denmark (DKP) following their criticism of the Soviet intervention in the Hungarian Revolution of 1956. It is to the left of the Social Democrats, and gained 13% of the vote in 2007, but dropped to 4.2% in 2015.

People's Party to negotiations. This was a temporary political defeat for the parliamentary left. Any attempt to reject collaboration with right-wing populists had become history and the left was assisting the right in gaining power and influence. The signal was given that the Danish People's Party is a party worth collaborating with.

The acceptance by Danish People's Party to this collaboration and the lack of ability of the left to set the agenda had two enormous consequences. First of all, the recognition of the Danish People's Party by the other parties gave legitimacy to the party and its policies. Secondly, the adaptation to the right-wing populist agenda meant that the policies of the Danish People's Party gained a wide audience and the party spread its influence far beyond its own ranks. Without the ideological support and the lack of opposition in the political field, the media and among the public, the political reach of the Danish People's Party would have been limited to its own core voters.

As mentioned above, not only did the parties of the centre recognise the Danish People's Party and are thereby gave respectability to the party and its ideology, but the parliamentary left also contributed to this process.

The far right threat minimised

In Denmark, there is a powerful tendency to identify the far right with Nazism, instead of recognising it as a political current with its own identity. That leads to minimising the problem and creates a conviction that racism and far-right ideologies have little importance in Denmark.

The idea of Denmark being a place that gave birth to 'tolerance' is part of this construction. The perception is of a tolerant people, supporting equality between the sexes or the existence of Christiania.[3]

---

[3] Christiana is a self-proclaimed autonomous neighbourhood, or commune, of about 850 residents in Copenhagen that was established in 1971. A special law, the Christiania Law of

In some ways, this perception of tolerance has a real basis, but it is problematic as it creates the generalisation of an image of Denmark. Less progressive aspects of the welfare state are seldom presented. In 2004, a survey revealed that two out of three respondents believed to live in the best country of the world. At that time, the right-wing coalition government, supported by the Danish People's Party, had been in power for three years and was pushing the laws and using rhetoric that was influenced by the DPP. Did the two out of three respondents in this poll welcome this move to the right, or are facts and perceptions being ignored in order to maintain the illusion of Denmark being the best country in the world? It is probably a combination of both. In this context, it is important not to forget that the danger of racist and discriminatory rhetoric is being minimised, or tolerated under 'freedom of speech', thereby being depoliticising the threat from the far right.

In 2010, the Danish National Centre for of Welfare Social Research carried out a research on discrimination, the results of which are summed up by Tina Gudrun Jensen[4]: 'The general results of our studies have been that there is very little focus on those topics out and about. It is something about the way in which we, in Denmark, are being controlled by an equality ideology that tells us we are all alike and there are no differences in the way we are being treated'.

By pretending that we are all treated in the same way, discrimination becomes subtle. This is about negative hidden expectations and prejudiced behaviour that ethnic minorities are confronted by and have to deal with, when applying for a job or for a place at college. Studies show that most of us downplay that racism and discrimination is happening and that when we have to recognise

---

1989, which transfers parts of the supervision of the area from the city of Copenhagen to the state, regulates the area.

[4] Tina Gudrun Jensen is a Professor at the University of Copenhagen and a researcher at the Danish National Centre for Welfare Social Research.

it, we then blame the individual rather than everyday social or institutional practices. '

Racism exists in Danish society but is not addressed as a collective or institutional problem, instead it becomes an individual problem. In this way, the perception of the Danish tolerance is maintained.

The Danish People's Party is very successful in areas where the number of migrants is actually relative small. This fact shows that prejudices and racism are alive when the targeted victims are not present. The prejudices are being defined, interpreted and reflected by the political agenda of the parties and by the media, and ordinary people then adopted them, whether they know an immigrant or not.

A study carried out in 2010, *Migration and integration policy in Denmark and Finland - a special Nordic way?*,[5] concludes that there is a kind of welfare populism in Denmark and Finland that sees the welfare and the social security system, and their set of values, being threatened by immigration. The survey conclude that the Danish and Finnish welfare models are closed systems in which the states and the societies have difficulties in dealing with immigration and in some cases ignores it. As the author puts it: 'On the basis of the study, it is obvious that Denmark and Finland as role models for other countries, is not a reality in regards to the field that has been investigated.' According to the report, the claim is not true that Denmark and Finland are role models for other countries to follow when it comes to migration and immigration policies.

It is time to adjust the national as well as the international perception of Denmark according to the reality, and there is one sentence that could describe Denmark today: 'Welfare? Yes! But not for everyone.'

---

[5] *Migration und Integrationspolitik in Dänemark und Finland - ein nordicher Sonderweg?* Jenny Bonin, May 2010, University of Rostock, Germany, http://d-nb.info/1005814902/34.

A nationalism that claims not to be one

It is striking that in Denmark there is a positive view of the country and its population. When challenged, there is a refusal to admit that this has something to do with nationalism. Peter Bejder and Kim Boye, in their book about Danishness,[6] write:

> Nationalism is something negative. You stress your own country, your own population or own cultures. However, that is not how the Danes do. For us, it is more like a national feeling. National feeling is something positive. It's also called love for your country – love for your fatherland.

That a positive national feeling contains a potential exclusion of others and necessarily must include negative consequences is being ignored.

Peter Gundelach does not share these considerations: 'Saying that something is Danish means that other things are not.'[7]

We are already witnessing that the adoption of positive values, and then transforming them into 'Danish values', is part of a process of Danish self-identity. Pia Kjærsgaard, leader of the DPP and Member of Parliament, says that: 'cosiness, spontaneity and good mood are characteristics we often identify as being Danish. We are a nation with a sparkle in the eye and a good mood.' Pointing out things as positive in this way makes it clear not only what being Danish is, but also points out what is un-Danish and thus not positive.

The law defines very well who is Danish, who is not, and who may be. The very restrictive immigration policies indicate who can get through the eye of the needle to become a member of the Danish community, however there are no guarantees. Not even your birth is a

---

[6] *Dansk, Danskere og Danskest - Om Danskhed* (Danish, Danes and *'Danskest'* - About Danishness), by Peter Bejder and Kim Boye Holt, 2004.

[7] Peter Gundelach is Professor of Sociology at the University of Copenhagen.

guarantee to becoming a Dane, as demonstrated by expressions like 'second' and 'third' generation immigrant. If a person with such a label commits a crime, they face the risk deportation to a country where they were not born or ever lived, but their family once upon a time, had originated.

It is not the development of a strong right-wing populism that makes Denmark different to other countries like Italy, Switzerland and the Netherlands. What stands out is the image of normality accompanying this development and the ability of the Danes not to look at themselves. The tolerant, open and progressive Denmark does not exist in this form today.

An organised smear campaign against refugees and immigrants is unfolding without provoking an outcry and being seen as a scandal. No-one is committing suicide by making with racist statements and caricatures of ethnic minorities. There is a process of 'positivation' of your own past and the present that allows an uncritical identification with your own state and your own people. Positive values like tolerance and equality become so-called 'Danish values', and proclaimed as a basic element of society, and which all Danes understand as Danish values. Contradictions and failures of society are not discussed, and if they are, these are exclusively being blamed on 'foreign' cultures.

The right-wing populist project of Danish People's Party to push public opinion to the right is certainly promoted by a conscious media strategy, but it would not have had not succeeded if there was no social pre-conditions. One can certainly fear that the right-wing drift has only begun. Recent opinion polls show the Danish People's Party at the same, if not higher, level as the Social Democrats. It could be an easy victory for centre-right parties and Danish People's Party.

Postscript: the DPP after the 2015 elections

Michael Voss

The outgoing governmental coalition, headed by the Social Democrats, suffered a stinging defeat in the elections held on 18 June 2015. But so did the Conservative Party, the leading party of the right-wing opposition. The winners were parties outside the political mainstream.

The 2011 election brought a centre-left governmental coalition to power, headed by the Social Democrats. The moment the new government was formed, it began disappointing its electorate as it was sticking to the economic policies of the EU Commission and of the previous government

Confronting each other in the 2015 election campaign was the media-dubbed 'Blue Block' and 'Red Block'.

The Blue Block consisted of five right-wing parties: the Conservative People's Party (*Konservative Folkeparti*), the liberal party (*Venstre*), the nationalist and xenophobic Danish People's Party, the new ultra-liberal party Liberal Alliance and the Christian Democrats.

The Red Block was that of the parties that supported the leader of the Social Democrats and outgoing prime minister Helle Thorning-Schmidt in her bid to form a government: the Social Democrats, the social-liberal party 'Radikale', Socialist People's Party (part of the government until 2014), the Red-Green Alliance and the completely new party The Alternative. In Danish parliamentary tradition there is no explicit political support implied in supporting a party leader for prime minister.

With a narrow majority, the Blue Block won the elections. Altogether, the three parties that took part in the former governmental coalition had suffered a defeat, losing 12 seats in a Parliament of 179. They were punished for pursuing neoliberal austerity policies. The two junior partners of the outgoing coalition government, the Socialist People's Party and the Radikale party, suffered most heavily: they lost more than half their previous votes.

The big winner of the elections was the Danish People's Party. It increased its share of the vote from 12.3% to 20.1%. This has come as a tremendous shock not only to the left wing and other progressives, but also to the whole political establishment.

The DPP built itself on nationalist, anti-migrant and anti-refugee policies. They had a big influence on this issue on the right-wing coalition government from 2001 to 2011 without being part of it.

Over the years they have succeeded in setting the political agenda, and have influenced both the other right-wing parties, as well as the Social Democrats and the Socialist People's Party, in a way that turned the recent election campaign into a competition as to which party is most 'tough on refugees'.

But xenophobia is not enough to understand the growth of the DPP. Over the years, it has projected itself more and more as a party that supports welfare and the public sector. In the 2015 election, the DPP campaigned for growth of the public sector.

The DPP also promised to improve unemployment benefits that they themselves helped cut in 2010. On this issue they actually took a position to the left of the Social Democrats.

This is fundamental in understanding the success of DPP. It has taken up policies that have been abandoned by the Social Democrats and has therefore been able to win huge numbers of former SD-voters.

The Red-Green Alliance increased its votes from 6.7% to 7.8%, improving its result on the 2011 elections in which the party had tripled its share of the votes. The radical and anti-capitalist left has never been so strong in Parliament. The RGA in particular was not dragged down along with the governmental parties by being identified with the government's austerity policies.

France: Pétain's children

Commission Nationale Anti-Fasciste, NPA

Translated from the French
by Bernie Gibbons and Bill McKeith

> *'I'm going into this battle. And take my union gun.*
> *We'll end this world of slavery*
> *Before this battle's won. You're bound to lose.*
> *You fascists bound to lose!'*
> 'All You Fascists', Woody Guthrie

Introduction

During an online interview given on 2 October, 2013 to the weekly *L'Express*, Marine Le Pen stated: 'We are absolutely not a right-wing party, those who think this are making a complete error of analysis.' She continued: 'I reject still more the formulation of far right', before threatening 'legal action' against those who characterised her party, the Front National (FN), in this manner.

Dominated by the hegemonic position of the Front National for forty years, the French far right presents a problem for the anti-fascist and social movement with its longevity and ability to rebuild itself when apparently reduced to silence. Despite the splits and strategic confrontations which have sometimes seemed to have grip it, the French far right has succeeded in maintaining itself on the political scene.

How has this current, completely discredited after the Second World War because of its collaboration with Nazi Germany and its active participation in the Vichy regime, successfully pulled off the feat of creating the conditions for unity around a 'nationalist front', and becoming an unavoidable element of the French political landscape, to the point where Sarkozy, Copé and part of the UMP (*Union pour un Mouvement Populaire*) adopt the language of the FN to demagogically seduce its voters – in spite of the inadequacies of its programme and its absence of a stable social, economic and political line?

We propose here to review the premises of the creation of this unique 'nationalist compromise'. Adapting a supposedly anti-systemic discourse against successive majorities, the Front National has consistently sought to intervene in the political debate to inject the two themes on which it is based: national preference and immigration, two facets of the same authoritarian and anti-social project. After having covered the history of the Front National, which the rest of the European far right envies to extent of often holding it up as a model, we will study the 'myths and realities' of the changes which have followed the election of Marine Le Pen as party leader in January 2011. Finally, after some semantic considerations – 'fascist'? 'populist'? 'far right'? – we will lay out the tools of struggle against a political chimera which has developed out of the inertia of left forces, which alone can provide the real social alternative.

1   The FN of Jean-Marie Le Pen

1.1   Prehistory of a small group (1945–1972)

Fallen into disgrace, struck by national opprobrium because of its participation in the Vichy regime, after the Second World War the French far right sought to make itself heard by the French people. Seizing on the wars of decolonisation, it defended the nation and its colonial empire by supporting the army in Indochina in the 1950s but above all by involving itself in the early 1960s in the fight for 'l'Algérie française' notably via the terrorists of the OAS (*Organisation Armée Secrète*). The military defeats of the army, the recourse to torture in Algeria and a series of terrorist incidents soon led public opinion to reject this discourse and its accompanying practices.

In parallel, the far right sought to involve itself in the internal political scene. It sought to anchor itself among small traders and artisans, initially by supporting the campaign of Pierre Poujade, candidate of the UDCA (*Union de Défense des Commerçants et Artisans de France*) in 1956, then that of Maître Jean-Louis Tixier-Vignancourin 1965[1]. This quest for political credibility did not convince the public and led again to crushing defeats.

At the same time, but in another register, numerous small groups[2] emerged in the youth and student milieu in reaction to the growing influence of the far left. A succession of organisations, whose principal mode of expression remained physical violence, occasionally made newspaper headlines.

Noting the political impasse into which these different strategies had led, Dominique Venner[3] published 'Pour une critique positive'[4] in 1962. This text, sometimes considered as foundational, sought to rethink far right strategy and would lead to the creation in 1963 of Europe Action then to that of the GRECE (*Groupement de Recherche et d'Études pour la Civilisation Européenne*, 1969), ancestor of the Nouvelle Droite.

This current sought to update the fundamentals of the far right, notably around a so-called 'differentialism' or 'ethno-differentialism'. According to this theory, GRECE stressed the specificities of each 'race' and no longer the superiority of one over the other, and thus

---

[1] A sympathiser of Action Française and deputy in 1940, Tixier-Vignancour voted full powers to Pétain and became deputy general secretary of Information under Vichy. After 1945 he became the quasi- official lawyer for the far right, defending former Vichy collaborators then the most hardened partisans of Algérie Française (J-P. Gautier, Les extrêmes droites en France, Syllepse, Paris, 2009).

[2] Small groups of political activists, e.g. *Jeune Nation* (1949), the *Fédération des Étudiants Nationalistes* (FEN, 1960), *Occident* (1964), the *Mouvement Jeune Révolution* (MJR, 1963), *l'Œuvre Française* (1968), the GUD (*Groupe Union Droit*, 1968) and so on.

[3] Dominique Venner is an ex-member of *Jeune Nation* who achieved a posthumous notoriety through his suicide on 21 May 2013 at Notre-Dame cathedral in Paris.

[4] Published by 'Politique Éclair', supplement number 98, 28 August 1962.

defended the need for each to develop in isolation with a view to maintaining its existence: if everyone kept to themselves the races would be well looked after. This optic led in practice to a rejection of 'racial mixing' and a firm condemnation of 'cosmopolitanism'.

GRECE did not think of itself as a political party but wished to practice 'metapolitics'[5] and what it called a 'Gramscianism of the right' by imposing its ideas on the traditional right and thus coming to power. In fact, several leaders of this current would occupy posts of responsibility in right-inclined newspapers or magazines.[6]

This new perspective of action led to the birth of ON (*Ordre Nouveau*), which emerged in 1970 from the ashes of the 'muscular' *Occident*[7] movement. ON had the ambition of broadening its field of intervention beyond the simple use of the iron bar and would rapidly envisage participating in elections. Conscious of the disastrous image the movement had, ON was at the origin of the *'Front National pour l'Unité Française'*, a structure of an electoral nature set up with the perspective of contesting the parliamentary elections of March 1973. The whole of the far right was asked to leave differences aside, and take part in the venture. It responded almost unanimously – the royalists of *Action Française* politely declined the offer – and agreed on Jean-Marie Le Pen as spokesperson.

1.2   From small group to mass electoral party

Then aged 45, Le Pen already had a long career on the far right. In 1955, he enlisted as a volunteer for Indochina but only arrived after the defeat of Dien Biên Phu. Back in France, he was active alongside Pierre Poujade (UDCA) and at 27 was elected to the National

---

[5]   Metapolitics as understood by the *Nouvelle Droite* is a strategy which aims to intervene in the cultural and ideological fields, prior to the seizure of political power. In France the theorisation of metapolitics has above all been done through GRECE, with the work of Alain de Benoist, Jacques Marlaud and Pierre Le Vigan.

[6]   Notably in *Figaro magazine*, before being removed from it in the early 1980s.

[7]   An organisation dissolved in November 1968 because of its abundant use of violence.

Assembly in 1956. He soon broke with Poujade and became committed to Algérie Française. He would later be accused of himself having practiced torture. In 1963 he founded SERP (*Société d'Études et de Relations Publiques*), publisher of, among other things, discs of Nazi songs, and in 1965 organised the presidential campaign of Tixier-Vignancour.

Le Pen then participated in the creation of the Front National, which was born on 5 October 1972, at the Salle des Horticulteurs in Paris. This front sought to incarnate the 'popular, social and national right' which alone could 'bar the road to the Popular Front' and 'throw the thieves out of power'. Le Pen, now a media star, advanced the theme of immigration, the principal angle of attack of the FN's politics – then as now: 'uncontrolled immigration ... threatens the jobs, security and health of French people'. He denounced a political majority which had 'betrayed the wishes of its voters' to the benefit of 'Marxist trades unions'. This allowed him to conclude that 'when the adherents of the liberal right have given way, the only right is now ours: the national right.'[8] The discourse, which also paid homage to the army, was smooth and the usual hardware (Celtic crosses, coshes and helmets) henceforth became more discreet.

Despite the efforts in presentation and the desire to pose as a genuine alternative to the 'system', the March 1973 election was a failure which led to a rapid resurgence of the specificities of the different factions, notably between *Ordre Nouveau* and Le Pen's supporters. ON returned to activism and violence. On June 21, 1973, the far left decided to prevent the holding of an ON meeting against 'uncontrolled immigration' and clashed with the security forces protecting the meeting. The evening ended with wounded police, but above all the dissolution of the *Ligue Communiste*[9] (later refounded as the *Ligue Communiste Révolutionnaire*) and ON. Ordre Nouveau

---

[8] 'Pour un Ordre nouveau', April 1973, 'Qu'est-ce que la droite nationale ?', Le Pen.

[9] French section of the Fourth International and precursor of the Nouveau Parti Anticapitaliste.

would continue to hold rallies and created the 'Faire Front' committee,s then, in November 1974, the PFN (*Parti des Forces Nouvelles*), which became the main competitor of the Front National for the decade which followed. Meanwhile, Le Pen reorganised the FN leadership around his cronies.

If the PFN aimed for an immediate rapprochement with the traditional right,[10] the FN opted to play the card of independence. Its programme stressed the classic themes of the far right: anti-Marxism, an end to trade union monopoly power, the death penalty, opposition to abortion, denunciation of a right which implemented the policies of the left, while maintaining always the theme of immigration as sole explanation of the social crisis which already loomed on the horizon: 'One million unemployed, is one million too many immigrants!'[11].

The journey through the political desert would continue for the French far right for a few more years. Lacking a sufficient number of signatures,[12] Jean-Marie Le Pen (FN) and Pascal Gauchon (PFN) were both unable to run as candidates in the presidential election of May 1981 which saw the victory of François Mitterrand, candidate of the Socialist Party.

The hope which this victory created for the 'people of the left' was as great as the disappointment which followed. Incapable of resolving the crisis, the left government soon imposed an austerity policy from which the far right would benefit. In 1983, Jean-Pierre Stirbois, then general secretary of the FN, was elected to the municipal council of the town of Dreux (Eure et Loir) with 16% of the vote.

The strategy of independence finally paid off and the FN was henceforth hegemonic on the far right. It was the end of the line for the Parti des Forces Nouvelles and its desire to build links with the

---

[10] The PFN participated in the presidential campaign of Valéry Giscard d'Estaing in 1974.

11 Speech made during the parliamentary elections of March 1978.

[12] A candidate for the presidential elections must achieve a minimum of 500 'sponsorships' from elected representatives.

traditional right: the FN's main competitor was a small group by 1986 and has never recovered.

Over the following 15 years, the FN imposed itself on the French political landscape. In 1984, it won 11% of the vote in the European elections which gave it 10 members of the European parliament. In 1986, through the proportional voting system introduced by François Mitterrand, 35 FN deputies entered the National Assembly. Two years later, at the presidential elections of 1988, Le Pen scored 14%. In the 1994 European elections, 11 FN MEPs were elected. The rise peaked in 1995, when Le Pen scored 15% at the presidential election.

1.3   Electoral victories and strategic crises (1990s–2000s)

Dirty hands, low profile: The FN in power

Despite often impressive electoral scores, the possibilities offered to the FN to put its programme into effect were to be be rare. The dreamed-of opportunity presented itself at the municipal elections of 1995, when four towns in the south of France fell into its hands. Vitrolles, Marignane, Orange and Toulon were the laboratory towns and each sought to put the FN programme into effect. The Front intended to demonstrate that it was able to govern.

Eminently symbolic, preferential treatment for French nationals ('national preference') was rolled out locally with preference for natives of Toulon, Orange etc. and from the arrival of Catherine Mégret at Vitrolles town hall. A birth allowance of 5,000 francs reserved to children of French parents or residents of the European Union was established from January 1998. Condemned for 'discrimination' by the court of Aix-en-Provence, the law was declared by the council to be bad – so it was necessary to 'elect many FN deputies to the National Assembly to change it'. This discrimination was also implemented by the other FN town halls in a less spectacular fashion. Accommodation certificates, necessary for visa requests, would be issued much more rarely and binational marriages were blocked.

In fact it was familial rather than national preference which was being implemented. All key posts were given to relatives; nepotism and clientelism become principles of management in FN municipalities. Among the most symbolic, Catherine Mégret[13] replaced her husband as mayor of Vitrolles, André-Yves Beck[14] become communications attaché, Mario d'Ambrosio, responsible for the death of Ibrahim Ali in Marseille in 1995, was hired on his release from prison, and so on. Meanwhile, subsidies to houses in neighbourhoods, associations and other structures deemed hostile were reduced. In Toulon, budgets allocated to associations which were active around immigration issues were re-assigned to military veterans or pieds-noirs, the grant to the Jewish community centre was abolishd but that of the Cat Lovers' Society was increased by 40,000 francs, while *Secours Populaire* obtained 8,000 francs. The same went for the FCPE (*Fédération des Conseils de Parents d'élèves*), an association committed to fighting AIDS (an 'association of homosexuals'). In Toulon again, the budget for educational supplies and sport fell by 25% and that for social affairs by 10%. In Marignane, the mayor Daniel Simonpieri boasted that 'no Maghrebian, no foreign person or person of non-European foreign origin uses our services. That should be the dissuasive effect of the FN label.'

Austerity for some...

Having made lower taxes one of the major axes of their campaigns, the FN municipalities wished to be exemplary in this area. As there were no small economies to be made, all means were good: cuts in the budgets for roadworks, refuse collection, public lighting, reduced

---

[13] Wife of Bruno Mégret, former number 2 and ideologue of the FN, who was a candidate in Vitrolles but was deemed ineligible.

[14] Troisième Voie, Nouvelle Résistance.

heating in schools, school canteens reserved for children whose parents could both prove they were in employment, and so on.

However, there was no austerity for the FN entourage, as witnessed by the familial expenses claimed in Vitrolles by the Bompards man and wife – spa, perfumes, cigars, musical instruments, bedding. Benefits in kind also flowed: housing provided free of charge, 33 courtesy cars acquired between 1998 and 2001. In Toulon, staff costs increased by 31% and by 30% in Marignane and Vitrolles. While the numbers employed in education fell, police and security forces grew rapidly.

The much heralded tax cuts were a fiasco: in Marignane, Orange and Toulon, local taxes increased and the regional accounts department issued a stinging report on the management of Marignane and Vitrolles. In 2001, Toulon was in debt. Incapable of drawing up a budget, the FN councillors resorted to private consultancies.

Culture on the scrapheap

A certain number of symbolic actions were also taken. Vitrolles became 'Vitrolles en Provence'[15] and the Provencal flag was replaced by the old royal flag of the Comtes de Provence. Streets were renamed: the Avenue Salvador Allende became the Avenue Mère Térésa, the Place Nelson Mandela the Place de Provence, and so on.

The FN town halls were also extremely active in the area of culture and applied their 'civilisational' concept of art: no more 'Rap-tag-Lang' culture, priority to folklore! Funds previously for 'living culture' was switched to 'heritage'. in Orange, Jacques Bompard suspended the financing of the opera and classical music festival Les Chorégies; the Sous-marin concert hall in Vitrolles was closed; Régine Juin, head of Les Lumières cinema, was dismissed[16]; the 11th comic book festival in Orange had to be relocated after 56,000 francs was

---

[15] The change was overruled by the prefecture.

[16] After refusing to cancel a series of short films on the theme 'Love in a time of AIDS'.

demanded to hire a venue, and so on. As an alternative there were competitions of every kind: fanfare, tea dance, singing, and a Feast of the Pig! All with the aim of immersing youth in 'Toulonais culture.'[17]

In the libraries, newspapers like *Le Monde* and *Libération* were suppressed and replaced by the likes of *Présent, Identité, Éléments, Krisis* and the works of Brasillac and Julius Evola. Librarians who quit under pressure were replaced by relatives of the municipal teams.

Twenty years later, there is complete silence from both the FN and the media on this pathetic yet instructive sequence.

Strategic crises

Despite a significant activist growth from 1995 to 1998, the changes of orientation and impasses of Le Pen's strategy of independence led to an unprecedented crisis in the party. A split in the winter of 1998-99 brought about an implosion of its activist apparatus. Bruno Mégret, the FN number 2 and its chief ideologue, promoted the idea that the 'strategy of the grand alternative' (hostility to both the left and the traditional right) would not bear fruit, and it was necessary to consider alliances with the traditional right, at least at the local level. Encouraged by the existence in Italy, since 1994, of a right–far right coalition government (*Forza Italia* led by Silvio Berlusconi, and the post-fascist MSI which had become the *Alleanza Nazionale* in 1995, as well as the Northern League), he implemented a policy of alliances, following the regional elections of 15 March 1998, in several regional councils (successfully electing presidents of regional executives, such as Charles Million in Rhône-Alpes).

Convinced he was the 'providential man' who the people would turn to at the fateful hour and afraid of losing control of his own party, Le Pen then dismissed his 'executive office' which he nicknamed 'Nabot-léon' together with several of his associates and launched a huge purge against this 'small minority of extremists, activists and

---

[17] See 'Le Toulonnais' (municipal bulletin) (number 17 December 1996).

perhaps even racists'. After losing the battle for the name 'FN' in the courts, the expelled minority regrouped inside the FN-Mouvement National, subsequently the MNR (Mouvement National Républicain), a direct competitor of the FN. Shedding its excessively far right attributes, it aspired to governmental posts. But the split had political results – Mégret had attracted both neo-Nazi youths and the most hardcore 'radical' activists (including MNR candidate Maxime Brunerie, who shot at President Chirac on 14 July 2002), and young well-educated cadres who were anxious for access to power, two milieux that found it hard to coexist since Mégret, in their eyes, lacked leadership qualities. Ten years later, the MNR had become a small group and Mégret had officially retired from politics, while Jean-Marie Le Pen, even if he was no longer FN president, was still in command of the ship.

Thus the 'historic' FN survived this split, albeit at the price of a reduction in activists (from 42,000 to 15,000 at the end of 1998), the majority of its cadres and half its elected representatives, becoming an empty shell, an electoral vehicle with hardly any activity outside of election periods. In this respect, even if the hegemony of the Front and its leader on the far right was confirmed, the idea of it going into the second round of the presidential election would have been dismissed as fantasy.

The end?

On 21 April, the results of the first round of the presidential elections produced a major surprise for the country: the FN beat the PS (*Parti Socialiste*) and thus made it through to the second round to face the candidate of the right, Jacques Chirac. The Front had won 4.8 million votes or 16.86% of votes cast. If Jacques Chirac won 82% of votes cast in the second round, 5.5 million votes were nonetheless cast for the far right candidate.

The Mégret split had repercussions for the organisation. Nicolas Sarkozy did not have much difficulty in capturing the FN electorate in

2006-07, with the FN vote falling to 10.5% at the 2007 presidential election and to 4.3% in the parliamentary elections of June 2007. While in 1986, 35 deputies were elected to the National Assembly, the FN had neither deputy nor senator in 2011[18]. At the European level, they elected 11 MEPs in 1994 but since that never had more than three until the 2014 European elections

This fall in the number of deputies and thus subsidies together with the departure of financial backers weakened the FN apparatus through the 2000s. The Paquebot, the immense headquarters in the wealthy Parisian suburbs, had to be sold and the organisation moved to a much more down-market neighbourhood. The traditional Bleu Blanc Rouge fête has not taken place since 2006 and 'Français d'Abord', the official party newspaper, ceased publication in 2008. In addition, the organisation suffered from a lack of structure and the weakness of its local implantation. In spite of the breakthrough of April 2002, unforeseen by anyone including the FN, votes polled by the hegemonic organisation of the far right would progressively decline through the decade.

2   The FN of Marine Le Pen

Conscious of the disastrous image the party still had, a new team set to work after the defeat of 2002 to reconstruct a far right discourse and restructure the FN apparatus. But it was only when the dynastic and familial succession appeared possible to Jean-Marie Le Pen that the party would restore itself as a movement around Marine, elected FN president at the Tours congress on 16 January 2011. After some splits on the right rejecting the drive for 'ideological modernisation', she set about remobilising a party which had broken down.

---

[18] A result which is also explained by the adoption of proportional representation for the parliamentary elections.

2.1   The programme

The FN's social and economic programme

What is the social and/or economic programme of the Front National? The reply is that there isn't one, really. The main party of the far right has no real coherent discourse in the area, there is no more or less immutable 'body of doctrine' (which would be possibly adapted to social developments), nor any clearly project crystallised around programmatic pillars. On the contrary, the FN's promises in the economic and social area often appear to depend on which public the party addresses, with party being capable of changing discourse and image according to the terrain on which it finds itself or the interests of its audience. Thus, on the party's website, economic and social themes are much more often illustrated by interviews with Marine Le Pen – whose content has a variable geometry – than by clear programmatic content.

Nonetheless, there is a real programmatic pillar, called 'national preference', also known as 'national priority' or 'citizen's priority'. The meaning of the formula is clear: privileges should be reserved by law for French nationals: a sort of structural discrimination applied to access to employment, social services, housing or pensions.

In an interview given to the newspaper *National Hebdo*[19] immediately after the FN's Strasbourg congress which appeared on 10 April 1997, Jean-Yves Le Gallou explained: 'national preference is the nuclear core of our programme' – the core being what is stable in an atom, with the rest (in this case the electrons) being in movement around it. The image was rather well chosen. While the idea of 'preference' according to nationality – leading to discrimination against immigrants – remains constant, the rest of the programme varies over time, which presents an immense advantage to the FN.

---

[19] At the time more or less directly owned by the party (40 % of share capital), the newspaper went bankrupt in 2008. Today, its role is played above all by media sympathetic to the FN on the Internet, in particular the site *Nations Presse Info* (NPI).

When it plans meet all its promises on the back of non-nationals, there is little risk of disappointing its voters (who by definition have nationality) – at least, not before coming to power, with results which are less good for those voters than promised. Awaiting the implementation of its programme, the party can defend virtually everything and its contrary, to all layers of the electorate: it is the non-nationals (who don't have voting rights) who will pay!

Thus, in principle, the party of the far right – in the manner of historic fascism which operated in a comparable way at this level – can claim to be the defender of property for those who have any, but also the party of social revenge for those who don't. It can claim to be the party of conservation and of movement, the expression of anger but also of the defence of existing privileges.

Nonetheless, over the years the FN's discourse and programme at the social and economic level have sometimes known profound modifications, notably because they were, at each period of recent history, marked by a principal tendency.

Benefiting from the betrayals of a PS newly come to power, from 1983/84 the FN became a mass electoral (although not a mass activist) party. Faced with the 'socialism' threatening the country, its first successes were built on a base conquered from the conservative right. The FN's first electoral breakthroughs were possible thanks people who turned away from the traditional right, expressed at the time in the RPR (*Rassemblement pour la République*) and UDF (*Union pour la Démocratie Française*). These were essentially middle class or petty bourgeois layers, composed of small employers, artisans, traders, farmers or the liberal professions. The main motive for their discontent in relation to the RPR/UDF right was that the latter, in their view, no longer sufficiently defended small capital against big capital (or against the workers' movement). On the basis of movements of concentration of capital, induced by the modernisation of the economic apparatus, but also by the opening of frontiers inside the EEC (European Economic Community), these social layers felt their existence threatened by the steamroller of more productive big capital. When the PS/PCF (*Parti Communiste Français*) left came to power in May 1981, facilitated by the beginning of the erosion of the social bloc of the traditional right, this fear of the future took a more ideological turn: The Reds want to ruin us! In a state of 'moral panic' combined with economic fear, these social layers saw their world threatened with upheaval. Thus they took to the street, just as the left or trade union forces began to desert it (should we undermine our comrades who are in government?). Demonstrations called by the right marked 1982 and 1983. Jean-Marie Le Pen participated himself in some of these, such as that on 13 September 1982 called by the *Syndicat National du Patronat Moderne et Indépendant*, whose leader at the time, Gérard Deuil, admired Pétain. But in 1984, it was a more 'cultural' and ideological mobilisation which gave a meaning to, and heartened, the whole: the right and the far right took to the streets for a mass mobilisation in defence of the 'free school', in other words, the privileges of private and religious education. Any similarity with certain current mobilisations, in 2012 or 2013, is obviously not fortuitous.

At the time, the social and economic discourse of the FN which accompanied this initial electoral anchorage was crystal clear: with Reagan as the model, the FN was a defender of economic liberalism, of the right of the strongest applied to the economy. The essence of the discourse was: Down with the unions, Down with taxes – this did not require much effort from Jean-Marie Le Pen, who had begun his political career as a Poujadist deputy in 1956 – and Down with state intervention in the economic sphere. The Labour Code should be pruned. Employees' organisations? Vicious hostage takers. When, on 15 February 1982, an employers' militia violently attacked a cheese factory occupied by strikers at Isigny in Calvados, Le Pen declared his 'total support'.

The orientation of the discourse would evolve in following years. A double movement was involved. First, the middle and petty bourgeois layers, electorally won in the early 1980s, remained, despite all disputes between the FN and the traditional right. Attracted by certain electoral promises or certain measures addressed to them, some of them turned – at least periodically – back to the RPR and the UDF. Second, the cadres and intellectuals (who do indeed exist) of the far right would make a strategic wager at the end of the 1980s: the Soviet bloc was showing cracks, then followed break-up of the old 'bipolar' world order. These cadres rejoiced: 'It's the end of Communism, the disappearance of Marxism and trade unions influenced by it, there is no longer any progressive alternative to the existing regime.' In any case, that is what they affected to believe. It thus became possible and necessary to address more vigourously the popular classes and wage earners who had until now identified with the left on the basis of a division of the political world in terms of class cleavages which, according to the far right, no longer had any meaning. The conclusion was: 'The alternative to the system, the expression of social anger, is now us. And us alone!' Some layers of the electorate, disappointed by the parties of the left – PS or PCF – would indeed vote for the FN from the beginning of the 1990s.

The public discourse started to change rapidly. The FN congress in Nice at Easter 1990 was held around 'social and ecological' themes. To journalists who expressed astonishment at seeing the FN downplay its priority themes of 'immigration' or 'law and order', the organisers effectively responded: we have already won in those areas, others do the work very well in our place, so we are turning towards new horizons. On 1 April 1990, a seminar in Paris was devoted to the question of national preference, raising notably the idea that the RMI (*Revenu Minimum d'Insertion*), the basic guaranteed income created in 1988, could be reserved to nationals or EEC residents. The main organiser was a young RPR careerist aged 35, a certain Nicolas Sarkozy.

However, the few symbolic gestures by the FN in the 'social and ecological' direction in no way modified its programme, which remained ultra free market. The main proposal for wage earners at the time was the 'deferred wage', based on the idea that wages could be increased without affecting capital. This would be done by paying workers their 'deferred wage' directly at the end of the month, in the form of unemployment, pension or sickness contributions. Employees would thus be very happy, seeing the sum indicated on their pay slip increase. A small problem: in the event of accident, inability to work, or unemployment, they would not be insured!

Confronted – under pressure from the left and trade unions – with the flagrant contradiction between their real programme and their new 'social' discourse, the leaders of the FN began to modify their proclaimed programmatic ideas. Until now, the party had fiercely opposed the social gains of the recent period – introduction of the fifth week of paid holidays (in 1982), creation of the RMI and so on. Starting from the campaign for the regional elections of 1992, and the programme for the March 1993 parliamentary elections (the '300 measures for France'), things changed. The FN was now, at least officially, a guarantor of social rights, low wage-earners and – at least – of the maintenance of the minimum wage by – promoting the conservation or improvement of these social gains through the introduction of 'national preference'. The latter would take the form of installation of separate social security funds for immigrants, who would thus have still have the right to contribute but would receive different payments (because, of course, 'in their countries of origin to which they will retire, life is much cheaper).

Another subject was added during the 1990s, which remains central to the social and economic discourse of the FN: that of job relocations, which relate in the most general way to changes in the international division of (capitalist) labour, and are presented as the main cause of all social problems. They are held to explain both the decline of the nation and the problems of workers faced with unemployment and pressure on their wages, supposedly as a result of globalisation and immigration – capitalism itself obviously not being responsible for these problems. Thus the FN's then chief ideologue (Bruno Mégret) was seen personally distributing leaflets outside the gates of the Moulinex company in October 1996, when relocations of jobs were announced.

This remains the main basis of economic discourse of the FN under Marine Le Pen. The party had, from the split between the partisans of Le Pen *père* and Mégret in the winter of 1998–99, become a purely electoral option which no longer innovated, either in the area of activist initiatives or in terms of the content of its discourse. When Jean-Marie Le Pen created a vacuum around himself to avoid his leadership of the party being challenged, the FN had lost its activists. For a decade, he could no longer benefit from the electoral capital previously acquired, his 'brand' being already well known. It was only from 2010–11 and the arrival of Marine Le Pen as its leader that the FN began to seriously mobilise once again. However, for the moment it only updated its social and economic recipes of the 1990s, with a suppler discourse. It would thus increasingly use the term 'globalisation' (used also by other forces to describe changes in the international division of labour, an objective economic reality). Le Pen *père* had spoken more of 'globalism', a more ideological term supposedly corresponding to 'globalisation', but which could also absorb other phenomena such as universal human rights, internationalism, or the imagined (Jewish and Masonic) 'world conspiracy'.

At this level, Marine Le Pen has recentred the public discourse, trying to make it appear more 'objective', even if she sometimes herself uses the term 'globalism'. Also, the current FN president has a 'positive' message for government employees, for whom her father had reserved an open contempt (except for the police and the military). Whereas Jean-Marie Le Pen had cultivated detestation of the non repressive public services and above all public education – he preferred private confessional schools – his daughter has adopted a discourse of defence of the state. Witness, for example the creation of the FN collective Racine, made up of state school teachers in October 2013; or, again in 2013, the call for members of the territorial civil service to agree to serve in future FN municipalities.

However, the real novelty of the period opened several years ago does not lie in the behaviour of the FN itself. It resides above all in the crisis of 2008–09, with all its consequences, which could open new unexpected opportunities for the far right, in France and internationally.

The far right: new faces, new territories, new methods

For some years now, the far right has been on the offensive in some unexpected areas: around social issues, secularism, anti-Zionism, the Internet, ecology and autonomy. Advancing in disguise, it can fool sections of youth and the workers' movement and dull anti-fascist vigilance.

Social questions. The pro-sovereignty right and practically all the far right now identify with anti-globalisation: from Nicolas Dupont-Aignan[20] to Serge Ayoub[21] via Marine Le Pen, all denounce Chinese competition and industrial relocations. The FN has passed from Reaganite neoliberalism of the 1980s to the defence of pensions in 2010 and a defence of factories against globalisation 'which use slave labour to manufacture for sale to the unemployed' (Marine Le Pen). Some small groups even claim to be anti-capitalist (*Egalité et Réconciliation*). After the case of Fabien Engelmann[22], the recent media agitation on the far right candidacies of trade union activists confirms the need for work to fight against the diffusion of fascist

---

[20] Former UMP member, now leader of Debout la Republique (DLR), mayor of Yerres in Essonne.

[21] Former skinhead, founder of the now disbanded Jeunesses Nationalistes Révolutionnaires (JNR) and Trosième Voie.

[22] Former trade unionist, mayor of Hayange in Moselle since April 2014.

ideas inside the workers' movement. Faced with this far right hiding behind a social discourse, trade union vigilance must be renewed and permanent.

Secularism. This is not traditionally a value the far right refers to; indeed some of them seek to destroy it (notably the Catholic traditionalists of the Manif pour Tous). However, some far right currents (FN, *Bloc Identitaire*) use secularism as a respectable rampart of their anti-Islam crusade. This mixing of messages has seduced a part of the secular movement ready to leap into an alliance of convenience. Thus the organisation Riposte Laïque, created by former left activists, uses an ultra-secularist discourse to conceal a solely anti-Islam offensive with racist connotations. This new packaging of an old discourse could seduce a fraction of the teaching or feminist milieus, in a European context where Islamophobic movements have the wind in their sails.

Anti-Zionism. If the anti-Islam discourse is very much dominant on the far right, there is also a current (Egalité et Réconciliation, Dieudonné[23]) which takes solidarity with the Palestinian people as a pretext with the sole objective of developing anti-Semitism and/or Holocaust denial. Making its electoral appearance with the 'anti-Zionist list' led by Dieudonné in the European elections of 2009, this current has been responsible for some surprising convergences: interviews with the spokesperson of the CBSP (*Comité de Bienfaisance et de Secours à la Palestine*) in far right publications, a public debate between far right 'intellectuals' and the Iranian ambassador, proximity to Shiite groups or elements of the UOIF (*Union des Organisations Islamiques de France*), 'Day of rage' demonstrations and so on.

---

[23] Dieudonné is a french comedian, close to the FN and holocaust deniers. He is known for making anti-Semitic jokes and has been condemned for incitement to racial hatred. The French state banned one of his shows.

Increasingly physically present in Palestine demonstrations, these groups could discredit the necessary solidarity with the Palestinians.

Ecology. The ecological project was long neglected by the FN, confined to a hollow discourse around defence of animals and the French countryside, with an anti-pollution discourse centred on agriculture (see the FN's Green Charter of 1985) giving the impression of the far right having an old fashioned approach to this subject. In a few years, while maintaining the fundamentals of animals and land (the association of Brigitte Bardot with the FN, the association 'Terroirs et Productions de France', a presence on demonstrations by wine cultivators), the far right has been able to take advantage of these growing concerns. Some currents which have worked on these questions for a long time are particularly in synch with the emergence of a radical critique of industrial society: rebalancing of the economy, the idea of *enracinement*, the AMAP (*Association pour le Maintien d'une Agriculture Paysanne*) of the *identitaires*, promotion of negative growth by Alain de Benoist, and so on.

Autonomy. Inspired by the German model, the autonomous nationalist movement is characterised by a systematic adoption of the functioning (independent groups, black blocs) and imagery (personal appearance and visuals) of the autonomist far left. It also subverts anti-fascist slogans, for example taking up an old slogan of the anti-fascist movement Scalp to transform it into 'No minarets in our neighbourhoods, no neighbourhoods for the minarets'. Since its activists are particularly violent, as shown by the series of aggressions against demonstrations and activists of the social movement (including comrades of the NPA, *Nouveau Parti Anti-capitaliste*) in the Nancy region, they should be unmasked as authentic fascists.

Internet. Use of Facebook by the *identitaires*, of Youtube by Kemi Seba (a phony FN press agency), success for certain blogs: the far right has massively used the Internet and social networks in search of new prey, sometimes very successfully. Pioneers in this area, the *identitaires* have built themselves to a great extent through the effectiveness of their webmasters, the systematic use of video, the multiplication of sites and a great ability to react. Also, Marine Le Pen has made the Internet a major issue in her electoral campaigns.

The far right is on the offensive in other sectors: music, stadiums, and charity initiatives. These new concerns of the far right, whether the result of pragmatism and opportunism (FN) or assumed political theorisation (*identitaires*, Soral) should be integrated into our everyday activism and all should be vigilant in unmasking them.

2.2   Marine Le Pen's cadres: The new and the old

The old guard:

Jean-Marie Le Pen presents to his daughter the permanent risk of an uncontrolled gaffe, a little crass phrase which will be taken up across the media: a risk much greater than anything that might be said or written by some obscure municipal candidate who can be immediately expelled. Jean-Marie Le Pen is the only person Marine cannot get rid of. As shown by his recent 'excesses' about 'Monseigneur Ebola' who would 'settle the immigration problem in three months' or his implicitly anti-Semitic remarks on the singer Patrick Bruel, he can in an instant ruin the patient efforts of his daughter to 'de-demonise' the party, a strategy which he has moreover on occasion publicly disavowed. The 'transformation' of the Front will thus not be total and changing of the name of the party, for example, will not be possible so long as he remains politically and physically present. Still an MEP, he remains popular among activists and still has a certain influence (to block an alliance with the *identitaires* for example) even if he is no longer the undisputed *chef*. He still has loyalists in the leadership such as Marie-Christine Arnautu, Louis Aliot, Edouard Ferrand and numerous local leaders.

Louis Aliot, a Le pen loyalist, is the author of the purges and de-demonisation. He detests the radicals and former Mégret supporters who he suspects (with reason) of being intelligent fascists in suits and ties. Aliot is virtually a moderate in comparison! A rather calm figure, this ideal son-in-law of Jean-Marie Le Pen is now responsible for training FN candidates and trying to keep an eye on the Le Pen 'babies' to ensure no gaffes are made. And there is a lot of work to do.

Marie-Christine Arnautu, parachuted into Nice for the municipal elections (by the decision of Jean-Marie Le Pen, against the advice of his daughter), is the last representative of the *solidariste* tendency of the Front. This far right 'workers' defence' current disappeared with the death in 1988 of its main leader Jean-Pierre Stirbois, the FN's number 2, with whom Arnautu was very close. Today vice-president of the FN, she is responsible for social affairs in recognition of her *solidariste* past.

Bruno Gollnisch has become marginal in the party, even in his bastion in Lyon. In two years, he has gone from being the quasi-designated 'dauphin' of Jean-Marie Le Pen to somebody who nobody in the political bureau wishes to listen to any more. He seems to have much more free time now. Although very much present on the Manifs Pour Tous, he had competition at this level from Marion Maréchal-Le Pen. As an MEP since 1989, contacts with the European 'brother parties' forms his last area of liberty. Even here, Marine Le Pen has sidelined him to turn towards more presentable parties. His third place on the European election list for the South Eastern constituency could even remove Gollnisch definitively from the European parliament in the event of bad results, which would put an end to his political career.

Alain Jamet has replaced Roger Holeindre as the last dinosaur who participated in the foundation of the Front. He seems content with this role as an extra, from the time when he relaxed his grip over the FN in Hérault. He has rallied to Marine Le Pen without conviction. Like all the old-timers he counts for less and less in a party where the youngsters are rearranging things.

The political advisors in the shadows

Philippe Olivier: a former Mégret supporter and brother-in-law of Marine Le Pen, Olivier is a radical ideologue who likes dirty tricks, such as the fake leaflet issued in the name of Jean-Luc Mélenchon (*Parti de Gauche*) in Hénin-Beaumont. He wages a personal war against the UMP mayor of the town of Draveil, where he lives.

Emmanuel Leroy: a former member of Ordre Nouveau and the PFN (*Parti des Forces Nouvelles,* a small neo-Nazi group), he is not shy about mixing with the most anti-Semitic elements of the far right. It should be said that he worked for a long time in the Ogmios bookshop, the principal centre of diffusion of Holocaust dernial in France. He has contacts in Russia.

Both are ideologues influenced by GRECE, very radical but also smart enough to hide it. They employ an anti-globalisation discourse against a left converted to neoliberalism and are responsible for writing many of Marine Le Pen's speeches (including that made at the Tours Congress) and edited her book-programme *A Contre Flots.*

These two 'Zionism obsessives' are joined in their delirium by **Christian Bouchet** (a former member of many small groups, now FN leader in the West and head of the municipal list in Nantes) and **Laurent Latruwe** (a FN journalist who has authored a book on the SS Skanderbeg division).

The apparatchiks

Three former Mégret supporters control the apparatus: the '3 Bs'.

Steeve Briois, a worker's son from the Pas-de-Calais, secretary general of the FN since 2011, joined the party at the age of 15, and was for a while a Mégret supporter. Briois has applied to the FN of Hénin-Beaumont a militant discipline inherited from the Communist Party: posters, leafleting, ward heeling and permanent presence on the ground. It's hard to know if he can extend this success to other regions. Elected mayor of Hénin-Beaumont in March, Briois incarnates the 'turn to the people' characteristic of the FN in the North-East, with a superficially highly social discourse and, behind the scenes, a well understood clientelism.

Nicolas Bay, responsible for the federations, while originating from the Catholic traditionalist current, has built links with the *identitaires*. While he has softened his image a little, he has for a long time flirted with the most hardcore far right elements.

Bruno Bilde was, like the other two, involved in the project of professionalisation of the party undertaken by Mégret in the 199s. He seems recently to have been excluded from the leadership of the Front. In disgrace?

The '3 Bs' are more enforcers than deciders: their political influence on Marine Le Pen is very weak and their grip on the apparatus often more theoretical than real.

Michel Guiniot, Dominique Martin and **Jean-François Jalkh** complete this apparatus which is distinguished by neither its competence nor its efficiency. If the Front has activist teams in some areas, in most regions activity is often non-existent and cadres are of very mediocre quality. However, the constant inflow of members and accession to posts as municipal councillors, indeed mayors, should change things in a party which is no longer short of money.

Chevènementistes gone to the dark side

Paul-Marie Coûteaux: another political chameleon who began the presidential election of 2012 supporting Nicolas Dupont-Aignan before rallying to Marine in extremis. Since then, this excitable ex-Chevènementiste, ex-royalist, and ex-Gaullist has on several occasions failed to quit a Marine Le Pen who tired of his permanent blackmail ('Keep me or I resign') from the beginning. A fantasist who was captured by the cameras of Canal Plus television while inventing false contacts at the end of 2013, his micro-party SIEL (*Souveraineté, Indépendance et Libertés*) is only an empty shell of whose existence even FN activists are unaware.

Florian Philippot: nicknamed 'the darling', he is the principal guru (the equivalent of the journalist, historian and fomer President Sakozy advisor Patrick Buisson for Marine Le Pen) and head of the European elections list in the East. An ENA (*Ecole Nationale d'Administration*) graduate in a party of general intellectual poverty, he has invented a *Chevènementiste*[24] past to hide the fact that he has always been on the right. He is a candidate for the municipal elections in Forbach. 'The man who whispers in the ear of Marine Le Pen' is mainly responsible for the turn to the 'invisibles' as well as the distance kept from the Manif pour Tous movement. His dizzying ascent (he became number 2 in less than two years) has provoked jealousies in the political bureau and resignations in Moselle, after his parachuting into Forbach where a dissident even ran against him in the parliamentary elections. Philippot has been much opposed internally (by Jean-Marie and

---

[24] Supporter of the ideas of Jean-Pierre Chevènement, founder member of the Parti Socialiste and minister in its governments 1981-2000, opposed to European federalism, founder (2008) of the Citizen and Republican Movement.

Marion Le Pen notably) during the Manif pour Tous events. However, he has toned down his 'pro-sovereignty and anti-euro' discourse to accentuate denunciations of immigration, music to the ears of the FN electorate.

Bertrand Dutheil de La Rochère is the only real former *Chevènementiste* (he was head of Chevènement's cabinet). However, this nobleman is not really from a left family background: his niece is Ludovine de La Rochère (spokesperson of the Manif Pour Tous) and his daughter is head of the FN list in the 13th *arrondissement* of Paris. Claiming to be a 'left patriot', he is above all a rightwing bourgeois who strayed leftwards.

Some other self-styled *Chevènementistes* (**Bruno Lemaire, Yannick Jaffré**) form a thin layer of 'left' weathervanes who have come to seek well-paid posts with the FN.

Experts ... in fantasy

In its search for presentable experts, the FN has experienced some big disappointments (Alain Soral, Laurent Ozon) and is probably prepared for others (notably the conspiracy theorist Aymeric Chauprade whose speculations on the role of Mossad in 9/11 do not help the credibility of the party). If there is at least one paternal tradition that Marine Le Pen has maintained, it is that of rewarding her advisors with electoral mandates: that is probably why Aymeric Chauprade was made head of list for the European elections in Île-de-France.

The Front has even emptied the UMP's dustbins by recruiting Philippe Martel, ex-head of cabinet for Alain Juppé, who enjoyed fleeting celebrity as one of the fictitious employees of the city of Paris in the 1990s: an RPR full-timer, he collected a salary from the city without working there (Juppé and Chirac were sentenced for this large-scale fraud). That gives us an idea of how the FN will manage the municipalities it has won.

Mates from youth and business

Marine Le Pen has maintained some very special friendships from her years of study in the law faculty at Assas.

Frédéric Chatillon, former GUD (*Groupe Union Défense*) leader, is head of a number of companies which more often than not are merely letterboxes. He draws a large income from the Front by invoicing at inflated prices for services which are then repaid through campaign funds: one of his companies, Riwal, drew up invoices for €1.6million during the FN presidential campaign. Even Dieudonné profited from the arrangement by renting out his theatre, the Main d'Or (200 seats) to the FN at a higher price than the Zénith de Paris (6,300 seats)! During the 2012 parliamentary elections, the FN candidates ordered 'campaign kits' at €16,000 each supplied by Chatillon's company.

Philippe Péninque directs a financial consultancy and is known for having opened the Swiss account of the former 'Socialist' budget minister Jérôme Cahuzac in 1992. Péninque was also questioned and held for several weeks in 1997 in a drug money laundering case, also involving Switzerland. As adviser in 2007 to Jean-Marie Le Pen, he was responsible for the non-payment of a printer which led to a trial lost by the Front and severe financial penalties.

Axel Loustau runs a security company which is regularly used by FN, employing graduates of Parisian neo-Nazis circles like Baptiste Coquelle (GUD) or Daniel Mack (JNR) to protect electoral meetings, party premises or the 1 May demonstrations. The Loustau family has participated in the most violent fringes of the far right for several generations, like the Le Pens. These characters also have a grip over the micro-party Jeanne, intended to finance the Front: the ex-

Gudards, Axel Loustau and Florence Lagarde monopolise this formation. The last member of the GUD 'dream team', Jildaz Mahé O'Chinal, is also involved in all the money-making plans. De-demonisation is just a huge joke for them (unlike Alliot or Philippot who really believe in it): they are not afraid of violence or anti-Semitism, or keeping bad company (Dieudonné, President Bashar Al-Assad of Syria, the Holocaust denier Robert Faurisson) when there is money to be made. Among their activities is a free magazine distributed at Parisian boulangeries and cafés: 'Cigale'. The title of the magazine makes a word play on the Nazi salute: sieg heil.

Gilbert Collard: this political chameleon (who passed from *Lambertisme* to centrism via the PS) serves as a guarantee of de-demonisation. His incompetence and absenteeism from the Assembly blocked his FN candidacy in Marseille and in the European elections. This ex-lawyer who has never opened a brief became a furtive deputy noted for absenteeism. It should be said that when elected as a municipal councillor in Vichy in 2001 (for the Radical Party), he only attended one council meeting in seven years. Present in the Manif Pour Tous, he came above all for the television cameras rather than through ideological commitment. He has no network in the Front and is detested by his fellow parliamentarian Marion Maréchal-Le Pen as well as by Jean-Marie. Collard is prompt to denounce corruption, although this has not stopped him, once elected deputy member of parliament, from hiring his wife as a parliamentary assistant: integrity is a difficult combat.

Marion Maréchal-Le Pen, the 'favourite granddaughter', assumes a right of the right positioning, far from the 'neither right nor left' discourse of her aunt. She is very popular with the UMP electorate as well as the youth of the Manif Pour Tous. She was on all the demonstrations against gay marriage, referring to rioters arrested at the margins of these demonstrations as 'political prisoners' and also participating in the traditionalist Catholic pilgrimage to Chartres in May 2013: a fine example of secularism! A deputy for the Vaucluse, her stand-in is vice-president of the Ligue du Sud and her parliamentary assistant a former GRECE activist: in the South, could she be the spearhead of the alliance of the right (FN-UMP-*Identitaires*) while awaiting the 'bleu Marion' generation in 2022? Her personal objective is first to build a bastion in the Vaucluse where the FN achieves huge scores and where her discourse has widespread appeal on the right.

The different familial and political circles around Marine Le Pen constitute clans where hatreds and political or personal (even amorous) rivalries often prevent effective work: Aliot detests Philippot who detests Jean-Marie Le Pen who detests Olivier and they all neutralise each other ... provided this basket of crabs continues.

2.3   The FN's international links

The FN, like other far right parties, uses international relations above all to produce an internal political effect, in France. It is partly about comforting its supporters by stressing that its theses are shared by other formations in other countries. But it is also about obtaining a stamp of 'respectability' and 'de-demonisation', by finding international allies who do not have too unsavoury a reputation.

Alliance between far right parties for the European elections

Between 22 and 25 May 2014 (depending on the member country), the elections for the European Parliament were held. The far right hoped to use them to advance by obtaining significant votes. This proved possible thanks to the context of crisis and the mistrust felt by a significant number of people in Europe with regard to the current functioning of the European Union.

Because a European parliamentary group allows its members access to considerable resources – offices, assistants, interpreters and so on – and several million euros, the FN, strengthened by its results on 25 May, quickly sought to form a group which it would lead. Six formations had met in Vienna, Austria, on 15 November 2013 to prepare an alliance for these European elections so as to form a parliamentary group. The parties participating were the French FN, represented by its deputy Marion Maréchal-Le Pen, the Austrian Freedom Party (FPÖ), Italy's Northern League, the Vlaams Belang from Flanders, the Sweden Democrats (SD) and the Slovak National Party (SNS).

However, to form a group in the European parliament, according to the rules currently in force, at least 25 deputies are required from at least seven different member countries. Thus cooperation between six formations from different countries would be insufficient and a seventh party was needed to join this alliance – the Dutch PVV (Party for Freedom) led by Geert Wilders, an openly anti-Muslim formation which had until then kept its distance from parties like the FN whose links with historic fascism it did not share. Wilders thus met Marine Le Pen on 13 November 2013 in The Hague, after a first encounter on 22 April 2013 in Paris.

The alliance was perhaps unnatural, since Wilders, like his predecessor and compatriot Pim Fortuyn (killed in May 2002), is the most typical representative of this Nordic far right which is liberal in economic matters – whereas the FN and FPÖ have long since made a 'national-social' turn – and 'liberal' in the area of women's and gay rights, essentially threatened in their eyes by 'reactionary Muslims'. Wilders thus defends gay marriage whereas numerous representatives of the French FN demonstrated against 'marriage for all' in 2013 and 2014. However, 81% of PVV voters approved of its rapprochement with the FN, according to a poll in November 2013, while only 2% were opposed.

At their joint press conference, Wilders expressed his desire that the United Kingdom Independence Party (UKIP), which gained 27.5% and came first in the UK European elections, should join them following the European ballot. For the moment, UKIP – a party which stresses national sovereignty and which identifies in part with the heritage of Margaret Thatcher – is concerned not to appear as a party of the far right. In France, it has until now privileged an alliance with the *souverainiste* conservative Nicolas Dupont-Aignan, rather than with the FN.

Another party, the Danish People's Party (DPP), anti-immigration and above all anti-Muslim, declined the offer of alliance with the FN, which it described as too anti-Semitic, above all because of the prominence still enjoyed by Jean-Marie Le Pen. However, the DPP spokesperson, Søren Søndergaard, also said that in his view Marine Le Pen represented a different political viewpoint from that of her father, but that the weight of the latter remained too significant. A similar position was adopted by the nationalist and anti-immigration True Finns Party, which won more than 19% of votes at the last parliamentary elections in Finland.

Change of alliance – from the European Alliance of National Movements (AEMN) ...

Who is relatively 'respectable' and who is less so? Who can claim the label of 'de-demonised'? It is partly in these terms that the question of its transnational European alliances is posed to the French FN. Marine Le Pen no longer wishes to ally with parties which are in her view too 'extremist', like Hungary's Jobbik, an openly anti-Semitic movement with a paramilitary wing, the 'Magyar Guard' or the Greek neo-Nazi party 'Golden Dawn' (9.39% of the vote and three seats in the European parliament), whose extremely violent dimensions were shown with the killing of the musician Pavlos Fyssas in Athens on 17 September 2013.

However, on 19 January 2011, three days after becoming party leader, she had given another press conference in Strasbourg where journalists had asked her about certain authoritarian measures taken by the conservative nationalist party currently ruling Hungary, FIDESZ (Civic Alliance). Marine Le Pen then stated that the

Hungarian party 'closest' to the FN was *Jobbik* rather than FIDESZ, and it was with the latter that the FN had, in Budapest on 25 October 2009, launched the AEMN (European Alliance of National Movements), with three other *groupusculaire* movements:

The Italian Social Movement – Flamme Tricolore (MSI – Fiamme Tricolore), a residue of nostalgic Italian neo-fascists who rejected the 'post-fascist' transformation undertaken by Gianfranco Fini from 1995);

The Swedish National Democrats (ND), an extremist split from the Sweden Democrats (SD); the SD has parliamentary representation whilst the ND obtain around 0.1 % of the vote; and

The Front National de Belgique (FNB), a party of weak influence in francophone Belgium.

Finally, matching her words and her deeds, Marine Le Pen, who had said that the FN would withdraw from the AEMN in June 2011, used a press conference held inside the parliament on 23 October 2013, to ask the two other FN MEPs elected with her for the 2009–14 term, Jean-Marie Le Pen and Bruno Gollnish, to leave the Alliance, with the latter agreeing to abandon his presidency. The AEMN was then reduced to four main parties, two of them newcomers (the Swedish ND and FNB were crumbling away as organised forces, their activist substance being very weak). The two newcomers were the BNP (British National Party) from the United Kingdom, whose leader Nick Griffin became vice-president of the Alliance, and the ultra-nationalist *Ataka* party from Bulgaria. They now form the skeleton of the AEMN with Hungary's *Jobbik* and the residual Italian neofascists, but representatives of other far right parties can sometimes participate informally. Thus, for another party of relative electoral significance, the *Vlaams Belang* (Flemish Interest) from Flanders, things are more fluid. It is represented in the AEMN by a regional MEP from Flanders, Christian Vergoustraete, who plays a supporting role. But in general the far right parties with electoral strength in Europe – such as the Austrian FPÖ – tend rather to keep their distance from this alliance. The FPÖ, for example, does not wish to be associated too much with *Jobbik*, which is active in their neighbouring country.

...to the AEL (European Alliance for Freedom)

In the same way, the main reason for the FN's rethink on the AEMN, beyond reasons linked to image and the quest for 'de-demonisation', was the existence of another coalition, the 'Alliance Européenne pour la Liberté' (AEL, European Alliance for Freedom), whose main parties have a broader influence and which thus seems more promising to Marine Le Pen, who was elected as its vice-president on 8 November, 2012 alongside Franz Obermayr, representative of the Austrian FPÖ, who was elected its president. The latter had participated at the press conference on 23 October 2013 with Marine Le Pen when she announced the definitive divorce from the more 'radical' AEMN.

The pillars of the AEL are the FPÖ and the Vlaams Belang. The Swedish Democrats (SD), represented in parliament in Stockholm since the election of 19 September 2010 (with a score of 5.7%) have also joined it. This party, founded in 1988, passes itself off as relatively 'respectable' inasmuch as it is committed to the parliamentary road rather than violence, although its origins lie in the neo-Nazi milieux of the 1980s. The SD hosted a meeting of the AEL (closed to the press) in Stockholm, in October 2013, and on this occasion Marine Le Pen dined with its president, Jimmy Akenson.

But, apart from the SD, which, having scored 9.7% of the vote at the last European elections, hesitated to go into Sweden's September 2014 parliamentary elections as part of group formed around the FN, the other FN allies did not achieve the scores expected, the Slovak SNS missing out on entering arliament, with 3.6% of the vote, the *Vlaams Belang* dropping from 9.85% in 2009 to 4.14%, and the Northern

League falling from 10.2% to 6.1%. The FN must thus now choose, in order to form a group in the European parliament, between breaking the commitment made not to ally with openly Nazi or fascist parties and negotiating with the pro-sovereignty, anti-euro and anti-immigration formations which until now have sought to keep their distance from the FN.

Friendship with the autocrats' Russia...

In terms of foreign policy orientation, Marine Le Pen perceives the USA a priori rather as a rival, an over-dominant competitor to a France 'sovereign once more', according to her vision. Thus it is not illogical that, among the representatives of the US right she met on her visit to the country in autumn 2011, her primary choice as interlocutor was Ron Paul, who envisages a more isolationist 'America first' foreign policy. In the event of a political victory for Ron Paul's ideas (he was beaten in the Republican Party primary elections for the November 2012 presidential election), the USA would concentrate more on its internal problems and intervene less in the affairs of other countries, not for pacifist or anti-militarist but for nationalist motives. Russia, above all when governed by autocrats in the manner of Vladimir Putin, remains a point of anchorage in the FN's world vision. While opposition to the Putin regime and its allies grew strongly in late 2011, an authoritarian and nationalist 'strong state' in Russia offers a good guarantee in the eyes of most FN leaders.

It is true that the latter are not entirely in agreement in this area. One of Marine Le Pen's advisors, Emmanuel Leroy (an advocate of 'revolutionary nationalism' and the vision of 'EurAsia', who has cultivated contacts with Alexandre Douguine, the ideological 'pope' of the Russian 'New Right'), has dreamed for some years of a 'great eurasiatic space' and a 'continent stretching from Brest to Vladivostok'. This would guarantee a sort of economic autarky internally disposing of all essential raw materials, allowing a serious reduction of relations with other areas of the world – a little like the vision of Adolf Hitler, except that access to the natural riches of 'EurAsia' would not be guaranteed by military occupation of Russia, but rather a structural alliance with a 'strong regime' seen as stable, authoritarian, 'white' and racist – in short, as a good ally. This 'continental, Eurasiatic' vision was not at all to everybody's taste in the FN. Some leaders did not share what they saw as its over 'supranational' approach. Thus Leroy officially withdrew this ideological project in 2010.

The theme of an autocratic Russia as anchor point of an international policy remains present in the official vision of the FN. Marine Le Pen stated in a speech on 19 November 2011 in Paris: 'Our foreign policy axes would profoundly modify the destiny of our country and render possible its return to the first level: 1) The advent of a Europe of Nations, a sort of integrated command of NATO and the offer of a 'strategic' alliance to Russia, based on a deepened military and energy partnership... 2) The proposal of the formation of a pan-European Union of sovereign states including Russia and Switzerland ... Turkey will not be associated with this project.'

Neo-colonial Africa...

Certainly, the vision developed here is not solely on a 'EurAsia' axis. Marine Le Pen spoke the same day of relations to be developed with African countries in France's post and neo-colonial zone of influence, saying: 'We want to break with the corrupt Françafrique and establish the basis of an African policy founded on the one hand on a real respect for African national sovereignties, and on the other on strong support by the French state for French private investment in Africa and an end to the migratory flows towards our country.'

Here, on the rhetorical level, Marine Le Pen begins by proposing a 'break' with the practice of French neo-colonialism in Africa, commonly known for some years under the term 'Françafrique'. (Nicolas Sarkozy had also promised a 'break with Françafrique' in 2006 and early 2007, before quickly reneging on the promise once elected.) However, what she really envisages is a continuation of neo-colonial relations based on exploitation of the wealth of the former colonies, together with agreements on a halt to net immigration from these countries.

... and the Israeli far right

Transposing to France the modernisation of the European far right (on the model of the Dutch leader Geert Wilders), Marine Le Pen wishes to turn the page on anti-Semitism and her father's 1987 comment on the Nazi gas chambers being a 'detail' of history. For this, a trip to Israel was indispensable. If the FN could obtain a certificate of respectability from Israel, that would remove some moral barriers to its alliances on the right in France. But the main obstacle to this trip was Jean-Marie Le Pen. Despite contacts in Israel with the worst right wingers attracted by its anti-Islam discourse, the Front National remains supportive of Bashar Al-Assad, of the Iran of the Ayatollahs and of Dieudonné in France. If Marine Le Pen has understood that anti-Semitism does not win elections, she is finding it hard to deal with a Front where 'radical anti-Zionists' are still present (Frédéric Chatillon, Bruno Gollnisch and of course Jean-Marie Le Pen) and more influential than the 'pro-Zionists' (Louis Aliot, Michel Thooris).

2.4 Links with the right

Continually adapting its discourse to the electorate it seeks, the FN now seeks not only to win back disappointed Sarkozy voters of 2007 but also to seduce the victims of a crisis which has grown ever sharper over the past 30 years. To make the party a credible alternative, the new president is ready to get rid of the small groups and openly fascistic references; it also benefits from the growing complicity of governments in relation to this discourse over the past 30 years, notably concerning the theme of immigration which has become, thanks to the Front, a 'problem' across almost all the political spectrum.

While the 1998 split momentarily weakened the FN apparatus, its discourse came to contaminate the institutional right. The latter benefited from the decline of the Front, notably during the presidential elections of 2007 which brought Nicolas Sarkozy to power as the candidate of a UMP clearly influenced by the theses of the FN.

An insidious ideological contamination?

The influence exerted by the Front National goes well beyond the far right. At the national level, the parties of the traditional right have until now rejected technical agreements with the Front, but this position is much more nuanced locally as a result of either the political sympathies of certain elected representatives with such agreements or the possibilities that they offer for taking seats.

Right–FN electoral agreements first emerged in the early 1980s and they multiplied up to the early 2000s. During the regional elections of 1998, Charles Millon (Rhône-Alpes), Charles Baur (Picardy), Jean-Pierre Soisson (Burgundy) and Jacques Blanc (Languedoc-Roussillon), all then members of the centrist Union for French Democracy (*Union pour la Démocratie Française*, UDF), were re-elected through winning majorities composed with FN elected representatives.

Certain themes emphasised by the Front such as immigration or law and order have moreover found an echo not only in the rhetoric used by the political leaders of the right, but also in that of the left which succeeded it in power. Laurent Fabius, former Socialist prime minister, said in 1984: 'Le Pen poses good questions but gives the wrong answers to them.' In 1990, Michel Rocard, another Socialist prime minister, argued that 'France cannot play host to all the poverty of the world.' On 19 June 1991, Jacques Chirac, then mayor of Paris and president of the Rassemblement Pour la République, employed a populist rhetoric until then characteristic of the Front National.[25]

These short term strategies seeking to win back an electorate which had turned to the FN opened the sluice gates of state racism a little wider and contributed to banalising the theses of the Front. The arrival of a right which had overcome its 'complexes' on numerous questions, starting by those of ordinary racism, would constitute a precious aid in the propagation of the discourse of the far right.

As candidate of 'order in movement' in 2007, Nicolas Sarkozy, then Jacques Chirac's minister of the interior, seemed to seduce the FN electorate with a 'muscular' discourse. The votes which usually went to the far right now went to a candidate who promised to clean up the French suburbs 'with Kärcher' (a high-pressure street cleaner).

On 17 May 2007, the day after Sarkozy's election, the highly controversial 'Ministry of Immigration, Integration, National Identity and Solidaristic Development' was created. At national and international level, numerous voices condemned the collapsing of the terms 'national identity' and 'immigration' and the banalisation of racism resulting from an ethnic treatment of political, economic and social problems.

A tougher discourse and legal arsenal

Four months before the regional elections of March 2010, a 'debate on national identity' was launched with great media fanfare by Éric Besson, a Socialist Party defector who was now the new minister of Immigration, Integration, National Identity and Solidaristic Development. 'We must reaffirm the values of national identity and

---

[25] Speaking of 'the French worker who lives in the Goutte d'Or, a popular Parisian neighbourhood ..., who works with his wife and who, altogether, earns around 15,000 francs, and who sees on the landing alongside in his low income housing block, piled up, a family with a father, three or four wives, and about twenty kids, and who earns 50,000 francs in state benefits, without ever working! If you add to that the noise and the smell, of course the French worker on the landing goes mad ....' Speech in Orléans, 19 June 1991.

pride in being French' he had stated in October 2009 at the opening of this 'great debate' which was more than anything an open door to every kind of prejudice concerning immigration and Islam. Even the FN president characterised this debate as an 'institutional gadget' for purely electoralist ends.[26]

This new attempt to capture far right votes was crushingly defeated: in March 2010, the FN bounced back with 11.42% of votes cast, which carried it forward to the second round in 12 out of 26 regions, to the chagrin of the UMP.

Pursuing its course despite everything, the government introduced a law on the wearing of the burka, the 2,000 or so women wearing it supposedly representing a new threat to the Republic. The law banning the wearing of the burka on the national territory was adopted on 13 July 2010. Through this text 'against the concealment of the face', the presidential majority courted an electorate for whom Islam and immigrants more generally represent a permanent threat and the source of all evils. At the height of the financial crisis, it also allowed the government to focus the attention of the media and the people on an entirely different subject.

The next avatar of the impact of far right discourse on governmental activity was the xenophobic onslaught on Roma and travellers in the summer of 2010 and the law and order demagogy which followed. Previously upheld only by the far right, the link between immigration and delinquency was now proclaimed at the summit of the state. In his 'Grenoble speech' on 30 July 2010, Sarkozy stigmatised '50 years of insufficiently regulated immigration'.

In a series of interviews given to 'Le Monde' dating from 14 August 2010, FN cadres agreed that 'Sarkozy's statements on the relation between immigration and delinquency favour and give credibility to the FN.' They added: 'Sarkozy serves as an icebreaker for the Front and he is not conscious of it. ... That gives legitimacy to our

---

[26] *Le Monde*, 26 October 2009.

arguments ... that shows that our programme is not so bad, when the president has just adopted it.' Louis Aliot, former secretary general of the organisation added: 'We must keep up the pressure to make the right implode. The recomposition will take place around us, our ideas.' Far from being hidden, the strategy is open, and it paid off at the municipal elections of March 2014.

However, there are still significant obstacles to a UMP–FN alliance: the economic disagreements are huge between the two parties (on the return to the franc, protectionism and Europe), so the risk is great that the UMP would see a part of its moderate electorate flee to the centre or the PS. Also UMP local leaders are sociologically and culturally very different from FN activists, notably in the North and East.

2.5 The 'Manif Pour Tous' and the FN: je t'aime moi non plus!

For the whole of the right, the 'Manif Pour Tous'[27] events (eight months of mobilisation, three national demonstrations, each of around 400,000 people, thousands of local initiatives, satellite groups, hundreds of arrests – a right-wing May '68, according to the press) represented a heaven-sent surprise that nobody predicted, not even the organisers. But what were the real motor forces?

A few moments observing the demonstrations sufficed to grasp their class nature: the social diversity much vaunted by the organisers was in fact limited to the old conservative and reactionary (on this occasion, counter-revolutionary) society, brought together once more in a crusade for its alleged moral values.

---

[27] Campaign initiated in 2012 in opposition to proposed for a law enabling same-sex marriage. Its agenda widened to opposition to adoption by same-sex couples, against IVF treatment, in defence of the family and against the teaching of the notion of 'gender'.

A 'rank and file right wing' and the churches

The organisers of this right-wing social movement usurped and misappropriated left and progressive references: not only May '68 but also the Enlightenment, 1789, the Resistance, as well as recent workers' struggles and the Arab Spring. at that point, however, any comparison with mobilisations of workers and youth ends. Beyond demagogic borrowings, the true demands were those of the 'family, human dignity, the Christian civilisation of our country' and so on.

More pertinent than the references to May '68 is the analysis stressing the appearance of a 'rank and file right'. It is a fact that no party of the right (UMP, UDI) or far right (FN) has steered or led this movement. First, because the right is itself experiencing a crisis of leadership, as spectacularly highlighted by the Copé-Fillon battle for the UMP presidency; numerous demonstrators identified themselves as being 'disillusioned with the top-down right' and went onto the streets to show their frustration. Second, the various reactionary parties are themselves very divided.

The UMP and FN divided

If Copé and Sarkozy's supporters were fully involved (while nonetheless avoiding any commitment to abolish the law in the event of a return to power), Fillon, Juppé and other UMP leaders had a much more guarded position, even calling for demonstrations to stop after the law had been promulgated. Symptomatic of these divergences was the fruitless call of the pro-Copé vice-chair Peltier to beat Kosciusko-Morizet in the Paris UMP primary to punish her for abstention on this law.

Strong contradictions were also seen in the FN, partly the division into two camps in another 'war of the leaders' which had taken place at the January 2011 congress. The loser, Gollnisch, and in general the traditionalist wing of the FN, were in the front ranks of the protest with Marion Maréchal-Le Pen. But this was not true of Marine

Le Pen and her team (Philippot notably): centred on their strategy of combating the PS for the working class and popular electorate, they kept their distance, avoiding demonstrations and denouncing the debate on gay marriage as a 'diversion' of the 'UMP'. Marine Le Pen said several times that she did not wish to 'become the new Christine Boutin'[28]. However, there was nothing progressive in a discourse which suggested that the main problem was not homosexuality but Muslim immigration.

This position increased the margins of manoeuvre of a galaxy of more radical groups, neo-Nazi and others. The most media coverage was attracted by Printemps Français, which brought together elements from the *identitaire* movement but also distant descendants of a combative Catholicism which emerged at the end of the 19th century in reaction to state anti-clericalism, according to the historian and expert on the far right, Grégoire Kauffmann.

The Catholic hierarchy and its networks

Catholic fundamentalists have been very active in this reactionary eruption, among them the Lefébvriste dissidents of De Civitas linked to the Sacerdotal Fraternity of Saint-Pius X, as well as more influential forces recognised by the Vatican, such as the Fondation Jérôme Lejeune (whose head of communications, Ludivine de la Rochère, presided over the Manif Pour Tous), the anti-abortion networks of Marche Pour la Vie (including Albéric Dumont, who organised the big demonstrations) and the Alliance Vita of Christine Boutin and Tugdual Derville, another national spokesperson of the movement who is close to Opus Dei.

But the French church as a whole has been involved in the movement. Its parishes and very dense associative network, with the Confédération Nationale des Associations Familiales Catholiques et

---

[28] Leader of the Christian Democratic Party (*Parti Chrétien-Démocrate*), a social conservative party associated with the UMP.

Familles de France, were the main structure for the mobilisations. Some organisers of the movement, like the 'moderate' Frigide Barjot, began their activity in the JMJ (*Journées Mondiales de Jeunesse,* World Youth Days, initiated by Pope John Paul II). And it was the reactionary Popes John Paul II and Benedict XVI who awakened what we now see at work. As the editorialist of one of the journals of this movement, 'Catholic Renaissance', put it: 'We should understand that a new stage of the veritable war waged for two centuries against France and its Christian vocation is unfolding under our eyes', that is, an anti-1789.

The Catholic hierarchy controlled their marionette Barjot from beginning to end, starting with its two main figures, the 'primate of the Gauls', Philippe Barbarin, and the archbishop of Paris and then president of the conference of bishops of France, André Vingt-Trois. In his final speech to the latter assembly, made after the adoption of the law, Vingt-Trois said that this 'forced passage' could contribute to 'paralysing political life' and to a rise in 'violence'! 'Le Figaro' commented on 16 April: 'While the president of the bishops could have launched an appeal for calm, faced with tension and the tone of the demonstrators against marriage for all, he has encouraged them not to give up and to practice a sort of conscientious objection.' The radicals in the French church have continued to gain ground over the moderates for some years, particularly among youth.

The Manif Pour Tous, with its left wing (Frigide Barjot) and its right wing (Printemps Français) is first and foremost a layer cake of Catholic associations steered and framed by the church, representing the interests and values of the old bourgeoisie (aristocracy, military and religious hierarchy, Catholic right from Boutin to Buisson) opposed to a 'modern' bourgeoisie defending marriage for all (such as Pierre Bergé, Matthieu Pigasse or Nathalie Kosciusko-Morizet ['NKM'] on the right).

The responsibilities of the government and the PS

Many ask why opposition to marriage and adoption for all took on such breadth, when similar laws have been adopted with less difficulty in countries deemed to be ultra-Catholic, such as the Spanish state or Argentina. This is, first, because the open complicity of the Catholic church with Francoism and the Argentine military dictatorship means that it is still discredited and strongly rejected in those two countries, whereas in France the Church remains powerful, for eample in 1984 organising massive demonstrations for *'l'école libre'* and triumphing over the Socialist government. The French church was able to bring 260,000 people to Les Invalides (where the Manif pour Tous was later held) in 2008 for Benedict XVI's visit to France.

Also the causes are linked to the crisis, which exacerbates the frustrations of middle and small layers of the bourgeoisie, and above all to the policy of the government and the PS.

As if frightened by their own audacity, the government and PS ceaselessly retreated, in particular on medically assisted procreation. From Lionel Jospin, for whom the 'fundamental idea' is that 'humanity is structured between men and women' and 'not according to sexual preferences' to Ségolène Royal, who 'would not have given the name of marriage' via François Hollande's evocation of a 'freedom of conscience' for mayors, signs of indecision multiplied, encouraging opponents.

Cynically using their sole remotely progressive reform to divert attention from a social and economic policy entirely at the service of the employers, the governmemt chose consciously to delay the legislative process, giving the reactionaries more time to mobilise. After the demonstration of 27 January in support of the draft law, the Inter-LGBT, controlled by the PS, abruptly halted mobilisations on the pretext of letting the parliamentary process take its course. Faced with multiplying homophobic attacks, the few reactions on the street were of a minority nature, launched at the initiative of associations like Act-Up or through NPA activists.

Who will benefit at the political level from this reactionary wave which forged a new right-wing generation? The UMP, which has been restored and re-legitimated by the first great movement of opposition to a 'left' government and will have Manif pour Tous leaders on its lists? The FN, whose leaders have been able to appear alongside representatives of the traditional right and who will attempt to build on this in new areas in the municipal elections? The identity-based and neo-Nazi groups which, without really growing in size, have been singularly emboldened by occupying the streets, a dramatic effect of this being the murder of Clément Méric?

The local and European elections will give a picture of the new electoral relationship of forces. In the streets the right-wing reactionary Catholics (UNI, anti-abortion networks) and the far right (Marion Maréchal-Le Pen, *Action Française, Renouveau Français*) could increase their activity. A rightist social agitation like Manif Pour Tous, or an attempt by the far right to take over the Bonnets Rouges movement in Britanny, could be on the agenda.

2.6 The municipal elections of March 2014

The municipal elections are traditionally the worst elections for the Front National, which encounters difficulties in finding lists of candidates, in drawing up a local programme, an absence of 'notables' and incumbent representatives, and so on.

Anticipating the situation, the Front prepared for these elections well in adfvance, from the presidential election: a tour by Marine Le Pen in the provinces in 2013 ('Tour of the Invisibles'), nomination of Nicolas Bay and Steeve Briois as organisers for the elections, training of list heads (courses in Paris and in the provinces, Internet platform, a guide for elected representatives), replacement of many incompetent departmental secretaries, opening of several dozen election offices and so on.

The Front selected its candidates carefully (excluding for example the best known *identitaires*, Philippe Vardon and Pierre-Louis

Mériguet), but numerous scandals (racist Facebook pages of certain candidates, Nazi tattoos on others, a friend of Dieudonné on a list in Paris, candidates registered against their wishes and so on) indicated that they had not been too scrupulous in filling their lists. A significant number of recycled UMP members were candidates (in Paris 19e, Avignon, Digne-les-Bains, Reims, Strasbourg). Also, some FN list heads originated from the Manif pour Tous (Annecy, Saint-Malo) and even, discreetly, the *identitaire* movement (Le Mans, Chassieu) or Action Française (Paris 4e).

Finally, the FN had 596 lists covering nearly a third of the population. Indicative of the activist weakness of the party, rural implantation was still very week and the Front was unable to contest a certain number of towns where its vote in 2012 indicated a high probability of having candidates elected (Haute-Saône, Gisors, Mitry-Mory and others). Nonetheless, there were a total of 20,000 candidates.

In many towns 'phantom' or straw candidates did not campaign and had no local programme, but there was a real campaign and elaboration of a local programme in 'winnable' towns and areas of strength (Hénin-Beaumont, Moselle, Var, Vaucluse). Wishing to give an appearance of professionalism and good management, the Front did not wage an ideological electoral campaign and often presented a programme characteristic of the traditional right: tax reduction, video surveillance or extra police. There were few 'hard' proposals on immigration or Roma and an obvious desire not to shock the voters. Demagogy was not wholly abandoned, and there were various acts of aggression in Arcueil or Paris, and anti-mosque campaigns in Fréjus and Bordeaux, for example.

In the first round the FN received an average of 14.8% on in the towns it contested, coming top in 17 towns and scoring more than 30% in 26 towns of more than 10,000 inhabitants. A total of 323 Front National lists qualified for the second round (by scoring more than 10%). The FN seemed to return to its 1995 level and emerged strengthened from this first round, the most worrying fact being a real breakthrough in popular communes including Hayange (30%), Elbeuf (35%), Fougères (17%), Petit-Quevilly (33%), Argentan (20%), Forbach (35%), Echirolles (21%), Carmaux (23%) and of course Hénin-Beaumont and Marseille-Nord. These results validated the demagogic declarations of Marine Le Pen presenting herself as the 'voice of the people' or of Nicolas Bay that 'there are no longer any deserts for the Front.' On all the evidence, the crisis had benefited the FN. For months, it had fed off the despair of a part of the working class which sought simplistic responses to a daily life made unbearable by the measures taken by Hollande, the new 'president of the rich'.

In the second round, in addition to Hénin-Beaumont and Orange, taken the previous week, the far right won about 15 towns and villages including Fréjus, Béziers and Marseille 7 for the Front, Camaret and Bollène for the Ligue du Sud.[29] We should note the specific cases of the Ménard list in Béziers and the surprise victory in a quadrangular contest in Mantes-la-Ville, the Front narrowly missing victory in Saint-Gilles.

The FN won in the most depressed towns, which often combined a generalised corruption, barely concealed clientelism, higher than average unemployment and deep insecurity, by presenting itself as an alternative and a novelty.

The biggest setback for the Front was its failure to break up the traditional right. Whereas all the media predicted inter-round agreements between the FN and right-wing mayors, none took place. While this is explained in part by the high level of the UMP vote in the first round, we should also note the phenomenon of the clandestine 'useful vote'. A fraction of first round FN voters transferred to the right in the second round when a left victory seemed possible: this was the

---

[29] Founded by Jacques Bompard with other former members of the FN, the Bloc Identitaire, Parti de la France, and Mouvement National Républicain, with an implantation in Provence-Alpes-Côte d'Azur, especially northern Vaucluse, and in Languedoc-Roussillon.

case in Belfort, Tourcoing and Aubagne, where the Front lost half its vote between the two rounds to the benefit of the right, many FN voters choosing the 'useful vote' against a Communist mayor. The cynical calculation of the PS that it could use the FN to divide the right into three did not work, even if it allowed the Socialists to win in Strasbourg, Avignon and Clermont-Ferrand.

An always delicate issue for the FN will be keeping control of its elected representatives: after 1995, the party had practically no influence over the policies of its elected mayors, the party which adores order having a strong tradition of indiscipline. Will Marine Le Pen, who seems to have increased centralism in the party, be able to keep control and steer the FN town halls?

Another essential issue: to avoid FN voters becoming disappointed. Will the contradictions sharpen between FN elected representatives who want to be 'normal' and FN voters who want change, between the small trader who wants lower taxes and the unemployed worker who wants a return to the welfare state? By carrying out concrete local policies, the FN risks institutionalisation, banalisation and loss of its anti-systemic characteristics. Other groups to its right could then try to occupy terrain increasingly abandoned by the FN.

The European elections, however, saw the Front playing on defence of the people against globalisation, safeguarding jobs against relocations, and the electoral expression of popular anger against a left blind and deaf to the suffering of the masses.

First measures

For Marine Le Pen, there is no question of repeating the errors made 20 years ago. She has thus rejected the ideal of 'laboratories': in future, municipalities managed by the Front will develop a local policy and not implement ideological directives coming from above. She has said that this time there will not be any purges of libraries or municipal staff.[30] However, the FN has created a cell for recruitment of local government managers, intended to train voluntary staff to work in FN town halls.

The FN seems, then, to have based its municipal policy on the search for cuts in expenditure. In the new flagship town of Hénin-Beaumont, a vast plan for cuts starting from 2015 has been announced, together with a cut in housing tax of 10%, which, being based on a fixed percentage, benefits the wealthiest most. The Audit Office having shown its disapproval – Hénin-Beaumont has €30 million of debt for 26,000 inhabitants – the mayor, Steeve Briois, replied that he would 'look for subsidies in the appropriate place' (for example, the EU).

Cuts have already taken place, in subsidies paid to the local CGT (*Confédération Générale du Travail*) and FCPE (*Fédération des Conseils de Parents d'Élèves*) in Villers-Cotterêts and the end of the free provision of an office to the LDH (*Ligue des Droits de l'Homme*) in Hénin-Beaumont, for example. In terms of spectacular measures serving as ideological markers, the FN is far now more reticent than it was 20 years ago. However, as a good will gesture addressed to its most racist voters, it has already cancelled the commemoration of the abolition of slavery in Villers-Cotterêts, and forbidden left forces from commemorating the Nazi deportation of Jews in Mantes-la-Ville (whose mayor, Cyril Nauth, has said he will oppose a plan for a Muslim prayer room approved by the outgoing municipality), and nominated reputedly 'radical' far right personalities to leadership posts in Béziers.

Between an electorate which demands visible measures from elected representatives and the national ambitions of Marine Le Pen for respectability, the contradictions are numerous, with two newly elected FN mayors in Var[31] dipping into the public coffers already.

---

[30] 'To suppress posts, we expect that people will leave, through retirement or for other reasons'.

3   An end to fascism ... but not just that!

3.1   Fascism?

The exact political characterisation of a party like the Front National raises questions beyond purely etymological or semantic problems. 'To misname things is to add to the unhappiness of the world,' said Albert Camus; to mischaracterise a political phenomenon can lead to significant errors of analysis and strategy, above all for those who display a certain fetishism in relation to vocabulary, believing they have already analysed a social or political phenomenon if they attach the 'correct' term to it.

A term which should not be used simply for political abuse

The term 'fascism' can have its full political meaning only if one guards against using it as a simple insult. For decades individuals and political forces have used this word, sometimes wrongly: the (bourgeois) state is fascist, Nicolas Sarkozy is fascist, a military dictatorship is fascist, the boss is fascist, and so on. We even saw, in the late 1920s and early 1930s, the then largely Stalinised Communist parties describe their reformist-socialist adversaries and rivals as social fascists. Certainly, when this term was used, the real horrors of fascism were not known. Italian fascism was in power (since 1922) but not German Nazism, and the world had not experienced the Second World War or the extermination of the Jews of Europe. Nonetheless, this vocabulary contributed to a profound division of the workers' movement, facilitating the coming to power of the NSDAP (*Nationalsozialistische Deutsche Arbeiterpartei*, or Nazis) in Germany.

---

[31] 'Philippe de la Grange has increased his indemnity and that of his deputies by 15%. In Cogolin, Marc-Etienne Lansade has awarded himself a monthly payment of 1250 euros for his 'costs of representation.' *Le Figaro*, 24 April 2014.

In summary, it is unacceptable to use the term 'fascism' lightly, simply as an insult. The term so used would lose all its political meaning, and its use could even become dangerous.

A movement which does not boil down to 'support for capitalism'

If the term claims to describe a more precise political phenomenon, it must describe something distinct from the 'ordinary' forms of political representation of the bourgeoisie. Fascism should absolutely not be confused with liberal, conservative, Gaullist or Bonapartist forces, or indeed authoritarian and militarist forces (of the Pinochet type), which defend the interests of the bourgeois economic order. It constitutes, on the contrary, a specific mass movement. It has indeed played a role in safeguarding of capitalist ownership of the means of production, when this order was seriously threatened by an exacerbated world crisis and by the rise of the socialist and Communist movement. But this was neither its primary objective nor the slogan under which the fascist forces mobilised their base and often considerable crowds.

In any case, not all fascist protagonists were consciously agreed on this goal. Some fascist leaders, through pure demagogy or 'sincerely', explicitly rejected the idea of serving as the 'guard dog of the bourgeoisie'. A current particularly attached to social demagogy thus left the NSDAP in 1930, dissenting from Hitler's over-close proximity to big capital. A part of this current then formed small groups like the Black Front (*Schwarze Front*), another section later returning to the triumphant Nazi party. Although objectively opposed to big capital, there is no question of classing among progressive or democratic forces a current whose leaders professed nationalist, anti-Semitic, and anti-democratic ideas favourable to violence.

However, even if, unlike these leaders, Hitler, with his grasp of opportunities and the relation of forces at the time, chose an alliance with the big bourgeoisie when this became possible, this was not the case before he came to power (from 1920 to 1933). The salvaging of capitalism as an economic order, the objective historic result of inter-war fascism and the alliance made, in a context of exacerbated crisis, between the leaders of capitalism and the rising fascist movements, was not written in advance. Certain fascist-type movements spent more or less long periods in opposition over this period, without the big bourgeoisie relying on them, and their leaders could not be sure of the course of history, or predict the consequences of the 1929 crash. This is of course also true of far right movements after 1945, many of which spent decades in opposition and sometimes political marginality.

Fascism, as a political movement, is not then a simple representation of the interests of the bourgeoisie or one of its fractions, contrary to the discourse of some devotees – mostly Stalinist – of a vulgar Marxism, who present it as a simple 'agent of big capital'. Nor is it a force which would seek simply to insert itself in the parliamentarism of bourgeois democracy in a game of (peaceful) alternations of power. On the contrary, it is characterised by the genuine desire for a profound 'cleansing', a 'purification', a 'sweeping away' of the established order and its current representatives, in an optic of social and/or political transformation.

A specific dynamic

Historic fascism, that of the inter-war period, is distinguished by specific elements which enabled a specific dynamic. It appeared at a time when the 'social question' was massively urgent, shaking the existing capitalist system. The collapse of the old order after the First World War exacerbated this tension. If the workers' movement mobilised part of society on a class basis, other small sectors also entered into movement: employees without much class consciousness, petty bourgeois elements threatened with becoming declassed, traders, artisans or small employers ruined by the concentration of capital or the 1929 crisis, demobilised First World War soldiers unable to return to their old place in the social order. These forces did not necessarily share the same objectives as the organised workers' movement. Even inside the working class, or more broadly among wage earners, different political ideologies contested for hegemony: the attraction of the workers' movement with its different political expressions was real, even very strong, but it did not act alone on society. Nationalism, which had deeply impregnated the masses with the onset of the First World War, also acted as a powerful motor. Modern anti-Semitism, born in 1870–80 period and freed of the old purely religious basis of anti-Judaism to become an economically based discourse, the rich and the exploiters being presented in a racialised vision and systematically identified with the Jews, would also play its role.

In this context of social tension and political radicalisation, fascism fixes its task as that of competing with the workers' movement, by adopting a discourse in which certain aspects superficially resemble those of the latter. That is, up until the seizure of power; after that, as we know, the discourse gives way to repression of the workers' movement.

While in opposition, fascism denounced social misery, exploitation (not by capital, but, according to the context, by foreigners, by the powers that acquired a dominant position following the First World War, or by Jews and freemasons), the current order of things, that part of the intellectualised and feeble bourgeoisie, unlike the 'young and healthy forces of the Nation'. But it did so in the name of mobilising ideologies which do not refer at all to the class struggle or the objective of creating a classless society. On the contrary, the 'good, healthy part' of the bourgeoisie, with 'real national sentiments', is invited to form part of an alliance which will triumph over the forces of the old established order. Fascism thus tries to take the head of the mobilisation of society's discontented, to surpass in (apparent) radicalism the forces of the workers movement through recourse to phraseology.

To do this, it necessarily adopts forms of organisation which radically distinguish it from the political forces which normally represent the bourgeoisie (liberal or conservative parties). It organises in the street, in the popular neighbourhoods, sometimes in the workplace. It contests the workers' movement for public space and political space in the enterprises. Far from confining itself to the institutional, parliamentary and media spheres as do the classic bourgeois or reactionary parties, it seeks to mobilise society 'from below', like the revolutionary or reformist forces of the workers' movement, the trade unions and workers' associations. The objective is different of course: not to promote the individual and collective emancipation of the exploited, poor or oppressed, but to mobilise them and channel their energies into an organisation guided by a reactionary ideology.

Once in power, fascism will moreover often maintain similar forms of organisation, but they change their function: it is no longer simply about mobilising the masses to channel these same energies 'against the system' but of being the eyes, ears and hands of the new regime which tries to root itself in every neighbourhood, family, and unit of production, sometimes to detect opposition and if need be repress it, and sometimes to mobilise around the objectives of the new regime. That regime must, at regular intervals, show its ability to again mobilise the masses and appear in tune with them.

Fascism after 1945?

To sum up, a party or political movement which – like a classic bourgeois party – remains confined to the institutional, parliamentary and electoral sphere has none of the characteristics of the historic fascist movement. It could only be characterised as 'fascist' by removing any meaning from the term.

However, we should avoid another trap, that of adopting a definition which is too narrow and restrictive because it is too attached to historic forms of appearance which have necessarily been transcended. Thus, part of bourgeois French historiography has for a long time claimed that there never was any fascism in France – even under the Occupation and Vichy regime – because the characteristics supposedly necessary to fascism (the single party, the uniforms and so on) were not present in France at the time. In the country's political history, only the 'three rights' presented in the dull and apolitical book by René Rémond: the 'legitimist' (conservative, historically monarchist), 'Orléanist' (liberal) and 'Bonapartist' (subsequently Gaullist) right. This thesis, ardently upheld by some bourgeois historians, is grotesque in several aspects. [32]

Indeed, one of the differences between France in the 1930s and 1940s and the Italian or German models resides in the fact that the fascist far right in France never succeeded in creating a single political formation, and that it only owed its accession to power in 1940 to the military defeat of the country. That is due, above all, to the political defeats that the fascist far right had suffered, notably in 1934–36. The road to power by way of the streets or by parliamentary elections being barred to it by a powerful counter-mobilisation (around the workers' movement and its allies), the fascist far right had to await an historic opportunity to take power, and it was the German attack which provided it. But this does not in any way exclude characterising the political forces which came to dominate from 1940 in France – or a part of them – as fascists. Certainly, they also recruited in milieux which were simply reactionary and traditional, attached to the clergy of the Catholic church or the army, to Vichy whose regime was based on a composite alliance. Nonetheless, several of the political currents which dominated between 1940 and 1944 can be clearly characterised as fascist, whether in Vichy or in the Parisian collaboration where forces like the RNP (*Rassemblement National Populaire*) of Marcel Déat and the PPF (*Parti Populaire Français*) of Jacques Doriot were active. The latter sometimes sought to depend more directly on Nazi

---

[32] *Les Droites Aujourd'hui*, Louis Audibert Editions, March 2005.

Germany to bypass Vichy, which led to a radicalisation of the policies implemented.

A comparison with other countries in the same period shows moreover that none of the fascist or fascistic regimes followed exactly the same model. In Spain, during the seizure of power by Franco following the civil war from 1936 to 1939, there was no single party either: there was certainly the 'Falange', but it was far from having the same political weight in its camp as the Fascist party in Italy or the NSDAP in Germany. In Japan, the nationalist and militarist regime – which resembled European fascism and was part of the Axis alliance – was not based on any united mass party. The process which led to its installation took place principally inside the army.

For all these reasons, it would be wrong to adopt so narrow definition of fascism as to eclude its presence if one or some of these elements are lacking. The main victorious fascist movements all included certain elements which allow us to identify them – the existence of massive paramilitary forces (in the form of militias or the Brownshirts – *Sturmabteilung*, SA), uniforms, 'mass organisations', open terror against opponents, the dismantling of trade unions and the workers' movement, and so on. We will certainly not necessarily find all these elements in a directly comparable form in a different periods. We should, then, make a more specific analysis, including the dynamic in which a political force is located or that it seeks to create, abstracted from elements attached to a given historic period.

The FN, a fascist force?

The first thing to note is that the French FN, at the time of its foundation, placed itself firmly in affiliation with historic fascism, but Italian rather than French. When the FN was created in October 1972, the French far right was rather splintered, while in neighbouring Italy, there was a relatively powerful party (scoring around 10% of the vote), the MSI (*Movimento Sociale Italiano*) which gave activist and financial aid to the creation of the FN in France. The MSI was clearly of fascist affiliation and did not conceal the fact: it used the symbol of the tricolored flame (green-white-red), adopted from its foundation in 1946, as its logo. Immediately after the war, this symbolised, in the eyes of the MSI founders, 'the soul of Benito Mussolini which rises to the sky, from his coffin'. The French FN would adopt this same symbol from its foundation and still has it today. Perhaps not all its members know the exact origin of the symbol but the generation of the founders are not ignorant of it.

In the first years of its existence, the FN did not hide its links with the fascist past in Europe, and its roots are clearly based in part in this historic experience. The first leading ideologue of the FN from 1973 until his violent death in 1978, François Duprat, edited among other publications the *Revue d'Histoire du Fascisme*, a publication which was neither impartial nor scientific.

However, for the FN – especially after it became a mass party in electoral terms – to be definitively characterised as a 'fascist formation', other elements would need to be present. Theoretically, it could be said that it could not be currently characterised as fascist – because it lacks several elements – but it maintains the memory of the historic experience of fascism, for example as a form of goodwill in keeping the votes or financing of 'old timer' nostalgics. For a clearer political analysis we should look at the FN's concrete political dynamic and what the party seeks to promote.

We start here from the postulate that such a party could alternatively be characterised as an electoralist party which de facto is integrating itself into the game of bourgeois democracy (whether or not it clothes its strategy with a 'folklore' recalling fascism), or a party which is genuinely the bearer of a fascist dynamic. There are possibly mixed forms, all the more so in that a party like the FN is itself a composite alliance of diverse currents, but fundamentally the two tendencies are opposed. A purely electoral party having as its sole historic horizon participation in bourgeois democracy, and possibly governmental alternation inside of this framework, is different from fascism, which involves the search for a dynamic situated outside of the bourgeois state, attempts to create combat groups, build implantation in the popular neighbourhoods or workplaces, adopts a paramilitary logic, and so on.

During the first years following its initial electoral successes (1983/84), the FN behaved above all as an electoral force participating at local and regional level in 'managerial' alliances with the right: in the Dreux municipality, in regional councils in Montpellier and Marseille from 1986, and so on. At this time, it was very far from the world of labour – all the more so because, before its strategic 'national-social' turn from 1989/90 (following what it believed to be the 'death of Marxism' leaving it as the 'sole existing systemic opposition'), its economic and social discourse remained ultra-neoliberal; it had hardly any extra-parliamentary or extra-institutional focuses. Having been a small group until 1984, the party grew through members gained in the 1984–86 period who sought, rather, to build a 'harder' but 'respectable' party of the traditional right, integrated into the parliamentary game. Some members, even some elected representatives, were then lost in the following period, after the first anti-Semitic 'gaffes' by Jean-Marie Le Pen in 1987 and 1988.

However, the behaviour of the FN changed from the early 1990s, following the 'national-social' turn. The party now sought to build an alternative to right *and* left, following the supposed 'death of Marxism' and any left alternative after the fall of the Berlin wall. It positioned itself as 'against the system', with the perspective of making gains on the left equivalent to that of the 10-15% coming from the traditional right. FN strategists believed they could thus, unlike all the 'establishment' parties, reach a level in polls close to 30% and follow the trajectory of the Nazi party in 1930–32. In 1995-98, the FN had to recognise the partial defeat of this strategy, hence accelerating the search for some structures outside the institutions of the bourgeois state, through so called 'trade unions' (created in 1995–96 but not legally authorised as such from 1998[33]), tenants' associations in housing estates, and a multitude of satellite associations.

The dynamic the FN sought at this period – with both relative success and setbacks–– resembles that of the historic fascist movements on a much more modest scale, far smaller than the hundreds of thousands of proletarians enrolled in the Nazi SA around 1930. Cadres and leaders would, however, sometimes use 'revolutionary' and 'anti-system' rhetoric. In October 1996, emerging from a public meeting at Wagram in Paris, Bruno Gollnisch participated in an FN attempt to lay an (unauthorised) wreath under the Arc de Triomphe, leading to a confrontation with the police. Four days later, in Montceau-les-Mines (Burgundy), FN stewards – the infamous DPS (*Département Protection et Sécurité*) – attacked a counter-demonstration with considerable violence, exhibiting behaviour which mimicked a genuine fascist dynamic, even in the absence of the historic conditions of the overthrow by the far right of the bourgeois Republic.

The fact that the strategy did not really succeed was among the factors leading to the big split in the FN in 1998/99 and the implosion of its activist apparatus, which took at least a decade to overcome and whose effects are still felt. The loss of a good part of the activist and cadre base made the FN a purely electoral front from 1999 à 2010, living off the capital of a reputation accumulated previously.

It was only with the resolution of the question of the succession of Jean-Marie Le Pen, in 2010/11, that the party managed to rebuild a more powerful apparatus. For tactical reasons linked to the search for de-demonisation, the new president Marine Le Pen sought to avoid actions which were too apparently reminiscent of historic fascism. However, the new leader also updated the strategy of establishing the FN in the popular neighbourhoods, even if the method followed remained, for now, primarily linked to electoral mechanisms.

---

[33] Social Front for Employment (*Front Social sur le Travail*): FN-Police, FN-RATP, FN-Prisons, disbanded by law.

Meanwhile, the FN also continues to attract activists who seem fascinated by the idea of a resurgence of elements of fascism.

We could sum up by noting that the FN emerged from a historic affiliation with fascism, and that it continues to carry within itself the germs of such a political dynamic. Today, for reasons of political realism, the FN leadership is (re)building the party mainly in the electoral field. However, it actively rejects – and not solely because the other big parties refuse to ally with it – any logic of participation in an alliance for the 'banal' management of the bourgeois institutions. We would need to see how it behaved if the other parties (notably the UMP) changed their policy on alliances. If the opportunity to participate in a coalition really came to the FN leadership, strategic splits could not be ruled out.

Elsewhere in Europe

Some far right parties, comparable in many ways with the FN, have at times chosen to enter a governmental alliance. This was the case with the FPÖ (Freedom Party) in Austria (from 2000 to 2005, with participation in the executive), the Northern League and the 'post-fascists' in Italy (in 1994, 2001–06, and 2008–13, each time under the leadership of Silvio Berlusconi and with far right ministers). This was also the case with the DPP in Denmark from 2001 to 2011, and the Dutch PVV from 2010 to 2012, even if these two parties emerged from a different tradition than the FN. Also, in the Dutch and Danish cases, there was support without ministerial participation. These examples show that, at least in the political conjuncture of these experiences, governmental participation has not led to the transformation of the political order – that of bourgeois democracy – into regimes of the fascist type.

Compared with the case of the FN, that case of the Austrian FPO, founded in 1956 shortly after the Treaty of Neutrality (1955) between the Austrian Republic and the Allies ending their control of the country's political life, which they had occupied since 1945, is more glaring. Since the end of the Second World War, the Allied regime strictly monitored all attempts to recreate a political force in the wake of the defunct Nazi party. With the end of this regime of control, the FPÖ could emerge. Indeed, far from transforming the bourgeois republic into a regime of the fascist type – when it entered government, in February 2000, as the second biggest political party in the country (behind the social democrats, but 0.1% ahead of the conservative party to which it was allied) with 27% of votes cast – the FPÖ handled its participation in government lamentably, falling to 6% of votes cast at the European elections in June 2004. At the national level, its vote was around 10%. It was only with its return to opposition in 2005 that the party recovered (strongly) in terms of electoral scores.

To summarise, even if some of the activists and leaders of these political parties ardently wish it, they are not in a position to unleash a real fascist dynamic when the historic conditions are not right. We could consider that they constitute formations of fascist heritage, bearing within them themselves the germs of a fascist-type dynamic, but all of their potentialities cannot develop at the current time. A deepening of the crisis, a degradation of the political situation (notably with a quasi-disappearance of the left) could, however, change things.

Populism?

To remedy the difficulty resulting from this understanding, some political analysts and journalists have proposed an alternative term, 'populism'. With fairly fluid contours, this term is supposed to describe political parties which cannot be classified as fascist but which have certain traits distinguishing them from 'ordinary' bourgeois parties. However, the cure here is worse than the disease, the term 'populism' explaining even less than 'fascism' in terms of the current behaviour of these parties.

'Populism' is thus characterised by a systematic recourse to the 'people', as opposed to those at the top, the little against the big, the will to exploit every discontent more or less shamelessly. Indeed, to explain the political nature of parties like the FN by this (supposed) behaviour is at best to confuse the form of appearance with the profound nature, the conjunctural with substance.

It is obvious that a party like the FN, placed in opposition (at least at the national level) since its creation and thus enjoying an 'oppositionist's bonus', which has no government record to defend, uses a rhetoric which is anti-establishment. It is natural that it should seek, with this perspective, to use discontent with the existing order, or some of its aspects, against other parties. That is common, to various degrees, to all opposition parties and movements.

Those who systematically use the term 'populism' as a pseudo-explanation of a political behaviour often attach the label to forces of social opposition ('left populism') as much as to reactionary and racist forces ('right populism'). The term thus loses any explanatory force and becomes a simple label for forces outside the 'Republican Arc' of the 'respectable', reasonable, intelligent formations. Furthermore, in other places and at other times, the term 'populism' has been used to describe totally different realities from what it is used to describe in France today. For example, the Populist movement of the 1890s in the USA was a left and anti-racist political movement with a class character.

Worse still, the term and concept of 'populism' do not in any way explain the political behaviour of a party like the FN. Obviously, simple exploitation of discontent in no way explains the deep strategic changes in the history of the FN, such as, for example, its change from a Poujadist and ultra-neoliberal discourse (surely also a form of populism?) in the 1980s to a rather 'national-social' discourse from the 1990s onwards. While this turn allowed the FN to win new layers of voters, it repelled others, notably in the petty bourgeois layers who returned to the traditional right in 1993–95. Still more importantly, some of the FN's political turns have definitely not been accompanied by a search for increased popularity, nor have they in any way reflected a powerful current in public opinion.

When Jean-Marie Le Pen decided in 1990 to break radically with the traditional pro-Western (and pro-US) orientation of the FN in foreign policy and to take up the defence of the regime of Saddam Hussein in Iraq during the Gulf War, it was largely incomprehensible to the public, including FN voters, only a minority of whom agreed with it. This significant ideological turn was not motivated by a desire to reflect public opinion, which in 1991 largely supported the Western military expedition (not the case with the Iraq war of 2003). On the other hand, changes in the world situation after the fall of the Berlin wall, and the will to build a 'new principal opposition' against neoliberal capitalism under US domination which seemed to triumph in 1989, motivated the choice of the FN leadership, which had nothing 'populist' about it since this new position was quite unpopular. It was nonetheless a very important political turn in the history of the FN.

To summarise, the use of the term populism smacks of confusion rather than political explanation and it should be left to bourgeois commentators who are content with simplistic labels rather than analysing the dynamic of things.

The FN can then be analysed as a political formation carrying within itself the germs of fascism – a fascism adapted to its time, to the potentialities and limits offered by the epoch – but whose fruits have not yet blossomed. It is up to us to stop these venomous fruits from growing.

3.2 Other French far right groups and their links with the FN

In recent months, fascist small groups have been seething with activity. The breach opened by a security-oriented national discourse of the Patrick Buisson type developed over two electoral campaigns by Nicolas Sarkozy, Marine Le Pen's de-demonisation policy, and the cleansing operation within the Front National in line with this strategy, together with the coming to power of the left, have revived the activity of radical small groups to the right of an FN accused of betrayal.

The demonstrations against 'marriage for all' allowed these groups, characterised by the historian Danielle Tartakowsky as 'clandestine passengers', to ride on these mobilisations, win media visibility and practice their favourite sport, violence, all the more so in that the UMP, in some of its positions, incited them, hoping to draw future electoral gains from this.

These groups carried out spectacular actions to get media coverage and the card of respectability played by Marine Le Pen opened up activist space for them. Their goal is to occupy and hold the street like their ancestor *Occident*[34] in the 1960s. The killing of Clément Méric thus took place in a specific context.

Cities such as Lyon, Toulouse and Bordeaux have for some years been the theatres for this aggression. Competition is fierce between these small groups, the aim being to attract activists from competitors. Forbidden to march in the FN parade on May 1st, they organise their own cortège for the demonstration in honour of Joan of Arc.

Four main protagonists stand out: Renouveau Français, Bloc Identitaire/Génération Identitaire, Œuvre Française/ Jeunesses Nationalistes and finally the Jeunesses Nationalistes Révolutionnaires and Troisième Voie.

Renouveau Français, the 'movement for national rebirth', was created in 2005 and succeeded *Garde Franque*, responsible for an attack on sans-papiers who occupied the basilica of Saint-Denis. It is a counter-revolutionary, Catholic traditionalist movement led by Thibaut de Chassey (a shareholder in the company which markets wine on behalf of Dieudonné). It advocates a social Christian nationalist state, based

---

[34] *Occident* (1964–68) was founded by Pierre Sidos, founder also of Jeune Nation and œuvre Française.

on 'the traditional social order and classical civilisation'. It publishes a review, *Héritage* ('our national identity is above all our blood. Generalised racial mixing destroys diversity'). During the demonstrations against 'marriage for all', *Renouveau Français* participated alongside the Catholic fundamentalists of *Civitas*.

Bloc Identitaire and its youth structure, **Génération Identitaire**, emerged in April 2003 from *Unité Radicale*, dissolved after the attempted assassination of Jacques Chirac by Maxime Brunerie. The Bloc is led by Fabrice Robert and Philippe Vardon and controls an Internet press agency, *Novopress*. Its members can appear under various names such as *Projet Apache*. It has a women's section, *Les Antigones*, neo-pagan and fans of Sparta. It carries out anti-immigrant and Islamophobic campaigns, sometimes with Riposte Laïque. It characterises equal marriage as an 'anthropological revolution' and has been responsible for such operations as disruptions of Printemps stores in Paris to denounce the buyout of the company by Qatar, occupations of the national headquarters of the PS, and the building site for a mosque in Poitiers. The latter action led to the arrest of four activists and the creation of a support committee which included Robert Ménard, Jean-Yves Le Gallou and Pierre Sautarelle from the Fdesouche Internet site (*François de Souche/français de souche*). The Bloc Identitaire has not broken contacts with the Front National. Some of its members were present on FN lists or supported by the Front for the municipal elections of March 2014: in Béziers, on the list headed by Robert Ménard, and in Le Mans where Lois Noguès headed the list. This was also the case for Romain Espino, alias Romain Castel, a federal councillor from *Génération Identitaire* and a member of the Clan (hard core of GI) who headed the list of the *Rassemblement Bleu Marine* in Chassieu (Rhône), and was arrested after the occupation of the PS offices at the end of the 'Manif pour Tous' (26 May 2013). After a very rapid return trip to the Rassemblement Bleu Marine, Phillipe

Vardon headed a 'Nissa Rebella' list in Nice against the FN and its head of list, Marie-Christine Arnautu.

Œuvre Française and the **Jeunesses Nationalistes**, adepts of the Celtic cross, practice a division of roles: Yvan Benedetti, who succeeded Pierre Sidos, heads the adult organisation while Alexandre Gabriac leads the Jeunesses, created in October 2011. Both were expelled from the Front National for dual membership and for having actively supported Bruno Gollnisch at the last FN congress. They still sit on the Rhône-Alpes regional council. The two groups are nationalist, anti-Semitic and in the tradition of Pétain. Benedetti thus calls, with reference to Pétain, for 'a second national revolution because our nation and our civilisation are at stake'. Gabriac has a high media profile; a television team followed his trip to Italy to visit the tomb of the Duce, and Greece where he has contacts with Golden Dawn. He says he is 'neither more nor less anti-Semitic than Saint-Louis' (the king who forced Jews to wear a distinctive sign, forbade mixed marriages with them and expelled them). The Nazi salute is 'an Olympic salute'. Gabriac wishes to 'destroy one by one the vices which poison our race' (human rights and democracy).

Believing the FN 'expels real nationalists', Gabriac wanted to regroup in his new organisation 'many young orphans in a structure of fighting youth'. For him, the FN has become 'a den for all the turncoats once decried by Jean-Marie Le Pen'. He wants to 'retake France and recover the country'. The movement's motto is marked by Mussolini: 'To fight, to win – a duty'; for 'action without concession'.

Benedetti says: 'the French should be and remain masters at home and not foreigners on their own soil... A natural Frenchman can only come from a European origin, from a spiritual tradition and a common intellectual culture.' Benedetti and Gabriac called on 29 September 2012 for a 'revolt of the indigenous'. Gabriac considered that the death of Clément Méric[35] was simply an unfortunate incident: 'A TGV has just run over a traveller who crossed the tracks, the SNCF should be dissolved.' With the Greek neo-Nazis of Golden Dawn, financial support was organised for Esteban Morillo, the killer of Clément Méric. The OF has a women's organisation, Les Caryatides, grouping 'nationalist women' and identifying with the *National Revolution*. Worthy heirs of Pétain, they say that 'the place of women is dictated by the intangible law of the transmission of life'.

Jeunesses Nationalistes and *Œuvre Française* were dissolved by the government.This did not unduly bother Gabriac: 'We will reorganise otherwise ... nationalism will continue. Even if you cut the branches of the tree, you will not stop it growing.' Thus, Benedetti and Gabriac have reactivated the website *Jeune Nation* and toured the provinces to maintain the morale of the troops. During the 'Jour de Colère' demonstration of 26 January 2014, supporters of the two small groups marched behind the Caryatides. For the municipal elections of March 2014, they presented a list (Vénissieux Fait Front) which led to the filing of a complaint by the FN.

The final notorious small groups of the fascist milieu are the **Jeunesses Nationalistes Révolutionnaires** and **Troisième Voie** led by Serge Ayoub, who in 1985 appeared with his troops under the banner *'les Amis de Barbie'* (Klaus, rather than the doll of the same name). In 1987, with the neo-Nazi 'Klan' movement, he launched the first version of JNR and began a rapprochement with the *Troisième Voie* of J-G Malliarakis, an alliance of short duration (combining a theorist with the Kronenbourg boys proved difficult). Ayoub (Batskin) made contact with the Kop of Boulogne (the *kobistes*, of a home supporters' stand at Paris Saint-Germain football club) and published a fanzine, 'Pour le prix d'une bière'. In 1992-94, the JNR with F. Chatillon's GUD

---

[35] Clement Méric, a left-wing anti-fascist militant, was killed on the 5 June 2013 following a confrontation with the far-right Jeunesses Nationalistes Révolutionnaires. Two members of the JNR were prosecuted, but later released, and the organisation dissolved.

provided some of the security for an FN meeting at the Zénith indoor arena in Paris and did so for other big FN occasions. Batskin has a high media profile and was in demand for television broadcasts ('Ciel mon mardi', 'Droit de savoir', '52 sur la Une', and others).

The 1990s marked a high point for attacks and murders committed by supporters of these organisations: in 1995, at the margins of the FN May Day demonstration, B. Bouarram was thrown into the Seine and drowned; Régis Kerhuel (known as Madskin), Ayoub's right hand man at the time, and Joël Giraud were arrested for the murder of a young Mauritian in Le Havre, and there is a long list of other incidents. After the death of a S. Deyzieux, a far right activist, following a banned demonstration, Ayoub participated in a support committee which included the FNJ, GUD, JNR (Comité du 9 Mai or C9M) and in the demonstration with FN members (Le Gallou, Le Hideux and others).

After an eclipse, the mid-2000s saw Ayoub's return. With A. Soral he founded an 'espace convivial', Le Local in Paris's 15th arrondissement, a place of convergence and debate for all the small groups. He re-launched *Troisième Voie* and the JNR, which became his praetorian guard, answering only to the leader Ayoub (a reference for all fascists) and ensuring the protection of meetings organised by R. Hélie's review *Synthèse Nationale*, and providing security for the Joan of Arc demonstration, for example, on 12 May 2013. Ayoub has tried to build an implantation in working class milieux by launching a *Front Syndical Patriotique* and developing an anti-capitalist, anti-left, anti-employer and anti-globalisation discourse. He targets youth from the most impoverished classes and his ideology draws both from the Strasser brothers (founders of the German NSDAP) and Mussolini's fascists, whose slogan, 'Believe, Obey, Fight' has been taken up by Ayoub. Unlike its direct competitors (JN, OF, BI, RF), JNR and TV had a very discreet participation in the 'Manifs pour Tous'.

Put in the spotlight after the crime committed by Esteban Morillo, the two organisations became subject to a dissolution procedure. Anticipating the government's decision, Ayoub, who talked of a 'new Dreyfus affair', announced the self-dissolution of his two movements.

The efficacy of such measures can be questioned. In 1936, the Blum government dissolved the far right leagues but they rapidly reconstituted themselves, the *Croix de Feu*, for example, becoming the *Parti Social Français*. More recently, *Unité Radicale* became the *Bloc Identitaire*. To dissolve a group sends a message to the public and reflects the will of the government but this type of measure does not dissolve the ideas or individuals, who can adopt other structures.

The different small groups are marked by systematic resort to violence and are animated by visceral hatred of the Other. Rivalry is strong between them, reflected in the battle for leadership, a recurrent phenomenon on the far right. Even if their forces are weak, they represent a constant threat to democracy.

3.3 The FN and its avatars: far right parties to fight

The French Republic has many laws acting as safeguards against the policies and discourse of the FN and certain measures taken by this party have violated the constitution.[36]

Positions adopted by FN leaders and notably the provocations of its former president have moreover been repeatedly subjected to legal sanctions; testing public opinion, the political class and the media, the courts have regularly punished his racist[37] or revisionist flourishes.[38]

---

[36] The birth premium granted by Catherine Mégret was deemed discriminatory and the mayor of Vitrolles was given a three months suspended sentence, with a fine of €15,245 and two years' disqualification from office.

[37] One example among others: on 2 April 2004, the Paris criminal court sentenced Jean-Marie Le Pen to a €10,000 fine for incitement to racial hatred, because of what he had said in 2003 in an interview with 'Le Monde', where he stated: 'The day there are no longer 5 million but 25 million Muslims in France, they will be in charge.'

More recently, Le Pen justified the expulsion of a journalist from the FN congress in Tours on 16 January 2011 by saying: 'He complained it was because he was Jewish he was thrown out. You couldn't tell by looking at his identity card, nor at his nose.'

Under the permanent threat of suppression, the far right has incessantly denounced a legal system which restricts freedom of expression[39] and presents itself as the main victim of this. Thus the FN retains its supposed 'anti-system' logic. But it is above all a militant anti-fascist effort which will halt the advance of the ideas of the far right.

Panorama of different forms of anti-fascism

We present here, in fairly schematic manner, different approaches which could form the basis of an anti-fascist commitment.

A first approach could be summed up as: 'anti-capitalism first and foremost'. According to this conception, the class struggle and/or the final overthrow of capitalism will deal more or less automatically with the question of fascism.

Such a viewpoint, which exists in the camp defining itself (rightly or wrongly) as Marxist – above all in its dogmatic versions – would consider that anti-fascism is a legitimate cause, but does not merit a specific struggle beyond that against the capitalist ruling class.

It is found in different forms, notably in the thesis of 'secondary contradictions' present in part of the New Left after 1968, which affirmed that the main contradiction was between capital and wage labour and that secondary contradictions could be settled immediately before or after the revolution, such as the oppression of

---

[38] An example: on 18 March 1991, he was sentenced by the Versailles appeal court for 'banalisation of crimes against humanity' for saying: 'I am not saying that the gas chambers did not exist. I did not see them myself. I haven't studied the questions specially. But I believe that it is a minor point in the history of the Second World War.'

[39] This is notably the case with the Gayssot law of 13 July 1990 against racist, anti-Semitic or xenophobic speech. This law criminalises the denial of the existence of crimes against humanity. In October 2010, a petition for the abrogation of the Gayssot law and the release of Vincent Reynouard, a national socialist activist who was the author of a pamphlet disputing the existence of the Nazi gas chambers, was circulated.

women, racism, discrimination against immigrants, homophobia, and so on.

A related vision recognises the legitimacy of an active struggle against fascism but sees the latter as a simple form of organisation of the rule of the leading classes of capitalism, a simple expression of the interests of the (big) bourgeoisie. For example, the Third International, recognising the question of anti-fascism as a priority in 1934 following the serious defeat of the workers' movement in Germany by the Nazis, defined fascism in the following words of Georgi Dimitrov : 'Fascism is the dictatorship of the most reactionary, most imperialist circles of finance capital.' Historically, this definition explains absolutely nothing in relation to the genesis of fascism as a political phenomenon. The reality is much more complex, even if it is true that certain elements of capital can rely on the fascist movement, whether in opposition (to sideline or crush other movements which are progressive and potentially dangerous for capitalism), or when these movements come to power. Support for this tactical alliance, by which certain elements of capital can try to organise their survival, does not, however, explain the dynamic of fascist movements, notably when they are in opposition.

Above all, in their periods of opposition, these forces are not always supported by the most powerful elements of capitalism. And the ideological dynamic on which such movements rest often appeals to ideological residues from previous historic periods, whose prejudices are not necessarily functional as such for capitalism (capitalism can easily combine the exploitation of women as well as of men as wage earners, can perfectly well accept equal rights for gays, at least in certain political configurations). Also, frequently, a successful fascist movement attracts individuals or groups, fragments of political blocs, which have become detached from the left and the workers' movement – no longer believing, for example, in the victory of socialism – and are seduced by an ascendant fascism. People like Jacques Doriot, Marcel Déat or Alain Soral are far from being the only examples of such a drift. The author Zeev Sternhell even argues that such a capacity to converge left and right currents is the essence of fascism.

In a softer version, there is a political discourse which recognises an ideological specificity in the far right, but immediately adds: 'Above all, the problem is the crisis, and the rise of fascism is explained above all by the social and economic crisis. If the effects of the latter can be overcome, the far right will also automatically fall back.' It is obvious that a link exists between the two, and that far right movements are strengthened in a context marked by the crisis of capitalism, combined with the weakness of the more progressive movements opposing it. A dual political necessity should, however, be stressed: it is necessary to defend both the idea of a general struggle against capitalism, and that of a specific struggle against fascism, because it will not disappear all by itself (once installed in the landscape). The far right – a movement totally opposed to our objectives – could today nevertheless be strengthened rather than weakened by the crisis of capitalism and it also claims to have responses to the latter.

We find a somewhat different approach, less present in French anti-fascism than elsewhere in Europe – in the German-speaking countries for example, and in the 'radical anti-fascist' milieu, which avoid the social question like the plague and wish to establish a clear separation between the latter and anti-fascism.

This current is sometimes combined with a vanguardism, resting on the idea that the social question is already dominated by the hegemony of the forces of the right in society. Raising the social question in a degraded relationship of forces would then be grist to the mill of the fascist forces: to raise the social question means appealing to a resentment against money, and resentment of money is equivalent to anti-Semitism.

Such an approach is less strong in France, a country whose left is marked by a heritage of social struggles and by an aspiration – broadly shared within society – to egalitarianism. If we find such a vision in France, it is in milieux very distant from our struggles. By way of example, we can cite the book *L'Idéologie Française* by the young Bernard-Henri Levy who claimed in 1981 that there was a common ideological basis to the CGT, Vichy and the far right, which he called 'the French ideology': detestation of money, intellectuals and élites was the common denominator and would constitute the basis of fascism.

We find in this form of anti-fascism either an extremely pessimistic vision of social relations (such as is anchored in part of the German far left or ultra left after the reunification of 1990), or an acceptance of the propaganda of the fascist movements and the image they seek to give themselves. Often fascist movements cultivate a discourse marked by social demagogy, using forms of external appearance copied from the workers' movement. Thus the NSDAP chose the colour red, combined with black and white on its flag; it also chose to put the terms 'socialist' and 'worker' in its name to attract voters disillusioned with the defeats, impotence and divisions of the left. It is a demagogic operation of psychological warfare, even if fascist or Nazi activists sincerely believed in it. But a certain type of anti-fascism takes this propaganda as good coin, drawing anti-fascism towards the 'anti-totalitarianism' of the so-called *'Nouveaux Philosophes'* of the late 1970s, thus towards the rejection of any collective movement, whether it is the workers' movement or fascism.

Third, in France we often face so-called 'republican front' anti-fascism, though this is currently declining (because of the tactical choices made by the UMP and the PS), as shown by the municipal elections of March 2014.

This approach can consist initially in a simple defensive reflex against the worse evil. On the evening of 21 April 21 2002, many activists, including some on the far left, said, 'Faced with death, we provisionally choose disease!', meaning that, faced with a choice in the second round of the presidential election between Jacques Chirac and

Jean-Marie Le Pen, they would choose 'the thief rather than the fascist'.

That did not mean entering into an alliance: this was a tactical question at a historic moment, which lasted a fortnight. But in trying from this, as some political forces did, to found a more lasting political alliance, the logic of the so called Republican front began, attempting to define a link between values or political approaches, uniting the forces participating against a common enemy. Such an approach can be accompanied by anti-racism of a rather moral type (not criticising or not criticising very much, the dominant system), like that defended by SOS Racisme for example.

In 2014, this logic declined somewhat. It can be seen inside the Front de Gauche, in certain phases. Currently, the big parties, whether it is the PS or the UMP – seem rather to have come to the conclusion 'This doesn't correspond to our interests, because people no longer see our differences.' Which (the note is not devoid of logic) risks strengthening the FN rather than weakening it, because it can present itself as the sole remaining alternative to the 'UMPS'.

Fourth, there is a form of vanguardist anti-fascism, sometimes substitutionist (seeking to substitute its own activity for the existence of a broad movement), which is often characterised by the search for direct confrontation, physical if necessary, with the most visible fascist forces.

At the initial level, this is simply about organising urgent self defence against potential or actual violent fascists. Inasmuch as this responds to a visible need shared as broadly as possible, there is no reason to oppose it from our viewpoint. However, the more the methods of action stem from a minority and/or are detached from a need for immediate defence visible to all, the more they are liable to pose a political problem.

In a part of the anarchist and libertarian movement – within which however there are other more complex and nuanced approaches – such a line of march can be in vogue. It is sometimes accompanied by elaborate research on the individuals and structures which make up the different far right movements, with analyses which sometimes reach a high level, as in the publications of the SCALP-REFLEX/No Pasaran movement in the past. At the risk of caricaturing this approach, there exists in these political milieux a practice liable to make anti-fascism appear as a small group affair involving a small number of courageous individuals recognisable by a particular look, participating in a kind of gang war between bands of youths called fascists and anti-fascists, and losing its initial political meaning through tactical and strategic insufficiency. One reason for this is the risk that the fascists, if they are reduced to silence by direct confrontation without having lost their power of ideological attraction, can complain of 'persecution', playing the card of victimisation as enemies of the system, with the anti-fascists portrayed as tools of the powerful. Second, the existing relationship of forces must be taken into account. There have been historic periods, as in the early 1970s when the far right had a fairly limited mass audience, when one could say that fascism had to be crushed in the egg, but that is quite simply unimaginable today, when we face a camp which gains more or less 20% of the vote in France (and in Austria, Hungary, and elsewhere). It is impossible to ban any political expression of it simply by methods of direct confrontation in the streets.

Fifth, we find an approach characterised by the search for a kind of osmosis between anti-fascism and the social movement, in the broad sense of the term.

This type of anti-fascism tries to be a political expression of the social movement. Anti-fascism is here not seen (for example) as a marker designating a specific group of individuals, but as a field of struggle which should be occupied, on which the social and progressive movement should work, while linking with other fields of struggle. This is what some activists tried to do, for example, inside the

Ras l'Front movement (with various thematic commissions: 'family and moral order', culture, trade unions, and so on) in the 1990s.

The basic idea of this approach is that our political and social camp is not in a position – given the size and influence now achieved by the opposing camp – to win immediate 'military' or peaceful battles against the far right, or by preventing its public expression. That can be legitimate, of course, to the extent that it is about showing the rest of society that 'the far right is not a political force like any other, banal, without specific risk.' But it is insufficient when such a victory would not automatically reduce the ideological influence of the far right on a broader scale. It is necessary, then, to combine the rejection of the political expression of the far right with an alternative content to the solutions it claims to have for the evils of the existing system. When it proposes, for example, to respond both to the poverty of families and the difficulty of finding a job by the 'familial model' and 'the return of women to the home', we need to be able to respond to women who, because of difficulties encountered on the labour market, can be attracted by a discourse affirming that: 'the family context can be a consolation, a source of comfort, if moreover we are paid to regain confidence in this natural environment'. Thus, it is necessary to deconstruct this idea, to say why it is false, and repressive and that the family is also – above all in a situation of social crisis – a place of violence and oppression.

That can only be done if this response is supported in part by the principals concerned. Thus – to take another example – when the far right advances supposed solutions through a would-be 'social' discourse, the counter-offensive must rely on the support of trade union movements or collectives of workers in struggle, who seek to develop solutions which reject those advocated by the far right.

A context of crises, the radicalisation of discourse, and reactionary governmental policies, combined with this resurgence of the far right ('institutional' or activist) should today attract our vigilance, and the current absence of a mass structure at the national level should lead us to reoccupy the terrain of anti-fascism.

Neglected for several years, this struggle is now no longer the concern of a narrow fringe of activists. Indeed, if we are convinced that the far right has real destructive power and that it remains one of the enemies of the labour movement, this question should become once more a permanent component of our activism.

Educational work is needed first to reacquaint radical left activists but also for a broader campaign in mass organisations: parties, trade unions and associations should denounce the fraudulent nature and dangers of the far right discourse in order to marginalise them and limit damage caused by them. Anti-capitalist activists should in these conditions participate in the self-organisation of mass movements, in the context of demonstrations and public meetings. This struggle should take place in unity and should not be limited to anti-capitalists alone: the radicalism of our anti-fascist struggle cannot exist at the price of division. Without over-estimating the far right, nor under-estimating it, two errors should be avoided in the context of joint campaigning, that of thinking that any counter-initiative risks giving publicity to a far right which hardly needs it, and that of a bidding war between so-called radical currents seeking to be exemplary, which is often incomprehensible to a majority of those who support our cause. In this context, the joint declaration issued by the main trade union federations following the announcement by several trades unionists that they were on FN lists for the cantonal elections of March 2011– and the expulsions which followed – was a good response:

> The thesis of national preference is opposed to the fundamental values of trade-unionism. Exclusion, the rejection of the other, the inward turn of France and the closure of frontiers, the designation of scapegoats, the denunciation of immigration as being responsible for all evils,

are attitudes which, as history shows, can only lead to the worst... The trade union organisations CFDT – CGT – FSU – SOLIDAIRES – UNSA are determined to prevent the use of trade unionism by the Front National ... whose orientations are opposed to the values they support. The trade union organisations are also guarantors of the respect of these values inside their organisations and by their activists.'

The fight against the rise of reactionary ideas and the far right: the role of the NPA

We are faced with a considerable challenge: to reconstruct an anti-fascist consciousness, exposing the far right as the watchdog of capital before it constitutes a major obstacle to struggles, without crying wolf about fascism but without underestimating the danger the far right already represents for our social camp or, above all, what it represents as permanent potential danger.

The rise of the far right is for now essentially electoral, but the threat is very real. If the crisis worsens and threatens the conditions of existence of petty bourgeois layers, the latter could supply far right movements with troops and physically attack immigrants, trades unionists and left activists, to make them pay for the policy of the current government. In short, the fascists of today, like those of yesterday, are the enemies of the working class.

Thus, faced with the far right, our party systematically defends a politics independent of the state and bourgeois political forces. It is necessary to denounce 'republican fronts'. When the PS shamelessly calls for a vote for the right-wing candidate in the former constituency of Jérôme Cahuzac (a minister forced to resign over tax evasion), this can only strengthen the electorate of the FN and its propaganda about the 'UMPS'.[40] And we should renounce any form of electoral policy

---

[40] UMPS is the combination of the initials of the UMP (the party led by Sareskozy, now known as *Les Republicains*) and of the PS, the Socialist Party.

which under the cover of a 'front against the FN' means that revolutionaries and anti-capitalists do not contest elections. Purely moral denunciation, under an intransigent posture, conceals the abandonment by the PS of any political alternative to unrestrained globalisation and the inability of its leaders to offer any policy other than mass unemployment.

A radical left and anti-capitalist programme which restores hope to those who work is also a weapon against the Front National! We have no illusions in the will or ability of the bourgeois state to deal with the fascist or far right groups. Currently the legal, policy and military apparatuses are not heavily infiltrated by the far right, but examples, from Germany in the 1930s to Hungary and Greece today, show that in the event of development of the far right, the forces of repression are the most attuned to its progress and ideas. We need to develop a specific activity around the following objectives:

1. Deconstructing the political, social and racist programme of the FN by informing and educating activists, because to understand this party's fraudulent nature is to know it. For this, the work of the comrades in the CNAF is precious. We must strengthen it and make it better known in our organisation and outside it. To this end, we shall produce material (pamphlets, posters, leaflets).

2. At the everyday level, in our workplaces, in our trade unions, in the neighbourhoods, there is an ideological struggle to be waged against all the prejudices on which the far right relies, prejudices against immigrants, foreigners, the LGBTI, women, and so on. Taking the offensive against racism, notably Islamophobia and repression against Roma, with campaigns for an end to expulsions, the closure of detention centres, regularisation of the undocumented migrants, equality of rights including the right to vote in all elections, access to welfare for all as well as freedom of circulation and installation for foreigners, and so on.

In response to each attack or provocation from the far right, it is necessary to act as broadly as possible, seeking to win a majority of the population to this political fight. We seek to build the militant unity of all those attacked by the far right by stressing their common interests.

3. Our campaigns for the municipal and European elections have provided an opportunity to develop this struggle in sight of the whole population, both to denounce the fraud of Marine Le Pen, the millionaire heiress who poses as the representative of the people, and to defend a democratic, anti-capitalist, internationalist perspective.

4. We participate in the construction of unitary and permanent, local and national frameworks, which can also be networks of vigilance for anti-fascist intervention in the event of the public appearance of the far right in all its forms.

We wish to link all components and organisations – trade unions, political parties, the 'antifa' movement, Conex (National Coordination against the Far Right), Ras l'Front, and create the conditions for common work. In the trade union milieu, VISA (*Vigilance et Initiatives Syndicales Antifascistes*), despite its weakness, is a useful framework where our comrades can get involved. We fight for unions to take up the struggle against the far right in the neighbourhoods and workplaces by showing that the FN is the workers' worst enemy. We play a ful part in this struggle, which is inseparable from that against the austerity policies which lie behind the rise of reactionary ideas, the far right and fascist threats.

4   General conclusion

Although it has effectively exercised power only at a local level, the rhetoric and programme of the FN have become so widespread that the government of Nicolas Sarkozy drew on its ideas and even prided itself, following the presidential elections of 2007, on having weakened the FN by siphoning off its electorate.

Multi-faceted and even politically contradictory from one decade to the next and from one political majority to another, this party, unique in Europe, whose 14th congress ended on 16 January 2011 with the predictable victory of Marine Le Pen, has profited from the economic and social crisis which affects the population to varying degrees. With a social discourse aimed at the popular classes, the adoption of ecology, secularism and the republic as new areas of propagation hardly conceals its sole political project since its creation: national preference, or discrimination against non French nationals, which the FN wishes to write into the constitution.

The game of sorcerer's apprentice that the traditional right has played in power by manipulating the FN's theses has shown its limits in terms of electoral advantage, and tends to turn against itself. However, despite all the verbiage to the contrary, laws and draft laws persitently go in the direction of this constitutional turn towards legalising national preference.

The results of the most recent cantonal elections in March 2011 indicate that the siphoning of the FN electorate by the UMP has ceased. The new FN president's talent for a communication strategy has brought those disappointed by Sarkozysm back to the Front.

The effect of Marine Le Pen should not, however, be over-estimated and it still provides a smokescreen for the weaknesses of the FN apparatus. Since the split of 1998, the FN has undergone several crises and lost many cadre and activists (2004, 2009). Also, it still faces heavy debts. And although the FN 'primary' between Gollsnich and Marine Le Pen gave the FN the opportunity to win waves of new members, the party has still not reconstituted an efficient national activist apparatus, as is shown by its numerical weakness on its march on 1 May.

Should the radical left wait for this apparatus to become an effective matrix before posing the question of combat against the far right in France and Europe when the votes obtained by these parties increase disquietingly from election to election?

The political struggle of the far right essentially consists in highlighting ideas of national identity, heritage, tradition, of a congealed culture. It thus seeks to render obsolete and inoperative the discourse of class in favour of a nationalist discourse cutting in particular across the most popular social layers.

Left forces – political, campaigns, NGOs and trade unions – have always condemned declarations and initiatives of the right which are dangerous in as much as they banalise the ideas and demands of the far right. The declarations and opposition against attempts of the far right to infiltrate the social and particularly the trade union movement constitute a salutary first step, at least from the viewpoint of unity. But there is still no concrete and effective unitary framework to dismantle far right discourses, which have an unfortunate tendency to be transformed into governmental acts.[41] Going beyond simple moral opposition to make the anti-fascist struggle a class struggle, a united working class will finally expose the charlatanism of the FN.

To a 'national interest' which amounts to pure fiction, we should oppose our class interest – beyond cultural, 'ethnic' or religious affiliations. We should translate this concrete interest of all French and immigrant workers, documented or undocumented, politically in our daily and unitary combat for social, political, and legal rights, for freedom of circulation and settlement on territory on both a national and a European level. Lately neglected, the struggle against fascism and the far right should become a central component of our activism. By fighting for an alternative to capitalism, the greatest vigilance is thus imposed on workers who must denounce the fraud of the FN discourse everywhere it seeks to infiltrate. Finally, the political, social, cultural and associative left, and the trade unions should never forget

---

[41] To be convinced of this, it is enough to examine the latest drafts and proposals of the 'Besson' and 'Hortefeux' law: expulsion of Roma for ethnic reasons, generalisation of minimum sentences, differentiation of nationalities marking a dichotomy between 'French by origin' and 'French by papers', threats to the right to health care for migrants, narrowing of the right of asylum, and so on.

that, as Ras l'Front stressed at its creation in 1990, 'their advances are made from our defeats.'

5   The Front National – a provisional epilogue...

Marine Le Pen gradually took over the leadership of the Front National between its 2011 congress in Tours and the one 2014 held in Lyon. She established her authority by creating a team that is totally devoted to her, which includes Louis Aliot, Florian Philippot, Nicolas Bay and Steeve Briois. Since taking over the leadership of party, Marine Le Pen, in contrast to her father, has been engaged in an operation to 'de-demonise' the party by cleaning-up its language, trying to appear credible, and declaring that it is ready for government. She says that she 'wants to be able to change things... to return power to the people and put France on its feet again'.

The Front National has always demonstrated a great ability for adaptation and opportunism, at times being free-market neoliberal, while at others being state-interventionist. As Louis Aliot puts it: 'The Front National tries to adapt itself to the realities on the ground'. Under the new leadership of Marine Le Pen, it has presented itself as *Front National – Rassemblement Bleu Marine*.[42] Using that label, it has scored victories in council, department, Senate and European elections. Even if the Front National does not have a majority in any Department, it now is in control of a dozen towns across France.[43]

Although the terminology has changed, the fundamentals have not. 'National preference' which has been changed to 'national priority', remains at the heart of the Front National's rhetoric and is

---

[42] *Rassemblement Bleu Marine* (Navy Blue Gathering) is a play on the words for Marine (Navy as well as a person's name) and blue, which is the traditional colour for parties of the right.

[43] The Front National has 23 MEPs and controls the towns of Béziers, Fréjus, Hayange, Cogolin, Beaucaire, Villers Cotterets, Le Luc, Le Pontet, Hénin Beaumont, Marseille (7e sect.) and Mantes-la-ville.

'non-negotiable'. On demonstrations, the slogan is no longer 'France for the French' but 'we are at home'. The FN no longer argues that 'immigrants should be sent back to their shacks on the other side of the Mediterranean', but that there should be an 'organised return of immigrants from the Third World to their homeland'. There is a new coat of paint on the pillars which support the Front National's doctrine so as to appear more acceptable, but there is no fundamental change.

Both Jean-Marie Le Pen and his daughter, Marine Le Pen claim that France is threatened by the four 'I': *Immigration, Insécurité, Islamisme, Imposition* (Immigration, Insecurity, Islamism, and Taxation). Marine Le Pen wants to deepen the party's social roots by relating to those that are 'invisible and have been forgotten', that is workers including those in precarious employment, who have been rejected by the 'UMPS political establishment'. She therefore denounces in a populist and nationalist manner the useless and corrupt elites, and calls upon the 'real as opposed to the legal country' to rise up, as Charles Maurras[44] once said. She wants the Front National take up 'the real questions and problems of the French', to 'arouse the people', to become 'the only defence against the dangers that threaten France', and to be the real defender of national identity.

The programme of the Front National intends to be social and nationalist. It is against the 'glamorous globalisation', and instead calls for a 'moderate protectionism' and a pragmatic nationalism to 'produce French goods by French workers in French firms'. Marine Le Pen supports state economic intervention, in contrast to her father who backed free-market neoliberalism. Furthermore, she claims to be a defender of secularism (*laïcité*), but it is really a position from which to attack Islam, which she sees as 'a religion that is incompatible with secularism and democracy'. In the 1970s, the main enemy for the Front National was communism, in the 1980s it was immigrants, and since 2000, it is Islam and globalisation that are the 'totalitarianisms of

---

[44] Charles Maurras was a leader of the *Action Française*, the main far right party in the 1930s.

the 21st century'. Islam is described as a state within the state, and Islamophobia has replaced anti-Semitism in the language of the Front National.

In her attempt to make the FN respectable, Marine Le Pen must absolutely rid the party of its anti-Semitic skeletons. According to Louis Aliot, 'the 'de-demonisation' of the Front National only relates to anti-Semitism. This is what has to be dumped'. According to Marine Le Pen, the Front National is today the defender of the Jewish community, and today 'anti-Semitism is Islamic'. This explains her quarrel with Jean-Marie Le Pen. He is opposed to the strategy of 'de-demonisation' and has repeatedly made provocative anti-Semitic remarks, leading to his break with the President and his expulsion from the FN, even though he is its founder member.

On foreign policy matters, Marine Le Pen opposes the 'globalised interventionism' of NATO in the Middle East (Iraq and Lybia). She claims that 'the Arab spring is a real danger for France and Europe' because it will create 'a wave of Muslim immigrants' and will encourage radical Islamism in the Middle East and North Africa as well as terrorism internationally. She denounces the European Union as 'an agent of the destruction of the nation' which has put 'France under its tutelage' and wants to rebuild a Europe based on 'identity, which is autonomous, and in solidarity against the Islamic threat'. She is critical of US foreign policy and of the looming TTIP and is developing closer relations with Putin whom she sees as an opponent of the New World Order. For her, it is the European Union and the USA that have both thrown Ukraine into chaos, and the Kremlin should be supported in its actions in Ukraine.

The Front National is riding the wave of fears that it claims is to be found in France: 'globalisation, unemployment, Islam, Europe'. The party is now going down the road established by one of its former leaders, Bruno Megret: respectability and splitting the traditional right to overtake the UMP.[45] It has already achieved one of its objectives: it is no longer a party of protest. However, even though it claims to adhere to 'republican values', it is still a party of the far right which has the ambition to become a party of government.

Bibliography

Fascism and nationalism

Milza, Pierre, *Les Fascismes*, 2001.
Eric Hobsbawm, *Nations and Nationalism since 1780*, 2001.
Leon Trotsky, *Fascism – What It Is and How to Fight It*, 1944.
Ernest Mandel, *Du fascisme*, 1974.
Daniel Guerin, *Fascism and Big Business, 1938.*
Larry Portis, *Qu'est-ce que le fascisme?* 2010.

History of the far right in France

Jean-Yves Camus, *L'extrême droite aujourd'hui,* 1997.
Ariane Chebel d'Appollonia, *L'extrême droite en France: De Maurras à Le Pen,* 1992.
Déconstruire l'extrême droite, nouveaux monstres et vieux démons, Contretemps, no. 8.
Jean-Paul Gautier, *Les extrêmes droites en France,* 2009.
From 1945 to today; an updated version is about to appear in digital form.
R. Monzat, *Les voleurs d'avenir; Pourquoi l'extrême droite peut avoir de beaux jours devant elle,* 2004.
René Rémond, *Les droites aujourd'hui,* 2005.
Michel Winock (ed.), *Histoire de l'extrême droite en France,* 1994.
Good and fairly short history of the far right and the counterrevolution from de Maistre to Le Pen *père.*

---

[45] UMP-Union pour un Movement Populaire, rebranded in 2015 as Les Republicains.

Michel Winock, *La droite depuis 1789: les hommes, les idées, les réseaux,* 1995.

Front National

Dominique Albertini, David Doucet, *Histoire du Front national,* 2013.
Jean-Yves Camus, *Le Front national: Histoire et analyses,* 1996.
Jean-Yves Camus, *Le Front national,* Milan, Collection Essentiels no. 199897.
Charlie Hebdo, *Le Front national expliqué à mon père,* 2014.
Annie Collovald, *Le 'populisme du FN': Un dangereux contresens,* 2004.
Sylvain Crépon, *Enquête au cœur du nouveau Front national,* 2012.
Alexandre Dézé, *Le Front national: à la conquête du pouvoir?* 2012.
Fondation Jean Jaurès, Le point de rupture: Enquête sur les ressorts du vote FN en milieux populaire, 2011.
Monnot, Mestre, *Le système Le Pen,* 2011.

On the staff around Marine Le Pen

Ras l'front, *Petit manuel de combat contre le Front national,* 2004
Romain Rosso, *La face cachée de Marine Le Pen,* 2011
Michel Wieviorka, *Le Front national, entre extrémisme, populisme et démocratie,* 2013
VISA (Vigilance et Initiatives Syndicales Antifascistes), *D'une élection à l'autre, pas de pouvoir au FN... Barrage syndical antifasciste,* 2014
On the FN vote and its causes, an essay can be downloaded at http://www.jean-jaures.org/Publications/Essais/Le-point-de-rupture. Written before the presidential election, it is still relevant, with the best analysis on the vote.

Far right in Europe

Dominique Vidal, *Le ventre est encore fécond,* Libertalia, 2013.
L'extrême droite en Europe (Hérodote no. 144), 2012.

Specific subjects

Jean-Michel Barreau, *L'extrême-droite, l'école et la République, petits détours par l'histoire*, 2003.

Briganti, Déchot, Gautier, *La galaxie Dieudonné*, 2011.

Jean-Paul Gautier, *La restauration nationale: Un mouvement royaliste sous la Vème République*, 2002.

Valérie Igounet, *Histoire du négationnisme en France*, 2000.

ISA, *Le Front national au travail*, 2003.

Lebourg/Beauregard, *François Duprat, l'homme qui inventa le Front national*, 2012.

No Pasaran, *Rock Haine Roll*, 2004.

Filmography

L'extrême droite dans l'histoire. Du général Boulanger à Le Pen, 52 min., France 5, 2004.

Histoire d'une droite extrême (2 parties), William Karel, 1999.

Selective bibliography by the far right

François Duprat, *Les mouvements d'extrême droite en France depuis 1944*, 1972.

Enquête sur L'histoire (Maurras/La Cagoule/Drieu La Rochelle/Alain De Benoist) no. 6 : *L'âge d'or de la droite 1870–1940*, 1993.

The Far Right in Hungary

Adam Fabry

Introduction

In recent years, the Hungarian far right has become increasingly assertive. Paramilitary organisations, drawing on the symbolism of the infamous Arrow Cross, the Hungarian Nazis responsible for the murder of tens of thousands of Jews in the encircled Budapest of 1944-1945, are marching up and down streets around the country, threatening minorities. Meanwhile, inside the halls of the country's neo-Gothic parliament, sitting imposingly on the banks of the Danube, the openly fascist Jobbik party, whose members are renowned for their anti-communist, anti-western, xenophobic, anti-Semitic agitation, has entrenched its position as the third largest party in Hungarian politics. Such views are, however, not only limited to the 'far' right of political spectrum. Since being swept back to power in 2010, there has been a concerted campaign by the neoconservative FIDESZ-KDNP coalition, led by the very talented, but completely unprincipled and ruthless Viktor Orbán, seeking to restore the Horthy regime, named after the fiercely anti-communist and openly anti-Semitic Admiral Miklós Horthy, who ruled Hungary during the inter-war years. Statues of Horthy have been popping up in Hungarian squares in recent years and street names are being renamed after supporters of his regime. The preamble of the country's new constitution, known as the Fundamental Law, which was prepared by the government in less than a year and introduced in 2012 without any regard for non-conformist opinions, states that Hungary lost its self-determination from 19 March 1944 (the beginning of the Nazi occupation of Hungary) and 2 May 1990 (the formation of the first democratically elected parliament since 1945). Effectively, this equates the four decades of 'communism' with the nine months of German occupation as periods of 'alien rule' (at the same time, it explicitly restores the authoritarian Horthy regime, whose many crimes have thus been clinically separated from the 'crimes of totalitarianism'). How has this colossal shift to the right been possible in a country that, until recently, was widely considered as a 'poster boy' of neoliberal capitalism and parliamentary democracy? What are the similarities and/or differences between past and present incarnations of the far right in Hungary? And what is being done to counter the resurgence of the far right?

History and origins of the Hungarian far right

While the material and ideological roots of the far right in Hungary and elsewhere can be traced back to the pressures caused by the uneven and combined development of global capitalism from the middle of the 19th century onwards,[1] it was not until the end of World War I that explicitly far right movements and political parties began to influence Hungarian politics. As the junior partner in the Austro-Hungarian Empire, Hungary entered the war on the side of the Triple Alliance. Faced with a deepening economic crisis, increasing resistance by workers and ethnic minorities in 1917-1918 and the disintegration of the army, the dual monarchy collapsed and an independent, bourgeois-democratic Hungarian republic was declared

---

[1] On the origins of the far right internationally, see Saull, Rick, 'The origins and persistence of the far-right: capital, class and the pathologies of liberal politics', in Saull, Rick, Alexander Anievas, Neil Davidson and Adam Fabry (eds), *The Far Right in the Longue Durée*, London: Routledge, 2014, pp. 21-43.

on 16 November 1918.[2] The republic was headed by Count Mihály Károlyi, a progressive nobleman sand opponent of the war, who formed a coalition government consisting of social democrats and anti-war radicals. However, the new government faced enormous economic and political pressures. According to the punitive peace conditions dictated by the powers of the Entente (formalised under the Trianon Peace Treaty on 4 June 1920) Hungary lost more than 70% of its pre-war territory, including many of its historically most important cities (e.g. Pozsony/Bratislava, Kassa/Kosice, Kolozsvár/Cluj-Napoca), and nearly two-thirds of its population. In addition to the immense economic-, political- and psychological shock caused by the dissolution of 'historical Hungary', the Károlyi government also found itself besieged by Czechoslovak, Romanian and Serb forces, who, supported by the Allies, occupied parts of the country's territories. Unable to counter the multiple pressures facing the young Hungarian republic, Károlyi resigned from power on 20 March 1919.

One day later, on 21 March 1919, a new government coalition, comprised by social democrats and communists, was formed. Led by Béla Kun, a revolutionary Marxist of Jewish origin, the new government managed to rally the support of sections of the army, radical intellectuals, and ethnic minorities, through its promise that it would negotiate the reception of military assistance from the Soviet Red Army against occupying forces, while simultaneously introducing radical reforms. However, the Bolshevik leadership was unable to provide any support, as it was itself held down in fighting the Russian Civil War. Kun and the communist leadership decided to push ahead on their own. They proclaimed a Hungarian Soviet Republic in May 1919, introduced a number of radical reforms (e.g. abolition of aristocratic titles and privileges, separation of church and state, introduction of universal suffrage, the provision of freedom of speech

---

[2] On Hungarian politics from World War I to the Trianon Peace Treaty, see Romsics, Ignác, *Hungary in the Twentieth Century*, Budapest: Corvina Kiadó,1999, pp. 79-126.

and assembly, free education, language and cultural rights to minorities), and even managed to reclaim some previously occupied territories from Czechoslovak forces.

Countering the threat of Bolshevism: the Horthy regime

Faced with the dual pressures of territorial disintegration and socialist revolution, the supporters of the *ancien régime* decided to focus on fighting the latter more forcefully than the former. In the end of May 1919, they set up an anti-communist provisional government in the south-western provincial city of Szeged (at the time under French and Serbian occupation), and elected the last commander of the Austro-Hungarian navy, Admiral Miklós Horthy, as leader of the counter-revolutionary National Army. In early August, its forces stood by idly while French-supported Romanian forces marched on Budapest, the country's capital, which by then had already been abandoned by Kun and his fellow communist leaders. The Romanian military finally abandoned Budapest in mid-November 1919, enabling Horthy to majestically enter the capital on a white horse declaring it 'liberated' from communists and liberals. In retaliation for the Hungarian Soviet Republic's excesses, a brutal wave of 'white terror' followed, in which right-wing paramilitary groups, with tacit support from Horthy and the conservative elite, murdered between five to six thousand persons, most of whom where social democrats, communist and Jews.[3]

With the 'twin evils' of liberal democracy and communism defeated, the forces of the counter-revolution moved swiftly to restore 'law and order'. The Kingdom of Hungary was re-established on 1 March 1920 and Horthy was elected as its Regent. While the Horthy regime was officially a parliamentary democracy, with 'free' (albeit highly restricted) elections, it was effectively a semi-constitutional right-wing autocracy, in which the leader of the nation (Horthy)

[3] Sakmyster, Thomas, *Hungary's Admiral on Horseback: Miklós Horthy, 1918-1944*, New York, NY: Columbia University Press, 1994.

retained significant control over key decisions, including the right to appoint (and dismiss) ministers, convene (and dissolve) parliament, and command over the army. The main aims of the Horthy regime were twofold: 1) the restoration of economic and political 'stability' in Hungary; and 2) abolition of the unjust Treaty of Trianon and the re-establishment of 'historic Hungary' based on 'national-conservative', Christian values. During the inter-war years, these aims coalesced into a dominant conservative ideology characterised by virulent anti-liberalism and anti-communism, Magyar irredentism, and semi-official paramilitarism.[4] There was also a growing interest in (and semi-official support for) 'Turanism' (*Turanizmus*), a romantic nationalist movement dating back to the mid-19th century, which emphasised the common ethnical origins and cultural affinity of the Hungarians with peoples from the Caucasus and Central Asia (Turks, Mongols, Parsi, etc.) and called for closer economic and political collaboration as a means to counter the threats posed by Britain, France, Russia and neighbouring Slavic nations. Meanwhile, radical political parties – such as the Communist Party of Hungary (*Kommunisták Magyarországi Pártja*, KMP), renamed in 1944 to the Hungarian Communist Party (*Magyar Kommunista Párt*, MKP), or the Hungarian Social Democratic Party (*Magyarországi Szociáldemokrata Párt*, MSZDP) – and avant-garde intellectuals (Endre Ady, Attila József, Lajos Kassák) were considered 'enemies of the nation' and their work was either banned altogether or subject to

---

[4] Nationalist indoctrination was a key component of the education system in Horthy's Hungary. Schoolchildren were forced to learn irredentist poems and songs, such as the renowned 'no, no, never!' (*nem, nem, soha!*), from an early age. Meanwhile, young boys (usually aged between 12 and 21 years) who were not able attend school were enrolled in right-wing military schools, known as the 'paladin associations' [*leventeszervezetek*], were they received military training and a conservative education emphasising discipline, religious morality and love for the nation. Originally established in 1921, the paladin assocations gradually became key institutions of pre-military training under the Horthy regime. Following the Arrow Cross takeover in October 1944 young paladins were even thrown in to participate in the war.

persecution and state repression. Yet, the most conspicuous aspect of the national-conservative ideology that pervaded the Horthy regime was its institutionalised anti-Semitism, which, in 1921, prompted the introduction of the first anti-Jewish laws in 20th century Europe, the *numerus clausus*, limiting access to the university for Jewish students.

The conservative governments that ruled Hungary between the early 1920s and the early 1930s drew their principal support from the aristocracy and large landowners, who had dominated Hungarian society prior to the war, large parts of the national bourgeoisie and state bureaucracy, and far right sympathisers within the military and the country as a whole. The relationship between the official regime in Budapest and paramilitarism was particularly disconcerting. Indeed, according to the late British historian Mark Pittaway, '[t]he consolidation of [its] political authority relied on the development of a symbiotic relationship between the aristocratic governing elite and counter-revolutionary paramilitarism.'[5] Prominent far-right organisations, such as the Hungarian National Defence Association (*Magyar Országos Véderő Egylet,* MOVE) and the Association of Awakening Hungarians (*Ébredő Magyarok Egyesülete,* ÉME), which had originally been formed to counter the 'threat of Bolshevism', continued to play an influential role in Hungarian politics and wider society long after the defeat of the Hungarian Commune. These organisations had their origins in counter-revolutionary paramilitarism and despised not only 'socialism', but also liberal democracy, which they blamed for Hungary's defeat in World War I and the successive revolutionary tides that were sweeping through the country. Their leaders, whom included such notorious figures as the former paramilitary leader-turned politician Gyula Gömbös,[6] and

---

[5] Pittaway, Mark, 'Fascism in Hungary', in Fabry, Adam (ed.), *From the Vanguard to the Margins: Workers in Hungary, 1939 to the Present,* Leiden: Brill, 2014, p. 258.

[6] In 1919, Gömbös had been elected leader of the Hungarian National Defence Association (*Magyar Országos Véderő Egylet,* or MOVE), a paramilitary organisation comprised of right-wing army officers who strongly opposed the Hungarian Soviet

Sándor Keltz, one of the earliest representatives of eugenics in Hungary, were openly racist and advocated for the economic, cultural and social protection of the 'Hungarian race' against 'Jewish influence'.[7]

During Prime Minister István Bethlen's period in office (1921-1931), the influence of the far right on the Hungarian political system was successfully contained by Horthy and the conservative elite (although members of MOVE and ÉME briefly held posts in the 'national unity' government formed in 1922). As a result, explicitly far right parties failed to record any significant electoral breakthroughs in the 1920s.[8] Similarly, the two main newspapers of the far right, the *Nép* ('People') and the *Szózat* ('Manifesto'), struggled to attract a wider audience and were forced to close down in April 1926. However, the onset of the Great Depression after 1929 would hit the Hungarian economy hard and move the entire political system further to the right.[9]

The international financial crash of 1929 and the economic depression that subsequently followed resulted in sharp falls in the world market prices of agricultural goods, which, in an economy still heavily dependent on agriculture, like Hungary, caused severe social distress.[10] The immediate impact of the crisis was exacerbated by

---

Republic and felt that mainstream conservatives were not strong enough to oppose communism. See Vonyó, József, *Gömbös Gyula*, Budapest: Napvilág Kiadó, 2014, pp. 71-78.

[7] Vonyó, József, *Jobboldali Radikálisok Magyarországon, 1919-1944*, Pécs: Krónosz Kiadó, 2012, p. 202; id. *Gömbös Gyula*, pp. 106-140.

[8] For example, in the 1926 general elections the Guardians of the Race Party (*Fajvédő Párt*), which had been formed in 1923 under the leadership of Gömbös, suffered a devastating defeat and the party was disbanded in 1928. See Szinai, Miklós, 'A magyar szélsőjobb történelmi helyéhez', in Feitl, István (ed.), *Jobboldali radikalizmusok tegnap és ma*, Budapest: Napvilág Kiadó, 1998, p. 120.

[9] Pittaway, 'Fascism in Hungary', pp. 257-258.

[10] Between December 1930 and December 1932 the world market price of corn and wheat, two major export products for Hungary, fell by 60-70%, leading to significant falls in

staggering differences in land ownership,[11] affecting the agrarian proletariat and small landholders particularly hard. As the crisis deepened, it led to a significant fall in industrial production and falling living standards for Hungarian workers: by the height of the crisis, in 1932, industrial production was 24% lower than in 1929, while around one-third of Hungary's industrial workers were unemployed.[12] Meanwhile, budget restrictions imposed by the government to cut Hungary's mounting trade deficit and foreign debt caused job losses among the state bureaucracy, severely affecting the middle classes.

Lurching further to the right: the rise of Hungarian fascism

Fearing social discontent, Horthy moved further to the right, replacing the 'moderate' Bethlen with Gömbös as Prime Minister in 1932. Gömbös was an outspoken advocate of the so-called 'Szeged idea' (*Szegedi gondolat*). Also known as 'Hungarism', it was a distinct variety of fascism characterised by the idea of creating an 'organic' nation based on the borders of 'historical Hungary' and free of domestic 'traitors' (i.e. liberals, communists and Jews), underpinned by a 'national' capitalism based on agriculture and supported by a 'strong' state, under the ultimate authority of a strong, 'national leader' (*nemzetvezető*).[13] (As we shall see below, the protagonists of later reincarnations of fascism shared many of these ideas.) Following his appointment as Prime minister, Gömbös reorganised the ruling party

---

income from agricultural exports. See Berend, Iván T. and György Ránki, *The Hungarian Economy in the Twentieth Century*, London: Croom Helm, 1985, pp. 58-62.

[11] The distribution of land in Hungary was one of the most unequal in Europe. According to the 1935 census, more than 43% of the land was still in the hands of large landowners (owning more than 120 hectares). Meanwhile, 50% of the peasants owned only 10% of the land, while another 35% owned no land at all. Berend and Ránki, *The Hungarian Economy*, p. 54.

[12] Berend and Ránki, *The Hungarian Economy*, pp. 65-66.

[13] Mann, Michael, *Fascists*, Cambridge: Cambridge University Press, 2004, pp. 240, 243.

into a national, mass-membership organisation – the National Unity Party (*Nemzeti Egység Pártja*, NEP) – and placed far right supporters in key positions. Moreover, he removed senior officers from the army, many of whom advocated conservative positions, replacing them with far right sympathisers.[14] As the renowned sociologist Michael Mann argues,

> He [Gömbös] moved Hungary steadily towards fascism. He declared violence to be 'an acceptable means of statecraft ... to shape the course of history, not in the interest of a narrow clique, but of an entire nation.' He ... embraced corporatist solutions to national unity and moved closer to Mussolini. After Hitler's coup, he promised Göring he would introduce totalitarianism and he wrote to Hitler describing himself as 'a fellow racist'. He declared that his government would 'secure our own national civilisation based on our own special racial peculiarities and upon Christian moral principles.'[15]

Although Gömbös' rule ended prematurely (he died in October 1936 following long-term illness), and proved to be a disappointment for his supporters, Hungary crept further towards fascism during his term in power.

Two factors were key behind the gradual ascendancy of fascism. Firstly, prolonged economic depression at home together with the economic and geopolitical ascendancy of Nazi Germany (and, to a lesser degree, fascist Italy) from the mid-1930s onwards brought increasing support for fascist ideas and practices in society at large. Large sections of Hungarian public opinion, including sections of the ruling conservative elite associated with the Prime Minister between 1938 and 1939, Béla Imrédy, considered the rapid economic growth

---

[14] Pittaway, 'Fascism in Hungary', p. 263.

[15] Mann, *Fascists*, p. 243.

achieved by Nazi Germany – obtained through rising military expenditures and authoritarian Keynesian measures – as a successful model to be emulated by Hungary. The prestige of Nazi Germany was further strengthened following the *Anschluss* of Austria in 1938 because it raised the possibility that an alliance with Nazi Germany might enable Hungary to regain parts of its territory lost following World War I.

The second key feature behind the rise of fascism was the emergence of a unified, nation-wide movement that was explicitly fascist in character. This was, however, not a straightforward process. The early 1930s had witnessed the formation of a number of political organisations openly advocating fascist and national socialist ideas, including the Hungarian National Socialist Workers' Party (*Nemzeti Szocialista Magyar Munkáspárt*, NSZMMP), also known as the Scythe Cross Movement, founded in 1931 by Zoltán Böszörmény, a self-professed admirer of Hitler, or the Hungarian National Socialist Party (*Magyar Nemzeti Szocialista Párt*, MNSZP), founded in 1933 by the large landowner and former ruling party member Count Sándor Festetics. The NSZMMP was explicitly organised on the model of German National Socialists and even launched a failed insurrection against the Horthy regime in 1936. However, these organisations failed to attract any mass support and eventually disintegrated by the late 1930s.[16] This was due to a combination of internal personal struggles, state discrimination, and a failure to expand their membership base beyond conservative smallholders in western Hungary. Instead, it would require the emergence of a 'strong leader', embodied by a former army officer-turned politician, Ferenc Szálasi, to unite various factions of fascism under one banner. Szálasi's first party, the Party of National Will (*A Nemzeti Akarat Pártja*, NAP), was established in 1935, but the conservative government disbanded it two years later for being 'too radical'. The party was reconstituted two years later as the

---

[16] Vonyó, Jobboldali Radikálisok Magyarországon, pp. 200-216.

Arrow Cross Party-Hungarist Movement (*Nyilaskeresztes Párt-Hungarista Mozgalom*, NP). By then, it claimed 250,000 members – 2.7% of the Hungarian population, and significantly higher than the 1.3 and 1% held by the German Nazis and the Italian fascists prior to their rise to power.[17]

The party's iconography – headed by the infamous Arrow Cross – was strongly influenced by the German Nazis and it promoted a variety of National Socialism adapted to Hungarian conditions and concerns.[18] Its aim was the creation of an 'organic' national community, known as 'Pax Hungarica', based on the borders of 'historical Hungary', which incorporated all ethnic groups historically inhabiting the Carpathian Basin, under the leadership of Hungarian people. The only exception were the Jews, who, according to Szálasi, constituted an 'alien race' and 'had not earned the right to live in this moral-national community.' According to Szálasi, the future Hungarian state would be a 'work-based' (classless) society, comprising 'the peasant who sustains the nation, the worker who builds the nation, the intellectuals that lead the nation, the soldiers that defend the nation, and the women and the youth who guarantee the immortality of the nation.'[19] Under Arrow Cross rule, subaltern groups would be liberated from the 'service of Jewish big capital' and the state would 'secure the greatest earnings possibilities for ... those who want to work and are capable of work ... tillers of the land, farmers, and artisans alike'[20] These ideas seemed to resonate with the demands of significant sections of the Hungarian electorate. In the

---

[17] Figures are from Michael Mann, *Fascists*, pp. 237-238.

[18] Pittaway, 'Fascism in Hungary', pp. 257-258.

[19] Szálasi, Ferenc, *Út és cél*, 3rd edition, Buenos Aires, 1955.

[20] 'A Nyilaskeresztes Párt programja', in Gergely, Glatz, and Pölöskei (eds), *Magyarországi Pártprogramok, 1919-1944*, Budapest: Eötvös Kiadó, 2004, p. 104.

1939 general elections, the party won 25% of the votes,[21] while other parties took the combined far right vote above 50%.[22] The party performed particularly strongly in rural areas where, as Pittaway notes, 'a poor smallholder population was an especially significant element of local society', but it also made inroads among the working class, outpolling the social democrats in the industrial towns surrounding Budapest.[23] Having said this, as Mann points out, these figures nonetheless probably understate the popular support for far right ideas and parties in Hungary, 'Since only Hungarian men over 26 and women over 30 could vote, and young people were more fascist.'[24]

By the late 1930s, the Horthy regime was thus faced with mounting pressure both from abroad (Nazi Germany), as well as the ascendancy of pro-German, anti-Bolsheviks forces at home (both within the government and the military command, as well as in the Arrow Cross). Increasingly cornered (and keen to retain his grip on power), Horthy gradually abandoned any pretexts of democracy and moved to satisfy the far right at home and abroad. As a result, Hungary became an increasingly militarised and racist state as the Horthy regime openly aligned itself with the economic and geopolitical interests of Nazi Germany (a move that was considered to further Hungary's territorial aims against neighbouring states).[25] Meanwhile, between 1938 and 1942 the governments of Kálmán Darányi and Béla Imrédy passed further discriminatory laws against

---

[21] However, due to the disproportionate character of the electoral system, this only translated into 31 parliamentary seats (out of a total of 259).

[22] Mann, *Fascists*, p. 238. Compare figures with Paxton, Robert O., *The Anatomy of Fascism*, London: Penguin Books, 2005, p. 73.

[23] Pittaway, 'Fascism in Hungary', p. 267.

[24] Figures are from Michael Mann, *Fascists*, 2004, p. 238.

[25] This process became increasingly inevitable following the introduction of the Győr-programme in 1938, which provided one billion *pengő* for the development of armaments (to upgrade the Hungarian army, but also in order to satisfy German demand). As a result, the Hungarian economy increasingly took on the characteristics of a 'war economy'.

Jews, including restrictions on the number of Jews allowed to work in the public and private sectors, a ban on mixed marriages, confiscation of private property belonging to Jews, and being forced to serve as unarmed workers in military battalions.[26] Simultaneously with the demotion of Jews as second-class citizens, the regime also intensified the stigmatisation and discrimination of the Roma population, most of who belonged to the poorest sections of Hungarian society.

Although the Horthy regime refused to support Nazi Germany's invasion of Poland in 1939, it moved increasingly closer to the Axis Powers, regaining southern Slovakia in November 1938, Carpathian Ruthenia in March 1939 and northern Transylvania in September 1940. Finally, on 27 June 1941 Hungary officially entered World War II on the side of the Axis Powers, declaring war on the Soviet Union. But the war turned out to be a disaster and the country suffered enormous human and material devastation. According to conservative estimates by the Hungarian historian Ignác Romsics, around 900,000 Hungarians (6.2%) out of a population of 14.5 million died in the war, including some 350,000 soldiers (many of whom died due to the substandard quality of their equipment), while as many as 600,000 Hungarians – most of them soldiers, but also between 100,000-120,000 civilians – were displaced or fell into Soviet captivity.[27] However, the worst victims turned out to be Hungary's Jewish minority.

By early 1944, with Soviet troops advancing from the north and east, Horthy began discussions with the Americans and the British about an armistice. However, Hitler found out about the plans and, on 19 March 1944, Nazi troops invaded Hungary, in order to ensure continued Hungarian allegiance. While Horthy formally maintained his powers, he was effectively placed in house arrest, and forced to replace Prime Minister Kállay with Döme Sztójay, a former

---

[26] Mann, *Fascists*, p. 244; Pittaway, 'Fascism in Hungary', p. 269.

[27] Romsics, Hungary in the Twentieth Century, p. 216.

ambassador to Berlin and an outspoken supporter of the Nazis. Following the orders of the Nazi military governor Edmund Veesenmayer, a special *Judenkommando* was established in order to supervise the extermination of Hungary's Jews. Led by Adolf Eichmann, but enthusiastically supported by Hungarian authorities, it oversaw the deportation of an estimated 440,000 Hungarian Jews (virtually all of the Jewish population in the provinces) between 15 May 1944 and the end of June 1944.[28] Pressured from neutral (e.g. Sweden, Switzerland and the Vatican) and Allied governments (Britain and the US) to intervene, as well as with an eye to his own future (following news about the Normandy landings and fresh German defeats), Horthy eventually ordered the deportations to be halted in early July. However, for those that had survived, the worst was still to come.

In September 1944 the Red Army crossed the Hungarian border, prompting Horthy to reopen peace talks with the Allies (including the hated Soviet Union). However, Horthy's belated and amateurish attempt to break with Nazi Germany backfired. On 15 October 1944 he was removed from power by Hitler in a *coup d'état* and replaced with Szálasi, the notorious leader of the Arrow Cross. Szálasi established a 'national unity government', which pledged continued loyalty to Nazi Germany and to 'realise the goals of Hungarism'. The new government sought to resume the systematic liquidation of Jews, but was hindered from doing so due to the country's rapidly deteriorating infrastructure system. However, this did not stop the Szálasi regime from unleashing a brutal reign of terror against the remaining Jewish population. With much of the railway network destroyed, tens of thousands were forced walk on foot from Budapest to the Austrian borders in death marches, while many of those who remained were lined up in pairs alongside the banks of the Danube

---

[28] With a few notable exceptions, there was very little opposition to the deportations inside Hungary.

and simply shot into the freezing river (in order to save on ammunition, the Arrow Cross henchmen only shot one of the two victims). In total, more than 500,000 Hungarian Jews (approximately two-thirds of the total Jewish population) were murdered in World War II. In addition, between 10,000 and 50,000 Hungarian Roma also lost their lives as a result of the Porajmos.[29] As for Szálasi and other Arrow Cross leaders, they were eventually caught by Allied forces and returned to Hungary for trial.

The regime change of 1989 and the return of the far right

Following the end of World War II and the establishment of establishment of an anti-fascist, popular front government (backed by the Soviet Union) in 1945, far right ideas and parties were officially banned from Hungarian society. Many of its leaders, including Szálasi and Imrédy, were brought to trial by specially constituted People's Courts and executed. Registered members of the Arrow Cross were imprisoned or prevented to return to their pre-war jobs, while institutions, like the gendarmerie (csendőrség), that were considered to have supported the Nazi occupation and anti-Jewish measures were officially disbanded. However, anti-fascist retribution by the post-war Hungarian state and especially the leadership of the Hungarian Communist Party (Magyar Kommunista Párt, MKP) was selective. Following Stalin's orders no charges were brought against Horthy for his responsibility in war crimes, instead he was allowed to leave Hungary and lived the rest of life in exile, in Portugal. Meanwhile, as Pittaway notes, following 'the relaxation of regulations concerning internment in 1946, many 'little Arrow Crossists' were freed from the camps. Indeed, 'During the late 1940s large numbers of those who supported Hungarism's radical programme of reform joined or supported the Communist Party.'[30]

---

[29] Romsics. Hungary in the Twentieth Century, p. 213.

[30] Pittaway, 'Fascism in Hungary', p. 273.

New parties, old ideas: the far right in the 1990s

Since the 'regime change' (*rendszerváltás*) in 1989-1990 far right ideas and movements have gradually re-emerged in Hungarian society. This process has been facilitated by the weakness of 'progressive' democratic forces and the emergence of an uncompromising neoconservative right from the early 1990s onwards, which has shown a noticeable admiration for many of the ideas and practices that characterised the Horthy regime during the inter-war years (rabid anti-communism and anti-liberalism, respect for law and order, promotion of Magyar irredentism and the restoration a genteel, property-owning Hungarian middle-class). While the neoconservative right has taken several institutional forms since 1989 – from to the parties that formed part of the 'moderate' right-wing coalition between 1990-94 to the FIDESZ-KDNP coalition holding power since 2010 –, it has, similar to Horthy regime in the inter-war years, enjoyed a symbiotic relationship with far right parties and movements.[31]

One of the most vociferous and influential spokespersons of far right ideas in the 1990s was István Csurka, a well-known playwright during the Kádár regime and a founding member of the then ruling Hungarian Democratic Forum (*Magyar Demokrata Fórum*, MDF). Csurka vehemently opposed the policies pursued by József Antall's right-wing coalition government between 1990-94, in particular with regard to privatisation and the media. In the autumn of 1992, he published a lengthy article in *Magyar Fórum*, the MDF's semi-official weekly paper, blaming Hungary's problems on a conspiracy by external and internal 'enemies' of the Hungarian nation. These

---

[31] Rowlands, Carl, "Gypsies are Animals' – Racism on Hungary's Right', *New Left Project*, 1 February 2013. Available on: http://www.newleftproject.org/index.php/site/article_comments/gypsies_are_animals_racism_on_hungarys_right (last accessed on: 11 December 2013); Pittaway, 'Fascism in Hungary', pp. 274-275; Verseck, Keno 2012, "Creeping Cult': Hungary Rehabilitates Far-Right Figures', Der Spiegel, 6 June 2012. Available on: http://www.spiegel.de/international/europe/right-wing-extremists-cultivate-horthy-cult-in-hungary-a-836526.html (last accessed on: 10 November 2014).

'enemies' were a devilish coalition, which included the IMF, multinational corporations and leading Western states, such as the United States and Israel, as well as a cabal of Judeo-Bolsheviks and/or Judeo-liberals at home.[32] His position caused a political crisis within the ruling MDF, as it became evident that his ideas were supported by a substantial – though not a majority – of the party's members.[33] In fact, even after Csurka's expulsion from the disintegrating MDF, the conservative government organised a ceremonial reburial of Horthy's remains in his native village Kenderes on 4 September 1993. The event was broadcast on state television and was supported by Prime Minister Antall who hailed Horthy as a 'Hungarian patriot'. It was attended by leading members of the government including minister of justice István Balsai and minister of interior Lajos Boross.[34]

Following his expulsion from MDF, Csurka went on to establish the Hungarian Justice and Life Party (*Magyar Igazság és Élet Pártja*, MIÉP) in September 1993. The party's name was an allusion to the Party of Hungarian Life (*Magyar Élet Pártja*), the official ruling party of Hungary between 1932 and 1944. Ideologically, the party restated many of the political positions revered by Hungary's conservative elite during the inter-war years, including its self-identification as a

---

[32] Andor, László, Hungary on the Road to the European Union: A Transition in Blue, Westport, CT: Greenwood Press, 2000, pp. 49-52, 76-77; Drahokoupil, Jan, Globalization and the State in Central and Eastern Europe The Politics of Foreign Direct Investment, London: Routledge, 2009, p. 104; Hanley, Lawrence King, and István Tóth János, 'The State, International Agencies, and Property Transformation in Postcommunist Hungary', The American Journal of Sociology, Vol. 108, No. 1, 2002, p. 153; Pittaway, Mark, 'Hungary', in White, Stephen, Judy Batt, and Paul G. Lewis (eds), Developments in Central and East European Politics, Vol. 3, , Basingstoke: Palgrave Macmillan, 2003, p. 66. For the original document, see Csurka, István (ed.), Néhány gondolat és nyolc társgondolat, Budapest: Magyar Fórum, 1992.

[33] In January 1993, at the MDF's 6th national conference, Csurka openly challenged Antall for the leadership of the party, but lost with a narrow margin of 138 votes (536 in favour, 674 against).

[34] Perlez, Jane, 'Reburial Is Both a Ceremony and a Test for Today's Hungary', New York Times, 5 September 1993; Rowlands, "Gypsies are Animals".

'national-conservative', 'Christian' party, rabid anti-communism and anti-Semitism, and the aim of restoring Hungary's pre-Trianon borders.[35] However, MIÉP's social basis differed significantly from its historical predecessors – most of the party's support came from elderly, middle-class, urban voters, in particular those living in the historically wealthier Buda districts of the Hungarian capital. In spite of this, the party's radical nationalist and anti-Semitic rhetoric was capable of attracting limited electoral support. The party won 248,901 votes (5.47%) in the 1998 elections, which enabled it to send 14 deputies to parliament.[36] Four years later, in 2002, the party obtained nearly as many votes as in 1998 (245,326 votes), however, due to the higher overall turnout, it was not enough to get above the 5% threshold for parliament.

The 1990s also saw a number of attempts to resurrect explicitly Hungarist, national socialist ideas, by organisations such as the Hungarian Welfare Association (*Magyar Népjóléti Szövetség*, MNSZ) or the Hungarian National Front (*Magyar Nemzeti Arcvonal*, MNA). The MNSZ received much media attention in the mid-1990s, in great part due to its notorious leader Albert Szabó, who denied that Hungarian Jews were murdered in the Holocaust and, at a demonstration on 23 October 1996, called for 'Hungarian Jews to be excluded from key economic, political, cultural and state administration positions'.[37] However, the most enduring of these parties has been the MNA. Formed in 1989 by István Györkös, allegedly in response to requests from old fascist leaders who had been exiled during 'socialism', the organisation openly revered neo-Nazi ideology and symbols. In 1997 the MNA organised the first 'Day of

---

[35] Andor, Hungary on the Road to the European Union, pp. 50-52.

[36] Pittaway, 'Fascism in Hungary', p. 274.

[37] Vultur, Csaba and István Mága, 'Perek szélsőjobboldaliak ellen: itélet is meg nem is', *Magyar Narancs*, 19 February 1998. Available on: http://magyarnarancs. hu/belpol/perek_szelsojobboldaliak_ellen_itelet_is_meg_nem_is-61981 (last accessed on: 3 December 2014).

Honour' (*a becsület napja*), an annual neo-Nazi propaganda event held in memory of the (failed) attempt by Nazi German and loyal Hungarian troops to break out from Buda castle on 11 February 1945 (then under siege by Soviet troops), which brings together sister organisations from Hungary and elsewhere in Europe. Moreover, the party also organised regular paramilitary training exercises for its members in the village of Bőny, close to Győr in north-western Hungary. However, in recent years the MNA has been plagued by financial difficulties and internal splits, leaving the organisation relatively small (a presumed membership of 30 people) and ineffectual.[38]

Up until the mid-2000s then, although far right ideas had re-emerged in Hungarian society, parties that explicitly professed far right and Hungarist views had not managed to achieve any significant electoral inroads. This was the moment when Jobbik entered the political arena.

Far right renewal and the ascendancy of Jobbik

The origins of Jobbik date back to 1999, when a group of nationalist university students formed the right-wing Youth Movement (*Jobboldali Ifjúsági Közösség*, or Jobbik[39]). Following the defeat of MIÉP in the 2002 general elections it was transformed into a political party in October 2003 and changed its name to Jobbik – the Movement for a Better Hungary (*Jobbik Magyarországért Mozgalom*). At the time, it claimed 1,200 members.[40] According to its founding

---

[38] 'Hungarian National Front', Athena Institute, 7 July 2014. Available on: http://www.athenaintezet.hu/en/map/olvas/20#read (last accessed on: 3 December 2014).

[39] The party's name is actually a *double entendre*, meaning both 'the right' and 'the better'.

[40] Tóth, András and István Grajczár, 'Válság, radikalizálódás és az újjászületés igérete: a Jobbik útja a parlamentbe', in Enyedi, Zsolt, Andrea Szabó and Róbert Tardos (eds), *Új képlet. Választások Magyarországon, 2010*, Budapest: Demokrácia Kutatások Magyar Központja Alapitvány, 2011, p. 60.

manifesto, the party described itself as a 'conservative', 'national-Christian', 'radical' organisation, whose ultimate aim was to 'complete' the regime change of 1989 and 'to create a better and more just society'.[41] In the 2006 general elections it formed an electoral alliance with MIÉP, but only obtained 119,007 votes (2.2%) and thus failed to get into parliament. The alliance was broken shortly afterwards following internal disagreements. However, since then, the party has risen rapidly through the polls.

Jobbik became increasingly visible in domestic politics after the massive demonstrations against Ferenc Gyurcsány's socialist-liberal government (in which the party played an active role), which shook Hungary during the autumn of 2006. In subsequent months and years, the party became increasingly popular, after skilfully riding a growing tide of anti-Roma sentiment in Hungarian society. Jobbik's first major electoral breakthrough took place in the 2009 European Parliament elections, in which the party won 427,773 votes and arrived third, behind Fidesz and MSZP, with 14.77% of the votes. While the result shook the Hungarian political establishment, it enabled Jobbik to send three representatives to the European Parliament. Since then, the party has consolidated its position as the 'third force' in Hungarian politics. As the table below indicates, the party doubled its electoral support in the 2010 general elections, obtaining 855,436 votes (16.67%) and 47 seats in parliament. In the general elections held in April 2014, the party won more than 1 million votes (20.22%), behind the ruling Fidesz-KDNP coalition (44.54%) and the second-placed social-liberal unity coalition (25.99%). However, due to a recent change in the electoral system, this was only sufficient to obtain 23 out of 199 seats (11.55%) in the new, reduced parliament.

---

[41] Jobbik, 'Alapító Nyilatkozat', 24 October 2003. Available on: http://jobbik. hu/jobbikrol/alapito-nyilatkozat (last accessed on: 26 November 2014). See also Korkut, Umut, *Liberalization Challenges in Hungary. Elitism, Progressivism, and Populism*, New York, NY: Palgrave Macmillan, 2012.pp. 186-187; Tóth and Grajczár, 'Válság, radikalizálódás és az újjászületés igérete', p. 60.

Jobbik's electoral performance (European and national parliamentary elections), 2006-2014[42]

Elections	Percentage	No. of voters
EP elections, 2009	14.77	427,773
EP elections, 2014	14.67	340,287
Parliamentary elections, 2006	2.2	119,007
Parliamentary elections, 2010	16.67	855,436
Parliamentary elections, 2014	20.22	1,020,476

Note: In the 2006 general elections, Jobbik formed a coalition with MIÉP

Explaining the rise of Jobbik

So what are the causes behind the spectacular rise of Jobbik? Its rapid rise in popularity can largely be pinned down to three main factors: 1) the failure of neoliberal restructuring since in the last 25 years; 2) the demise of liberal democracy (and the centre-left who were its most ardent supporters); and 3) the ability of Jobbik to present itself as 'new' political force, offering 'radical' solutions to Hungary's economic, political and social malaise.

The failure of neoliberal restructuring

The regime change of 1989 was widely perceived as the *annus mirabilis*, when the wonderland of free market capitalism and liberal democracy was opened for Hungary and other 'socialist' states in Eastern Europe. As elsewhere in the region, Hungary's new economic and political elite (which often bore a remarkable similarity with the

---

[42] Source: Hungarian National Election Office (*Nemzeti Választási Iroda*). Available on: http://valasztas.hu/ (last accessed on: 18 November 2014).

old one) embraced neoliberal policies of accumulation, including the introduction of radical austerity measures, liberalisation of trade and financial markets, privatisation of previously state-owned enterprises, and the marketisation of public resources. This was in the hope that these policies would contribute to economic growth and higher living standards, a 'return to the west', while simultaneously leading to the development of a strong, domestic bourgeoisie supportive of liberal-democratic values. The hopes of the time were well summarised by Miklós Vásárhelyi, an author and former press secretary of Imre Nagy, the reform-minded Stalinist leader of the Hungarian Revolution of 1956. In 1989 he told a *New York Times* reporter:

> First of all there will really be a Europe again. The countries of Central and Eastern Europe will finally get an opportunity to unite with the West. We will begin to live under the same conditions. It will take time, but socially, politically and economically we will achieve what the Western countries have already achieved. The door is now open.[43]

With 25 years of hindsight, however, we know that this turned out to be a mirage. Rather than a fairytale, the neoliberal transformation of former Soviet bloc turned out to be a nightmare. While neoliberal restructuring produced some individual success stories, including former *nomenklatura* members-turned entrepreneurs who made fortunes on buying and selling western cars and consumer goods, or selling off previously state-owned enterprises to transnational corporations, it has deepened class, racial and regional inequalities in Hungary and elsewhere in the region. The arrival of foreign capital, new technologies, and the gradual transition to a post-Fordist economy, based on finance and services, rendered existing skills and

---

[43] Vásárhelyi, here quoted in Gwertzman, Bernard and Michael Kaufman, *The Collapse of Communism*, New York, NY: Random House, 1990, pp. 225-226.

infrastructure obsolete and many unskilled workers redundant. In total, more than 1.3 million jobs (almost one-third of the Hungarian workforce!) disappeared during the first five years of the transition. Structural adjustment measures introduced between 1988 and 1995 destroyed more economic assets than did World War II.[44] According to the Hungarian sociologist Zsuzsa Ferge, the biggest losers of the regime change in Hungary were those who were,

> ... low on all types of capital – economic, cultural, social, psychological or other. They were probably never among the best off, but in the former system most of them had gained existential security and some sort of, perhaps token, self-esteem ... More concretely, among the losers we find the unemployed ... many of the unskilled and semi-skilled ... village-dwellers (peasants); families with children, who are losing family benefits and childcare services; and, as result, some women.[45]

The entrenchment of mass unemployment led to declining living standards and the emergence of mass poverty, with almost one-third of the Hungarian population (nearly three million people) living in poverty by the early 2000s.[46] According to the sociologists János

---

[44] Fabry, Adam, 'End of the Liberal Dream: Hungary since 1989', *International Socialism*, No. 124, 2009, pp. 71-84; Szalai, rzsébet, *New Capitalism – And What Can Replace It*, Budapest: Pallas Kiadó, 2008; Tamás, Gáspár M., 'Counter-revolution against a counter-revolution', *Eurozine*, 2007. Available on: http://www.eurozine.com /articles/2007-09-18-tamas-en.html (last accessed on: 28 December 2013).

[45] Ferge, Zsuzsa, 'Introduction', in Ferge, Zsuzsa, Endre Sik, Péter Róbert, Fruzsina Albert, *Social Costs of Transition. International Report*, Budapest, August 1997, p. 4.

[46] Eurequal, The State of Inequality in the Central and Eastern Europe: Desk Research on Hungary, Oxford: Eurequal, 2006, p. 2; Fóti, Klára (ed.), Alleviating Poverty: Analysis and Recommendations. Human Develop-ment Report for Hungary, 2000-2002, Budapest: Institute for World Economics of the Hungarian Academy of Sciences and United Nations Development Programme (UNDP), 2003, p. 56.

Ladányi and Iván Szelényi, the most significant aspect of poverty in post-transition Hungary was the creation of an 'underclass' comprised of permanently unemployed people with no proper access to health care, education, and social security.[47] Making matters worse, welfare protection and provisions have been strenuously cut by successive governments in Budapest, irrespective of where they stand on the political spectrum. The increasing retirement of the state from welfare provision has also been accompanied by an increasingly explicit and formalised stigmatisation of the 'lazy' unemployed and 'undeserving' poor in public discourse. As János Lázár, an influential politician within the ruling FIDESZ party, bluntly summarised the domi nant worldview of the contemporary Hungarian ruling class, 'he who has nothing, is only worth as much'.[48]

While many unskilled workers and sections of the middle class also fell into poverty, the Roma population, who constitute Hungary's largest ethnic minority accounting for 3.2% of the population in 2011, was hit particularly hard.[49] Following the years of (enforced) full employment under 'actually existing socialism', the unemployment rate among Roma people skyrocketed, with only 30% of the Roma being employed by the mid-1990s.[50] As early as 1997, Martin Kovats, a British researcher on Roma politics, painted a dramatic picture of the situation facing many Roma families in Hungary:

> The last ten years have been a disaster for the majority of Hungary's Roma population. Most of those who had work

---

[47] Ladányi, János and Szelényi, Iván, *A kirekesztettség változó formái*, Budapest: Napvilág Kiadó, 2004.

[48] 'Fidesz parliamentary leader apologises for 'poverty remarks'', Politics.hu, 21 March 2011. Available on: http://www.politics.hu/20110321/fidesz-parliamentary-leader-apologises-for-poverty-remarks/ (last accessed on: 11 December 2014).

[49] Központi Statisztikai Hivatal (KSH), *Hungary Population Census 2011*. Available on: http://www.ksh.hu/nepszamlalas/tablak_demografia (last accessed on: 11 December 2013).

[50] Fóti, Alleviating Poverty, p. 21.

have become unemployed, and young people coming through are denied opportunities. Half-hearted government policies to improve the social and economic position of the Roma have failed to halt the rapid rise in Roma poverty. Neither have they addressed poverty-related problems such as falling standards of education, anxiety, poor health, crime, prostitution, etc. The scale of problems is mounting and they have to be addressed if Hungary is to make any long-term social, political or economic progress.[51]

The situation has, as we shall see below, only worsened since. Today, Roma people in Hungary face not only the dual challenges of institutionalised discrimination and impoverishment, but are also increasingly facing direct threats to their lives from fascist vigilantes.

In addition to the entrenchment of class and racial inequalities, the third main feature of Hungary's neoliberal transformation has been the intensification of regional inequalities. While the historically more developed regions around Budapest and north-western Hungary have 'surged ahead' thanks to the arrival of foreign investment, much of north-eastern Hungary, where much of the country's heavy industry and mining was concentrated prior to 1989, has either failed to 'take off' altogether or struggled badly. In a striking parallel to the areas of Britain that experienced the greatest job losses in manufacturing and the mining industry under Thatcherism, these are today the areas of Hungary that exhibit the highest levels of unemployment, poverty, and related social problems.

While the picture depicted above is hardly a rosy one, the situation has deteriorated further since the onset of the global economic crisis in 2007-8. Although not as badly hit as the Baltic States, which suffered the worst recessions in the EU, the Hungarian

---

[51] Kovats, here cited in Andor, László and Martin Summers, *Market Failure: A Guide to Eastern Europe's 'Economic Miracle'*, London: Pluto Press, 1998, p. 123.

economy was nonetheless badly affected. The first wave of the crisis, following the collapse of US investment giant Lehman Brothers in September 2008, caused a run on the Hungarian *forint*, which depreciated sharply against major foreign currencies.[52] This hit members of the already 'squeezed middle class', who had taken out large loans in *euros* and Swiss *francs*, particularly hard.[53] The second wave, following the onset of the 'Great Recession', led to a destructive downwards spiral of declining production and trade, increasing bankruptcies and rapidly falling levels of employment. In 2009, the GDP contracted by 6.8%, while official unemployment soared from 7.4% in 2007 to 11.4% by February 2010, the highest figure for 16 years.[54] The negative impact of the crisis was exacerbated by successive rounds of austerity measures, initially introduced in 2009 by the semi-technocratic Bajnai government and – despite official claims to the contrary – continued by the Orbán regime since it came to power in 2010 (at least on this point there is near-total agreement between the regime and the parliamentary opposition), in the hope that this would 'rebalance' the Hungarian economy and enable the country to regain its 'credibility' among foreign investors. As a result, living standards of ordinary Hungarians have deteriorated. Real wages decreased in 2007 by 4.6% and, after a negligible rise of 0.9% in 2008, fell again in 2009 by 4.5% (the third steepest fall in the region after Latvia and

---

[52] In October 2008, the value of the *forint* fell from 240 to 280 against the Euro, a fall of 17%. Marer, Paul, 'The Global Economic Crises: Impacts on Eastern Europe', *Acta Oeconomica*, Vol. 60, No. 1, 2010, p. 21.

[53] Prior to the crisis, 1.7 million Hungarian citizens had taken out loans in foreign currencies. Now, the Hungarian government estimated that 10-15% of these loans were 'endangered' (i.e. liable to default). As a result, of the depreciation of the *forint* many borrowers had to sell their homes, while others faced hefty hikes in mortgage payments. See Bryant, Chris, 'Hungarians in Debt to Swiss Franc', *Financial Times*, 16 July 2010.

[54] I discuss the impact of the global economic crisis on Hungary in detail in 'From Poster Boy of Neoliberal Transformation to Basket Case: Hungary and the Global Economic Crisis', in Dale, Gareth (ed.), *First the transition then the crash: Eastern Europe in the 2000s*, London: Pluto Press, 2011, pp. 203-228.

Lithuania).[55] Meanwhile, poverty rates have skyrocketed. According to recent figures from Eurostat 33.5% of the Hungarian population, i.e. *circa* 3.3 million Hungarians, lived 'at risk of poverty or social exclusion' in 2013 – an increase of 500,000 people (from 28.2%) since 2008.[56]

The crisis of liberal democracy (and the centre-left that supported it)

The deepening crisis of (neoliberal) capitalism, described above, has been accompanied by increasing public disillusion and outright rejection of liberal democracy. This process, which was predicted long ago by a small, but courageous group of radical intellectuals[57] (since then confirmed by a plethora of studies[58]), had already begun long

---

[55] WIIW, *Current Analyses and Forecasts 6: Will Exports Prevail over Austerity?*, prepared by Astrov, Vasily, Mario Holzner, Gabor Hunya, Kazimierz Laski, Leon Podkaminer et al., July 2010, Vienna: Vienna Institute for International Economic Studies (WIIW); Onaran, Özlem, 'From transition crisis to the global crisis: Twenty years of capitalism and labour in the Central and Eastern EU new member states', *Capital & Class*, Vol. 35, No. 2, 2011, Table 1, p. 217.

[56] Official data also show that a growing number of Hungarian workers live in poverty (calculated as 60% of the median income in Hungary, eg. HUF 65,000 per month). See Napi.hu, 'Drámai adatok Magyarországrólígy terjed a szegénység', 14 August 2014. Available on: http://www.napi.hu/magyar_gazdasag/dramai_adatok_magyarorszagrol _igy_terjed_a_szegenyseg.585336.html (last accessed on: 23 August 2014). For the Eurostat figures, see Eurostat Statistical Database, 'People at risk of poverty or social exclusion' and 'Income distribution and monetary poverty'. Available on: http://epp.eurostat. ec.europa.eu/portal/page/portal/income_social_inclusion_living_conditions/data/main_ta bles# (last accessed on: 12 September 2014).

[57] See for example, Szalai, Erzsébet, 'Az újkapitalizmus intézményesülése – és válsága', *Kritika*, 1-6 April 2004; Tamás, Gáspár M., 'Megbukott a rendszerváltás', *Népszabadság*, 29 February 2004.

[58] Pew Research Center, Two Decades After the Wall's Fall: End of Communism Cheered but Now with More Reservations, Washingtond, DC: The Pew Research Center, 2009; Tóth, István G., Bizalomhiány, normazavarok, igazságtalanságérzet és paternalizmus a magyar társadalom értékszerkezetében, Budapest: TÁRKI, 2009.

before Prime Minister Orbán officially declared parliamentary democracy as *passé* earlier this year.[59] Indeed, cracks in the hegemony of liberal democracy were already visible before the revelations of former Prime Minister Gyurcsány's infamous 'lie speech' in September 2006, which led to massive anti-government protests that were brutally repressed by the police. The reasons for this are many, including the weakness of democratic traditions (in large part thanks to the suppression of three democratic revolutions during the course of the 'short 20th century' by conservatives and Stalinists alike), the absence of a genuine, popular democratic movement during the regime change in 1989, and the widespread disillusionment in liberal democracy since then (as evidenced by steadily falling participation in general elections since 2002, with almost 40% of registered voters opting to stay at home in the 2014 general elections). However, these trends are not only limited to Hungary, but are visible across the world.

The crisis has merely accelerated the demise of liberal democracy. According to one comparative survey, carried out in 2009 by the *Pew Research Centre*, a stunning 94% of those interviewed regarded the economic situation in the country as 'bad', while 72% said they were 'worse off now than under Communism'. These figures were significantly higher than those of many neighbouring countries, such as the Czech Republic, Poland, and Slovakia.[60] Moreover, they also revealed that Hungarians were not only disillusioned with the economy, but with politics too: more than three-quarters (77%) of Hungarians were 'dissatisfied' with the way democracy was working in their country, compared to 49% of the respondents in the Czech Republic, 46% in Slovakia, and only 39% in Poland.[61] The study also

---

[59] Orbán, Viktor, 'A munkaalapú állam következik', speech at the 26th summer university and youth camp in Tusnádfürdő (Băile Tuşnad), Romania, 26 July 2014.

[60] Pew Research Center, *Two Decades After the Wall's Fall*, pp. 3, 40.

[61] Pew Research Center, Two Decades After the Wall's Fall, p. 32.

showed an increasing opposition to EU membership in Hungary, with only 20% agreeing that EU membership was 'a good thing', while 43% were neither in favour, nor against, but almost one-third (28%) responded that it was 'a bad thing'. Hungarians were significantly more pessimistic towards the EU than most of their neighbours in the region, with 63% in Poland, 58% in Slovakia, and 45% in the Czech Republic holding a positive view.[62]

The main loser of this process has been the centre-left. Between 2006 and 2010, the approval rating of the ruling Hungarian Socialist Party (*Magyar Szocialista Párt*, MSZP) fell by more than 23% (from 43.2 to 19.3%), while its junior-coalition partner, the neoliberal Alliance of Free Democrats (*Szabad Demokraták Szövetsége*, SZDSZ), was completely wiped out altogether from the political map (it obtained a measly 0.25% of the votes in the 2010 general elections and the party was officially disbanded in 2013). The spectacular decline of the centre-left was in large part due to the fact that, when in power, these parties persistently pursued austerity policies that were diametrically opposed to their electoral promises (and, in the case of the socialists, also against the interests of their own electorate!), while their entire period in office (between 2002 and 2010) was marked by revelations of corruption scandals too numerous to mention. Support for the MSZP was further weakened by its association with former Prime Minister Gyurcsány, who, ever since the revelations of his infamous 'lie speech' in September 2006 and the massive anti-government protests that subsequently followed, has been considered a *personae non grata* by popular opinion in Hungary. As we shall see below, Jobbik has correctly and skilfully recognised the widespread public disillusion and anger with the regime change existent in Hungarian society.

---

[62] Pew Research Center, Two Decades After the Wall's Fall, p. 67.

Jobbik as a 'new', 'radical' alternative to mainstream parties

Contrary to most other far right parties in Europe, like the Front National in France or the ÖVP in Austria, Jobbik did not attempt to present itself as a 'respectable', mainstream political party. Rather, it has consciously and skilfully presented itself as a 'novel', 'radical' alternative to mainstream parties, based on a popular movement, including a strong, paramilitary wing – the Hungarian Guard (*Magyar Gárda*) –, and a radical rhetoric that openly advocates anti-Roma racism and anti-Semitism.[63]

Jobbik's ideology, as first formulated in the party's founding document in 2003 and later revamped in its 2010 and 2014 general election manifestoes, shows a strong ideological continuity with the basic ideas and principles that have characterised the Hungarian far right ever since the late 19th and early 20th century.[64] Its first feature is a rabid anti-communism and anti-liberalism, which not only considers the 'communist' regime that ruled Hungary between 1948 and 1989 to be illegitimate, but also contests the period that has followed since the regime change in 1989. In contrast to the centre-left and (at least until recently) the centre-right, Jobbik refutes the central tenets of the regime change – what the Hungarian Marxist philosopher G.M. Tamás has described as the 'triple shibboleth'[65] of free market capitalism, liberal democracy and unconditional allegiance to the 'west' –, and argues that the transition was fake and that 'hidden' continuities exist between the old regime and the post-1989 system.

---

[63] Fabry, Adam, 'Hungary: fascists on the march', *Socialist Worker*, No. 2198, 20 April 2010; Smith, Martin, 'What is Jobbik? The rise of Europe's biggest fascist party', *Dreamdeferred.org.uk*, 30 January 2014. Available on: http://www.dreamdeferred.org. uk/2014/01/jobbik-two-faces-of-fascism/ (last accessed on: 4 November 2014).

[64] Jobbik, 'Alapító nyilatkozat'; id. Radical Change. A Guide to Jobbik's Parliamentary Electoral Manifesto for National Self-determination and Social Justice, Budapest: Jobbik, 2010; and id. Kimondjuk. Megmondjuk. A Jobbik országgyűlési választási programja a nemzet felemelkedéséért, Budapest: Jobbik, 2014.

[65] Tamás, 'Counter-revolution against a counter-revolution'.

Hence, the party's main aim is to 'complete' the regime change of 1989 and 'to create a better and more just society'.[66] As the party's young and wily leader Gábor Vona makes clear in straightforward terms, this can only be achieved through 'radical' solutions:

> Radicalism isn't an ideology, neither is it a conception, it's a perspective. If a person is struck by a car, and suffers serious injuries as a result, and two doctors arrive on the scene, one of whom slaps the injured fellow square in the face, while the other says, 'Here, have a paracetamol', the injured party would surely tell both of them to get lost. Hungary over the last decades hasn't merely been struck by a solitary automobile, it has been positively mown down by dozens of freight trains … The Left just keeps slapping and kicking the patient regardless, while the Right just keep stupefying them with all sorts of well-meaning sanctimony. Let's be straight about it for once: they have deliberately and completely destroyed the country. What we need here instead of yet more slaps or painkillers is a radical – to continue the above analogy: a surgical – form of intervention.[67]

The second principle, following on from the first one, is the idea of 'national rejuvenation', which is to be achieved through the revival of national self-determination, the restoration of law and order, and the pursuit of nationalist economic policies aimed at increasing productivity. As stated in the party's founding document, Jobbik seeks to, 'protect […] Hungarian values and interests … and stands up against the ever more blatant efforts to eradicate the nation as the

---

[66] Jobbik, 'Alapító Nyilatkozat'. See also Korkut, *Liberalization Challenges in Hungary*, 186-187; Tóth and Grajczár, 'Válság, radikalizálódás és az újjászületés ígérete', p. 60.

[67] Vona, here cited in Kovács, András, "The Post-Communist Extreme Right: The Jobbik Party in Hungary', in Wodak, Ruth, Majid KoshraviNik, Brigitte Mral (eds), *Right-Wing Populism in Europe: Politics and Discourse*, London/New York: Bloomsbury, 2013, p. 226.

foundation of human community'.[68] In terms of foreign policy, this takes the form of an aggressive nationalism, which demands the 'reunification of a Hungarian nation unjustly torn apart during the course of the 20th century'.[69]

Internally, Jobbik fervently opposes all 'treacherous' and 'unproductive' groups in society, that is the political elite in general, but 'communist' and liberal politicians in particular, who have betrayed 'national interests', the unemployed and underemployed, pensioners, the sick and the poor, public sector workers, intellectuals and artists. In particular, however, it has singled out the Jews and the Roma – two of the largest minorities in the country and the traditional enemies of Hungarian fascists – as its primary targets. The party has often been accused of invoking anti-Semitic ideas and practices harking back to the darkest days of Hungary's inter-war history. For instance, in the run up to the 2009 European Parliament elections, Krisztina Morvai, now one of the party's MEPs, allegedly advised 'liberal-Bolshevik Zionists' to 'start thinking of where to flee and where to hide'.[70] More recently, in November 2012, the party's then deputy parliamentary leader and spokesperson on foreign affairs Márton Gyöngyösi, called for the establishment of a special registry of Hungarian Jews, especially members of the government and parliament, on the grounds that they 'pose a national security risk to Hungary'. Meanwhile, members of the Hungarian Guard have held countless marches throughout Hungary dressed in combat boots and black uniforms, and adopting symbols closely resembling those used by the fascist Arrow Cross in the 1930s and 1940s. The paramilitary group was banned in July 2009, but it was soon re-established under

---

[68] Jobbik, 'Alapitó nyilatkozat'.

[69] Jobbik, *Radical Change*, p. 20-21.

[70] Follath, Eric, 'Europe's Capital of Anti-Semitism: Budapest Experiences a New Wave Hate', *Der Spiegel*, 14 October 2010. Available on: http://www.spiegel.de/international/europe/europe-s-capital-of-anti-semitism-budapest-experiences-a-new-wave-of-hate-a-722880.html (last accessed on: 11 December 2014).

the thinly veiled name the New Hungarian Guard (*Új Magyar Gárda*). Such statements and actions have led to widespread condemnations in Hungary and abroad. However, Jobbik has vehemently denied any allegations of anti-Semitism or racism as either being the evil machinations of its political enemies and/or simply false.[71]

Jobbik has also managed to create a 'moral panic' about what it calls 'the Gypsy question'. In the party's 2010 electoral manifesto, it argued that '[t]he coexistence and cohesion of Magyar and Gypsy is one of the severest problems facing Hungarian society', which, if left unresolved, allegedly risked pulling Hungary into 'a state of virtual civil war'. In order to combat what it describes as 'gypsy crime' (an invented classification, which, however, has been accepted as *fait accompli* in public discourse), its 2010 electoral manifesto calls for 'the strengthening of the established police' and the foundation of a dedicated rural police service, or Gendarmerie'.[72] To prove its intentions, the party has held several confrontational rallies in Roma-dominated neighbourhoods in recent years, calling for harsher punishments for criminals, including the reintroduction of the death penalty. The rise of Jobbik has been accompanied by increasing physical attacks on Roma people. According to a recent report by the European Roma Rights Centre (ERRC) 48 attacks were carried out on Roma people and/or their property between January 2008 and December 2010. These included a series of racist, terrorist murders – unprecedented in post-World War II history of Hungary – carried out by a group of neo-Nazi sympathisers, which resulted in the death of nine Roma, including a five-year old boy, and left dozens of others

---

[71] Lebor, Adam, 'Jobbik: Meet the BNP's fascist friends in Europe', *The Times*, 9 June 2009; Moore, Matthew, 'Hungarian extremist running far-right website from UK', *The Daily Telegraph*, 10 November 2008; Stancil, Jordan, 'Jobbik Rising', *The Nation*, 29 June 2009.

[72] Jobbik, *Radical Change*, p. 11.

with severe injuries.[73] Following a long series of bungled investigations, the perpetrators were eventually arrested and sentenced to life in prison. However, as Keno Verseck writes in *Der Spiegel*, 'public reaction in Hungary has been minimal, and hardly any wider debate has arisen from the conclusion of the trial.'[74]

In terms of its economic policy, Jobbik's ideology is characterised by a pseudo-revolutionary radicalism, which condemns the dominant forces of neoliberal globalisation (i.e. transnational corporations, international financial institutions, the United States and the EU, etc.) for their 'colonialist' exploitation of Hungary. Instead, it advocates a so-called 'eco-social national economics', which 'defend[s] Hungarian industry, Hungarian farmers, Hungarian businesses, Hungarian produce and Hungarian markets', while at the same time protecting 'strategic national assets', such as land, water, natural gas, and forests, from transnational corporations. The party aims to restore economic growth by limiting economic dependence on the west and reorienting Hungary's foreign trade eastwards (through strengthening economic ties with China, India, Russia, Kazakhstan and Indonesia). In addition, it advocates for the introduction of a number of right-wing Keynesian policies – state-sponsored infrastructure programmes, tax incentives to domestic small- and medium sized enterprises, and the introduction of workfare schemes – in order to reinvigorate key domestic industries (agriculture, manufacturing and tourism) and the creation of new jobs. In order to implement such ambitious policies, the party advocates the return of a 'strong' state.[75] The fact that Jobbik's proposed policies are frequently described by the

---

[73] European Roma Right Centre (ERRC), *Anti-Roma Violence and Impunity*, Budapest: ERRC, 2011, p. 5.

[74] Verseck, Keno, 'Right-wing Terror: Hungary Silent over Roma Killing Spree', *Der Spiegel*, 23 July 2013; *id.* 'Neo-Nazis Get Life for Roma Murder Spree', *Der Spiegel*, 6 August 2013.

[75] Jobbik, *Radical Change*, pp. 2-3.

media, mainstream politicians and experts, as being 'anti-capitalist' only shows the level of confusion in society.

The social base of Jobbik

Having obtained more than 20% of the votes in the 2014 general elections, it seems obvious that Jobbik's appeal is not only limited to a small, ideologically motivated group of far right voters, but also to wider sections of the electorate. However, empirical analysis on Jobbik's voters provides a more complex picture. Firstly, it shows that, similar to far right parties elsewhere, men are more likely to vote for Jobbik than women (the gender distribution of the party's voters was 63-37% in favour of men). Secondly, in terms of their previous party affiliation, 70% of the party's voters were either old FIDESZ-KDNP or MIÉP-Jobbik voters (51% and 19% respectively), while the remaining 30% were former MSZP voters. Third, in contrast to the mainstream parties in Hungary, young and relatively educated voters are over-represented amongst Jobbik's voters: people aged 18-29 constituted the largest part of Jobbik voters (29%) in the 2010 general elections, closely followed by people aged over 50 (27%). At the same time, there was also a noticeable contradiction between the 'actual' and 'perceived' class position of Jobbik's voters: while the party's electorate was predominantly comprised of students, young unemployed or unskilled, private sector workers, most of them described themselves as belonging to the 'middle class'.[76] Moreover, there are also striking differences in terms of Jobbik's electoral support on a regional level. The party's stronghold is in north-eastern Hungary, where, as we described above, the impact of neoliberal restructuring has been particularly devastating and where there is a large Roma minority living in racially segregated areas with substandard infrastructure. Here, the party obtained around 30% of the votes in last year's general

---

[76] Kovács, 'The Post-Communist Extreme Right', p. 229. See also Tóth and Grajczár, 'Válság, radikalizálódás és az újjászületés ígérete', pp. 71-73.

elections and also won several mayoral posts in the local elections in autumn, including in Ózd, another former centre of 'socialist' heavy industry, where they thrashed the local Fidesz candidate. In contrast, in the historically more industrialised and 'better-off' north-western Hungary and Budapest, 'only' 10-15% of the voters supported Jobbik.[77] (Although this trend might be changing too. In what was hailed as a 'landmark event' by party leader Gábor Vona, Jobbik won the mayoral elections in Tapolca, located near Lake Balaton in western Hungary, in April 2015.)

In summary then, it appears that part of the reason behind Jobbik's success has been its ability to extend its appeal beyond the narrow ideological boundaries that historically characterised the far right in Hungary (law and order, nationalism, racism and anti-Semitism). As András Kovács writes:

> A young and mainly student-dominated group is overrepresented among Jobbik voters in every region of the country. The group of 'losers' is significantly present in the Jobbik constituency in the economically prosperous regions. However, in poorer areas with large Roma populations, a relatively well-educated, economically active and better-off group constitutes the core electorate. Thus, on the 'demand side' the common denominator of the different electoral groups seems to be neither 'loser' status nor a purely ideologically motivated choice (extreme nationalism, racism, anti-Semitism, etc). Though all these elements are widespread among Jobbik voters, *the binding element between the different groups of the constituency seems to be a strong anti-establishment attitude. Consequently, a key factor to the party's*

---

[77] Figures based on: Hubai, László, 'A 2014.évi választási metszetek településnagyság szerint', paper presented at conference on the 2014 general elections in Hungary, Institute of Political History, Budapest, 19 June 2014. See also: Kovács, 'The Post-Communist Extreme Right', p. 229.

success has necessarily been an ability to successfully unite these electoral groups with different motivations and expectations.[78]

Countering the far right...

When Jobbik first entered parliament in 2010, the mainstream political parties, media and liberal commentators alike believed that its radical rhetoric would eventually fade away. However, this turned out to be a very naïve view. Instead, the opposite has happened. In recent years, Jobbik has cemented its position as Hungary's third largest party (recent polls even put it in second place, in front of the socialists). Indeed, under the authoritarian Orbán regime key points of the party's manifesto – from its demands of increasing 'social and economic autonomy', through its thinly veiled attacks on minorities, to its open veneration of the Horthy regime – have become integrated into government practice and wider public discourse.[79]

Simultaneously with the growth of Jobbik a plethora of minor far right and paramilitary groups – including the above mentioned New Hungarian Guard, the Hungarian National Guard (*Magyar Nemzeti Gárda*), the Sixty-four Counties Youth Movement (*Hatvannégy Vármegye Ifjúsági Mozgalom*), the Outlaw's Army (*Betyársereg*), the Movement For a Better Future-Hungarian Self Defence (*Szebb Jövőért-Magyar Önvédelem Mozgalom*) and the Guards of the Carpathian Homeland (*Kárpát Haza Őrei*) – have also emerged in recent years, which openly dismiss parliamentary democracy and proudly boast about their violent attacks on minorities. Most of these organisations maintain close relationships with Jobbik, but others have formed as a result of internal splits within Jobbik. For example, in 2012, a number

---

[78] Kovács, 'The Post-Communist Extreme Right', p. 230 (my emphasis).

[79] See for example, Berend, Nora and Christopher Clark, 'Not Just a Phase', *London Review of Books*, Vol. 36, No. 22, 20 November 2014, pp. 19-22; Nagy, András B., Tamás Boros and Áron Varga, 'Right-wing Extremism in Hungary', Berlin: Friedrich Ebert Stiftung, 2012, pp. 7-12.

of disgruntled ex-Jobbik and Hungarian Guard members led a (failed) attempt to establish a local version of the Greek neo-Nazi Golden Dawn party (*Magyar Hajnal Párt*).[80] While most of these organisations remain relatively small (their membership range from a dozen to a few hundred), recent reports by the Athena Institute, an independent institution based in Budapest that carries out research on 'extremist' groups, indicate that Hungarian far right organisations are successfully extending their activities to neighbouring Romania and Serbia, both of which have significant Hungarian minorities.[81]

Faced by what, following the Italian Marxist Antonio Gramsci, can be described as a protracted, relentless and highly successful 'war of position' from the right, the fragmented parties of the self-proclaimed 'democratic opposition' have proven to be completely incapable of mounting any resistance. After the recent general elections, the spiritless and cowardly leaders of the opposition and the increasingly disoriented liberal intelligentsia (to their great shame) officially abandoned any last pretences of resisting fascism and began to seriously discuss the idea of having a 'constructive dialogue' or 'debate' with Jobbik. They claim that 'the fascist party can no longer be kept in quarantine'. This is a claim, which is either based on a misconception, or a deliberate misrepresentation of facts, since Jobbik was never completely quarantined in the first place. Instead, they have begun talking of the need to pay more attention to 'problems of public security in the countryside' (a respectable translation for 'Gypsy crime'), in the vain hope that they will appear more credible than the

---

[80] Magyar Hajnal,'A Magyar Hajnal rövid programja', 19 November 2013. Available on: http://magyarhajnal.com/a-magyar-hajnal-rovid-program/ (last accessed on: 2 December 2014).

[81] Athena Institute, 'Successful Network Building in Serbia by Hungarian Extremists', 4 April 2014. Available on: http://www.athenaintezet.hu/en/news/read/268 (last accessed on: 3 December 2014); 'Hungarian Extremist Structures in Romania', 25 March 2014. Available on: http://www.athenaintezet.hu/en/news/read/266 (last accessed on: 3 December 2014).

fascists when it comes to the question of 'law and order'. As a result, the task of resisting the far right has fallen on civil society and there are a number of 'progressive' organisations, such as the Hungarian Association of Resistance Fighters and Anti-fascists (*Magyar Ellenállók és Antifasiszták Szövetsége*, MEASZ), the Hungarian Anti-fascist League (*Magyar Antifasiszta Liga*, MAL) and the Anti-fascist Network (*Antifasiszta Hálózat*), who regularly organise anti-fascist actions. According Mátyás Benyik, an anti-fascist organiser and leading member of Attac Hungary, '[we have] achieved a number of minor achievements, including the banning of the Hungarian Guard, prevention of far right events, raising public awareness about anti-Roma atrocities, or the protests against the erection of Horthy-statues or the infamous memorial to the victims of World War II at Freedom Square in Budapest.'[82] For now, however, these actions remain very small and completely ignored by the majority of society. The problem, as G.M. Tamás points out, is that, for now at least, civil society 'simply isn't anti-racist.'[83]

Conclusion

As this chapter has argued, the far right does not constitute an aberration, but rather an integral part of Hungarian history in the 20th century. Emerging as a reaction to the crisis of the liberal capitalist world order following World War I – accelerated in Hungary due to the territorial disintegration of the Austro-Hungarian Empire and the threat of Bolshevism following the establishment of the Hungarian Commune in 1919 –, far right and fascist parties existed in a problematic, but symbiotic relationship with the authoritarian Horthy regime during the inter-war years, before eventually rising to power in

---

[82] Electronic interview with Mátyás Benyik, 9 November 2014.

[83] 'Hungary: A Black Hole on Europe's Map', interview with Gáspár M. Tamás, by Jaroslav Fiala, *The Bullet: Socialist Project*, E-Bulletin, No. 979, 5 May 2014.

October 1944 (following the overthrow of Horthy in a Nazi-led *coup d'état*). Hence, the horrors associated with the short-lived Arrow Cross regime in 1944-1945 cannot be separated from the dominant practices of the Horthy era (as currently attempted by neoconservative politicians and intellectuals in Budapest), but ought to rather be considered as the culmination of far right politics in inter-war Hungary (in its most extreme form).

Since the transition to free-market capitalism and liberal democracy in 1989, there has been a resurgence of the far right in Hungary. While this phenomenon is, as indicated by other chapters in this volume, part of a broader political and ideological shift to the right globally, the distinct characteristics and seemingly broad appeal of far right politics in Hungary – epitomised by the spectacular ascendancy of the openly fascist Jobbik party – has, arguably, been closely interrelated with the deepening economic, political, and social crisis of neoliberal capitalism in recent years. Having said this, the entrenchment of Jobbik as the third largest force in Hungarian politics and wider society, has also been facilitated by the nebulous borders existing between the far right and the neoconservative Orbán regime and the weakness of anti-fascist forces in the country. Admittedly, the present political conjuncture looks dark in Hungary. However, this does not mean that resistance to the far right is hopeless. Rather, to paraphrase Samuel Beckett's famous quote, the slogan for anti-fascist forces in Hungary must be, 'Try again. Fail again. Fail better.'

Bibliography

Andor, László, *Hungary on the Road to the European Union: A Transition in Blue*, Westport, CT: Greenwood Press, 2000.

Andor, László and Martin Summers, *Market Failure: A Guide to Eastern Europe's 'Economic Miracle'*, London: Pluto Press, 1998.

'A Nyilaskeresztes Párt programja', in Gergely, Jenő, Ferenc Glatz and Ferenc Pölöskei (eds), *Magyarországi Pártprogramok, 1919-1944*, Budapest: Eötvös Kiadó, 2004.

Athena Institute, 'Successful Network Building in Serbia by Hungarian Extremists', 4 April 2014. Available on: http://www.athenaintezet.hu/en/news/read/268 (last accessed on: 3 December 2014).

— 'Hungarian Extremist Structures in Romania', 25 March 2014. Available on: http://www.athenaintezet.hu/en/news/read/266 (last accessed on: 3 December 2014).

— 'Hungarian National Front', 7 July 2014. Available on:http://www.athenaintezet.hu/en/map/olvas/20#read (last accessed on: 3 December 2014).

Berend, Iván T. and György Ránki, *The Hungarian Economy in the Twentieth Century*, London: Croom Helm, 1985.

Berend, Nora and Christopher Clark, 'Not Just a Phase', *London Review of Books*, Vol. 36, No. 22, 20 November 2014, pp. 19-22.

Bryant, Chris, 'Hungarians in Debt to Swiss Franc', *Financial Times*, 16 July 2010.

Csurka, István (ed.), *Néhány gondolat és nyolc társgondolat*, Budapest: Magyar Fórum, 1992.

Drahokoupil, Jan, *Globalization and the State in Central and Eastern Europe: The Politics of Foreign Direct Investment*, London: Routledge, 2009.

Electronic interview with Mátyás Benyik, 9 November 2014.

Eurequal, *The State of Inequality in the Central and Eastern Europe: Desk Research on Hungary*, Oxford: Eurequal, 2006.

European Roma Right Centre (ERRC), *Imperfect Justice: Anti-Roma Violence and Impunity*, Budapest: ERRC, 2011.

Eurostat Statistical Database, 'People at risk of poverty or social exclusion' and 'Income distribution and monetary poverty'. Available on: http://epp.eurostat.ec.europa.eu/portal/page/portal/income_so

cial_inclusion_living_conditions/data/main_tables# (last accessed on: 12 September 2014).

Fabry, Adam, 'End of the Liberal Dream: Hungary since 1989', *International Socialism*, No. 124, Autumn 2009, pp. 71-84.

— 'Hungary: fascists on the march', *Socialist Worker*, No. 2198, 20 April 2010.

— 'From Poster Boy of Neoliberal Transformation to Basket Case: Hungary and the Global Economic Crisis', in *First the transition then the crash: Eastern Europe in the 2000s*, edited by Gareth Dale, London: Pluto Press, 2011, pp. 203-228.

Ferge, Zsuzsa, 'Introduction', in Ferge, Zsuzsa, Endre Sik, Péter Róbert, Fruzsina Albert, *Social Costs of Transition. International Report*, Budapest, August 1997.

'Fidesz parliamentary leader apologises for 'poverty remarks'', Politics.hu, 21 March 2011. Available on:http://www.politics.hu/20110321/fidesz-parliamentary-leader-apologises-for-poverty-remarks/ (last accessed on: 11 December 2014).

Follath, Eric, 'Europe's Capital of Anti-Semitism: Budapest Experiences a New Wave Hate', *Der Spiegel*, 14 October 2010. Available on: http://www.spiegel.de/international/europe/europe-s-capital-of-anti-semitism-budapest-experiences-a-new-wave-of-hate-a-722880.html (last accessed on: 11 December 2014).

Fóti, Klára (ed.), *Alleviating Poverty: Analysis and Recommendations. Human Development Report for Hungary, 2000-2002*, Budapest: Institute for World Economics of the Hungarian Academy of Sciences and United Nations Development Programme (UNDP), 2003.

Gwertzman, Bernard and Michael Kaufman, *The Collapse of Communism*, New York, NY: Random House, 1990.

Hanley, Eric, Lawrence King, and István Tóth János, 'The State, International Agencies, and Property Transformation in

Postcommunist Hungary', *The American Journal of Sociology*, 2002, Vol. 108, No. 1, pp. 129-167.

Hubai, László, 'A 2014.évi választási metszetek településnagyság szerint', paper presented at conference on the 2014 general elections in Hungary, Institute of Political History, Budapest, 19 June 2014.

'Hungary: A Black Hole on Europe's Map', interview with Gáspár .M. Tamás by Jaroslav Fiala, *The Bullet: Socialist Project*, E-Bulletin, No. 979, 5 May 2014.

Jobbik, 'Alapitó Nyilatkozat', 24 October 2003. Available on: http://jobbik.hu/jobbikrol/alapito-nyilatkozat (last obtained on: 26 November 2014).

— *Radical Change. A Guide to Jobbik's Parliementary Electoral Manifesto for National Self-determination and Social Justice*, Budapest: Jobbik, 2010.

— *Kimondjuk. Megmondjuk. A Jobbik országgyülési választási programja a nemzet felemelkedéséért*, Budapest: Jobbik, 2014.

Korkut, Umut, Liberalization Challenges in Hungary. Elitism, Progressivism, and Populism, New York, NY: Palgrave Macmillan, 2012.

Kovács, András, 'The Post-Communist Extreme Right: The Jobbik Party in Hungary', in Wodak, Ruth, Majid KoshraviNik, Brigitte Mral (eds), *Right-Wing Populism in Europe: Politics and Discourse*, London/New York: Bloomsbury, 2013, pp. 223–234.

Központi Statisztikai Hivatal (KSH), *Hungary Population Census 2011*. Available on: http://www.ksh.hu/nepszamlalas/tablak_demografia (last accessed on: 11 December 2013).

Ladányi, János and Szelényi, Iván, *A kirekesztettség változó formái*, Budapest: Napvilág Kiadó, 2004.

Lebor, Adam, 'Jobbik: Meet the BNP's fascist friends in Europe', *The Times*, 9 June 2009.

Magyar Hajnal, 'A Magyar Hajnal rövid programja', 19 November 2013. Available on: http://magyarhajnal.com/a-magyar-hajnal-rovid-program/ (last accessed on: 2 December 2014).

Mann, Michael, *Fascists*, Cambridge: Cambridge University Press, 2004.

Marer, Paul, 'The Global Economic Crises: Impacts on Eastern Europe', *Acta Oeconomica*, Vol. 60, No. 1, 2010, pp. 3-33.

Moore, Matthew, 'Hungarian extremist running far-right website from UK', *The Daily Telegraph*, 10 November 2008.

Nagy, András B., Tamás Boros and Áron Varga, 'Right-wing Extremism in Hungary', Berlin: Friedrich Ebert Stiftung, 2012.

Napi.hu, 'Drámai adatok Magyarországról – így terjed a szegénység', 14 August 2014. Available on: http://www.napi.hu/magyar_gazdasag/dramai_adatok_magyarorszagrol_igy_terjed_a_szege nyseg.585336.html (last accessed on: 23 August 2014).

Onaran, Özlem, 'From transition crisis to the global crisis: Twenty years of capitalism and labour in the Central and Eastern EU new member states', *Capital & Class*, Vol. 35, No. 2, 2011, pp. 213-231.

Orbán, Viktor, 'A munkaalapú állam következik', speech at the 26th summer university and youth camp in Tusnádfürdő (Băile Tuşnad), Romania, 26 July 2014.

Paxton, Robert O., *The Anatomy of Fascism*, London: Penguin Books, 2005.

Perlez, Jane, 1993, 'Reburial Is Both a Ceremony and a Test for Today's Hungary', *New York Times*, 5 September 1993.

Pew Research Center, *Two Decades After the Wall's Fall: End of Communism Cheered but Now with More Reservations*, Washington, DC: The Pew Research Center, 2009.

Pittaway, Mark, 'Hungary', in White, Stephen, Judy Batt, and Paul G. Lewis (eds), *Developments in Central and East European Politics*, Vol. 3, , Basingstoke: Palgrave Macmillan, 2003, pp. 57-73.

—   'Fascism in Hungary', in Fabry, Adam (ed.), *From the Vanguard to the Margins: Workers in Hungary, 1939 to the Present*, Leiden: Brill, 2014, pp. 257-275.

Romsics, Ignác, *Hungary in the Twentieth Century*, Budapest: Corvina Kiadó, 1999.

Rowlands, Carl, "Gypsies are Animals' – Racism on Hungary's Right', *New Left Project*, 1 February 2013. Available on: http://www. newleftproject.org/index.php/site/article_comments/gypsies_a re_animals_racism_on_hungarys_right (last obtained on: 11 December 2013).

Sakmyster, Thomas, *Hungary's Admiral on Horseback: Miklós Horthy, 1918-1944*, New York, NY: Columbia University Press, 1994.

Saull, Rick, 'The origins and persistence of the far-right: capital, class and the pathologies of liberal politics', in Saull, Rick, Alexander Anievas, Neil Davidson and Adam Fabry (eds), *The Far Right in the Longue Durée*, pp. 21-43.

Smith, Martin, 'What is Jobbik? The rise of Europe's biggest fascist party', *Dreamdeferred.org.uk*, 30 January 2014. Available on: http://www.dreamdeferred.org.uk/2014/01/jobbik-two-faces-of-fascism/ (last obtained on: 4 November 2014).

Stancil, Jordan, 'Jobbik Rising', *The Nation*, 29 June 2009.

Szalai, Erzsébet, 'Az újkapitalizmus intézményesülése – és válsága', *Kritika*, 1-6 April 2004.

—   New Capitalism – And What Can Replace It, Budapest: Pallas Kiadó, 2008.

Szálasi, Ferenc, *Út és cél*, 3rd edition, Buenos Aires, 1955.

Szinai, Miklós, 'A magyar szélsőjobb tőrténelmi helyéhez', in Feitl, István (ed.), *Jobboldali radikalizmusok tegnap és ma*, Budapest: Napvilág Kiadó, 1998, pp. 114-122.

Tamás, Gáspár M., 'A rendszerváltás megbukott', *Népszabadság*, 29 February 2004.

— 'Counter-revolution against a counter-revolution', *Eurozine*, 2007. Available on: http://www.eurozine.com/articles/2007-09-18-tamas-en.html (last accessed on: 28 December 2013).

Tóth, András and István Grajczár, 'Válság, radikalizálódás és az újjászületés igérete: a Jobbik útja a parlamentbe', in Enyedi, Zsolt, Andrea Szabó and Róbert Tardos (eds), *Új képlet. Választások Magyarországon, 2010*, Budapest: Demokrácia Kutatások Magyar Központja Alapitvány, 2011, pp. 57-92.

Tóth, István G., 'Bizalomhiány, normazavarok, igazságtalanságérzet és paternalizmus a magyar társadalom értékszerkezetében, Budapest: TÁRKI, 2009.

Verseck, Keno 2012, "Creeping Cult': Hungary Rehabilitates Far-Right Figures', *Der Spiegel*, 6 June 2012. Available on: http://www.spiegel.de/international/europe/right-wing-extremists-cultivate-horthy-cult-in-hungary-a-836526.html (last obtained on: 10 November 2014).

— 'Right-wing Terror: Hungary Silent over Roma Killing Spree', *Der Spiegel*, 23 July 2013.

— 'Neo-Nazis Get Life for Roma Murder Spree', *Der Spiegel*, 6 August 2013.

Vonyó, József, Jobboldali Radikálisok Magyarországon, 1919-1944, Pécs: Krónosz Kiadó, 2012.

— *Gömbös Gyula*, Budapest: Napvilág Kiadó, 2014.

Vultur, Csaba and István Mága, 'Perek szélsőjobboldaliak ellen: itélet is meg nem is', *Magyar Narancs*, 19 February 1998. Available on: http://magyarnarancs.hu/belpol/perek_szelsojobboldaliak_ellen_itelet_is_meg_nem_is-61981 (last accessed on: 3 December 2014).

WIIW, *Current Analyses and Forecasts 6: Will Exports Prevail over Austerity?*, prepared by Astrov, Vasily, Mario Holzner, Gabor Hunya, Kazimierz Laski, Leon Podkaminer et al., July 2010, Vienna: Vienna Institute for International Economic Studies (WIIW).

Italy: a resurgent far-right and fascism

Checchino Antonini

While I am working, the television is often on. I usually do not even know what the programme is. I am sure that some of you do the same. The other day, I happened to notice a programme called 'Wife Swap'. Perhaps you also have it in Britain or other countries. It is true the 'revolution will not be televised' but TV is certainly globalised today.

In the programme, two women swap husbands and houses and each one changes the household routines and rules – who cooks, who washes the dishes, who cleans the house, how one dresses and even how leisure time is managed. It is always a case of traditional families with men and women who play a traditional role, a festival of stereotypes. This is already a worrying feature.

In the episode I saw when I began to write this article there was one of these wives who was examining the wine bottle collection of her 'new' husband – bottles decorated with the Duce's (Mussolini) image.

This woman had no particular reaction when she discovered that she had been living under the same roof as a fascist. Indeed bottles like this can be found in every souvenir shop and even in the motorway service stations, along with key rings, busts, tee shirts and pictures. Lots of Duce memorabilia is found alongside similar objects with the face of the pope. Sometimes Stalin's face crops up among the wine labels. The marketing experts say it is a niche phenomenon but nonetheless it is just as fascistic. The fascistic zeitgeist, the common sense notion of fascism current in Italy is in my opinion expressed in this anecdote.

Pier Paolo Pasolini wrote the following words in September 1962 about the spread of fascism among the younger generations, just 17 years after the Liberation of Italy:

> You do not have to be strong to stand up to fascism in its crazy or ridiculous forms: but you need to be very strong to confront fascism when it is seen as normal, as the codification – even in a light-hearted, ironic, socially acceptable way – of the brutally egoistic foundations of a society. Italy is rotting within a consumer society that is egotistical, stupid, uncultured, interested only in gossip, moralistic, coercive and conformist; letting yourself contribute in any way to this degeneration today is fascism.

My neighbour is under house arrest for trafficking hard drugs, he has a Celtic cross tattooed on his calf and a massive dog – bigger than me - that is called Dux. The dog owned by two Nazis that killed a comrade called Davide (Dax) ten years ago was called Rommel.

When Italy won the World Cup in 2006, Rome seemed like Nuremburg in 1937. The football terraces were teeming with fascist symbols and knives. Photos of our soldiers from the war zones worldwide are full of illegal fascist symbols. There are a few parties and organisations linked on a national level as well as about a hundred 'cultural' associations. These celebrate the fighters of the Italian Social Republic (also known as Republic of Salo), the puppet state that continued the war alongside the Nazis from 1943 to 1945. Other people identify with the ideological heritage of Julius Evola.[1] There are

---

[1] A Sicilian philosopher, occultist, political writer and spiritualist, Julius Evola was one of the major advocates of Traditionalism, a philosophy which replaced individual or

also small local groups, a few dozen Internet sites, a web radio, a fair number of football fan gangs (from the top division to the lower ones), dozens of musical groups from 'Nazi-rock' to 'Blackshirt singer songwriters'.

Furthermore, if you count the votes for the extreme right in the general elections of February 2013, we seem to be facing a problem:

Fratelli d'Italia	666,035 (1.95%)
La Destra	219,816 (0.64%)
Futuro e Liberta	159,429 (0.46%)
Forza Nuova	89,826 (0.26%)
CasaPound Italia	47,691 (0.14%)
Fiamma Tricolore	44,753 (0.13%)

Taken altogether, this is a bit more than 1,317,000 votes, or 3.58%. According to some analysts, between about 25% and 35% of their electorate have been attracted to Beppe Grillo's M5S, Movimento Cinque Stelle (Five Star Movement). Even as I write, Grillo is putting together an alliance with the British Nigel Farage of UKIP in the European parliament. Historical revisionism has become part of common sense thinking, through those agencies that form society's narrative – commercial TV, talk shows, and TV drama. But its virus also spreads through the ideological machinations of so-called historians and other pseudo intellectuals, as well as the agitprop of activist groups. Berlusconi, the ex-prime minister and TV magnate, stated that at the end of the day Mussolini sent the opposition into holiday camps. In fact they were islands and rural zones where political prisoners were sentenced to prison terms. The mayor of a city from central Italy posed for a photograph with a courgette poking out of his trousers to attack Gay Pride. The mayor of Verona, the city

---

collective motivation with an appeal toward an eternal order which included natural selection.

of Romeo and Juliet, posed for a photograph with a lion on a lead that supposedly was to be used to push out the migrants. In a neighbouring city another mayor welded iron bars onto the benches to prevent people from lying on them.

Pippo Baudo has been one of the best-known TV presenters for over 50 years. A few months ago he put out a false and revisionist version of what happened with the Fosee Ardeatine massacre. The Nazis killed 335 people there as a reprisal against partisan attacks. A village near Rome has inaugurated a mausoleum dedicated to Rodolfo Graziani, the army general and leader of the armed forces of the 1943 Social Republic and the butcher of the Libyan and Ethiopian peoples against whom he used torture and chemical weapons. In many cases fascist councillors in towns and cities have tried to change school textbooks in a revisionist way, for example describing as heroes those people who colluded with the Mussolini regime during the Second World War. From 2008 until 2013, the mayor of Rome was Gianni Alemanno, a 'post-fascist' who had been involved in violence in the 1970s. Over the previous four years he had taken on the payroll ex-fascist terrorists, NAR (Armed Revolutionary Nucleus) members, people from the Banda della Magliana (Magliana Gang), extremists from Forza Nuova (New Force) and the Terza Posizione (Third Position) - putting them into key, well-paid jobs.

The partial rehabilitation of fascism, with its culture of intolerance, has been facilitated by parties that present themselves as 'moderate' and which are part of the political mainstream. The overwhelming majority of their electorate is not Nazi, but believes they it is giving a good kicking to those parties, which are corrupt and ignore its needs. The same process has been seen in Italy with the Lega Nord (Northern League) the Allianza Nazionale (National Alliance) and partially with Grillo's M5S.

Steig Larsson, the Swedish writer well known for the Millennium trilogy, but before that a militant journalist, wrote about the fascists in his country in the following way:

> The most common propaganda message is that in one way or another the democratic politicians are all scoundrels who have enriched themselves on the backs of the people and have sold out or betrayed the country.

There are at least three generations of the Italian right wing:

a) Those who grew up with the Movimento Sociale Italiano (MSI – Italian Social Movement) and never accepted the change in the name of the party and the post-fascist evolution headed up by Gianfranco Fini (the architect of laws on drugs and against immigrants).

b) All those who passed through the radical right-wing groups of the 1970s to the 1990s from the Avanguardia Nazionale (National Vanguard) to the Movimento Politico (Political Movement).

c) The latest recruits, are young people involved in the so-called 'non-conformist occupations'. Some people have called these 'right-wing social centres', where neo-fascist ideology takes the form of a youth subculture with music and dances of extreme energy where you are chained up with other dancers ('cinghiamattanza') along with other communal rituals. Community is certainly a key word that is very attractive for the whole neo-fascist milieu. An idealised inter-class and hierarchical blood community, which is not chosen but a destiny, for people who love their own type and hate any diversity.

There is a photo of a demonstration of 700,000 people called by Berlusconi in 2006 which captures all this rather well: they were all there behind a banner with the words 'Anti-communists forever'. It was the birth of the 'plural right wing'. Berlusconi co-opted them into the coalition that governed Italy until the end of 2011. On another occasion Berlusconi has stated without a hint of irony that he 'fought communism like Churchill fought Nazism'.

For the first time in Europe the policies and the leaders of the far right became part of a government. What a legitimisation! While the extremist right-wing sects have little electoral support, some of their ideas have won a significant space in national politics, through more 'respectable' exponents. On a social level the most striking consequence of this state of affairs has been the development among the younger generation of a broadly xenophobic and neo-fascist subculture.

For many ex-'black' terrorists and thugs, Berlusconi was the bus to jump on quickly. Fascists always put themselves where the money is. But it was also a great opportunity to come out of the shadows. Berlusconi has the money to say whatever he likes and an army of journalists and TV producers who work hard to transform his revolting lies into gold. Within this stew of populism and liberalism many old rogues have found a home in Berlusconi's party, the PdL (Partito della Liberta -Party of Liberty) and also inside the Lega Nord (Northern League – set up by Umberto Bossi). Everyone remembers Borghezio, the Lega's MEP, now linked up with Le Pen, for his racist rantings such as 'we should disinfect trains where immigrants travel'. He comes from Ordine Nuovo (New Order) whose members actually put bombs on trains.[2]

---

[2] On 4 August 1974 a Ferrovie dello Stato train was bombed in the early morning hours killing 12 and wounding 48. The following day, Ordine Nuovo claimed responsibility and issued a public statement claiming that 'We took revenge for Giancarlo Esposti. We wanted to show the nation that we can place a bomb anywhere we want, whenever and

The Alleanza Nationale, the ex-fascists who formed the PdL with Forza Italia (Go Italy – Berlusconi's first political vehicle), and the Lega Nord have very much the same position on immigration. The Italian people, or even those of Padania[3], are a constituent part, along with other European peoples, of a civil, juridical, aesthetic, ethical and philosophical identity that does not deserve to dissolve itself or to be dissolved in an amorphous, pseudo-cultural mixture. The danger is defined as ' indiscriminate, multi-ethnic dirt' or a 'multi-cultural, disordered Babel'. While being part of a government that promotes neoliberal globalisation, it also paradoxically adopts a strident nationalistic tone. A number of heterogeneous positions are expressed: Vaticanphiles or secularists, pro-Arab or Islamophobic, anti-Semitic or pro-Zionist. However the references to tradition, homophobia, sexism and anti-communism remain the bedrock of its ideology, as well as collusion with the secret services of various countries, the mafia and the arms or drugs traffickers.

A series of violent incidents in January 2012 have revealed the links between the Roman criminal fraternity, the extreme right and the Sicilian mafia. It is an alliance which goes back thirty or forty years. Of course the right-wing government-imposed drugs prohibition is the best breeding ground for this narco-mafia.

The profile of the neo-fascists since the turn of the century is extremely diverse. It is an inter-class galaxy with strong bases in Lazio, Lombardy and the Venice regions. In the present crisis they have tried to give themselves an image that is more attentive to people's social needs. They attempt to make a political breakthrough in areas like education where formerly the far right were known for their gang-like, violent actions. Often they put themselves forward as 'neither on the

---

however we please. Let us see in autumn; we will drown democracy under a mountain of dead.'

[3] Padania is what the Northern League claim as their motherland – the northern regions.

right or the left.' Some groups try to use the social movements to impose their own policies and actions. For example they occupy houses and community centres and define them as 'non-conformist' occupations and they put them at the disposal of 'those in need', because they are ' Italian citizens'. Other groups just show off fascist symbols and organise military style parades in the streets, pubs and the stadiums. The real extremists organise violent actions – racist attacks on gypsy camps, against groups of immigrants or against rival right-wing groups with whom they fight in the streets and outside the universities.

We are dealing with a wide variety of groups who are often involved in fratricidal battles. People often belong to several groups at the same time and there is a fierce battle for hegemony. The average age of these activists is decreasing all the time but there are usually some leaders behind them who earned their spurs in the 1970s, during the violent period of street battles and the diffuse terrorism of the MSI youth at that time or of the Terza Posizione, which was an armed group. For the fascists of today, the veterans of Salo (the capital of the Italian Social Republic) are men of honour, faithful to the vows made by romantic heroes who fight for a lost cause. Today this lost cause is the fight against globalisation, immigration, the conspiracy of the big banks whether controlled by the Zionists or not. Saverio Ferrari, a leader of Osservatore Democratico (Democratic Observatory) in Milan and an analyst of neo-fascist phenomena who for many of us is both a comrade and an inspiration, has denounced the fact that in broad sectors of the Italian far right, there has been for some time a neo-Nazi evolution whose seriousness has not been sufficiently taken on board. There is a tendency to embrace ever more explicitly the historical, mythological and symbolic references of the Third Reich and not simply those of the twenty-year Mussolini period. This is not an abstract point. We are dealing with a new identity inevitably destined to produce dire consequences, within a society that is becoming more multi-ethnic and socially complex.

According to the specialists, the right-wing of the right is still a bit formless, relatively unstructured and in search of a strong, charismatic leader - someone capable of transforming it into an active, functioning counter-power. Nevertheless, in the almost messianic wait for this strong leader, nuclei of political soldiers ready for action are forming who get money from businesses and often from mafia groups trafficking in arms and drugs. In Lombardy nobody knows how the group that is winning hegemony is able pay a rent of thousands of euros a year for offices in the centre of Monza, while in Milan they operate out of the offices of a character well known for belonging to the Ndrangheta (the Calabrian mafia).

Saverio Ferrari's analysis is confirmed in the increase in the acts of violence committed. There have been hundreds of physical attacks, vandalism and some more serious criminal acts against their political opponents, immigrants, and offices of left wing organisations and of associations of partisan veterans. The most tragic case was in December 2011 in Florence with the murder of two Senegalese immigrants by Gianluca Casseri, a CasaPound[4] sympathiser.

We are seeing street fighting, scuffles with the police, hooliganism and vandalism inside and outside football grounds, in railway stations and motorway service stations. According to various intelligence reports, we are seeing a new type of football hooliganism where extremist politics is brought into sporting events. Sixty-three out of ninety-eight banners behind which the football supporters groups march are from the right or far right. We are talking about an army of 15,000 fans based in the most fanatical terraces of Italy (Lazio, Roma, Inter, Napoli, Verona, Ascoli, Padova, Catania).

Their military capabilities and cultural hegemony was seen when a policeman killed a fan in a motorway service station in November 2007. The match was called off in Rome and there were

---

[4] A more recent fascist group that took the name of Ezra Pound a great 20th century literary figure who had fascist views.

hours of urban guerrilla warfare with attacks on police stations, cars set on fire and violent confrontations even in other cities.

The neo-fascist imaginative narrative has for some time now been transferred into a Tolkienian world. Here the new right sees the realisation of its own 'conception of the world' in a fantasy framework. At the same time it also uses it to reconstruct a new 'sense of community', no longer based on old mythical stereotypes but on a new symbolic plot that can be absorbed more rapidly and more efficiently. Already in the 1970s, the MSI youth organised Hobbit camps, a sort of fascist Woodstock, with lugubrious, mythical military rites and a bonding similar to other youth subcultures, even like some on the left.

There is a catalogue of openly fascist songs and singers who are linked to the three most significant currents – Forza Nuova, CasaPound and La Destra.

The leader of Forza Nuova (New Force), Roberto Fiore, immediately gave his full solidarity to the Greek Golden Dawn leaders when they were arrested. Forza Nuova was established in 1997 after being briefly part of MSI-Fiamma Tricolore (MSI-Blazing Tricolour) – those people who had not supported the turn of Fini to Alleanza Nazionale. Roberto Fiore was one of the leaders of Terza Posizione at the end of the 1970s and Massimo Morsello was among terrorists sentenced for the 2 August 1980 Bologna train massacre.[5] Fiore and Morsello escaped to London in 1980 pursued by arrest warrants in connection with the inquiry on the Bologna massacre. They were sentenced for subversive association, robbery and being part of an armed group. The English authorities always refused requests for extradition to Italy despite their illegal entry into Britain and the falsification of documents.

---

[5] On August 2, 1980 a bomb exploded at the Central Railway Station of Bologna killing 85 people and wounding more than 200. The attack was attributed to a neo-fascist group of terrorists.

According to an investigation[6] by the Guardian newspaper this 'protection' was connected to the collaborative relations between Fiore, Morsello and the English secret services.

Once back in Italy as a result of the statute of limitations in 1999, they founded Forza Nuova with a programme of just a few basic positions. Number one was the removal of the abortion law combined with defence of the family and for demographic growth. Following that, we have 'the end of immigration and a human repatriation', the 'reactivation of the Church/state concordat of 1929', 'the abrogation of the Mancino and Scelba libertarian laws' (laws banning fascism) and the 'formation of corporations for the defence of working people and the national community'. What is clear is that they are looking to be the favoured partner of the Italian Catholic fundamentalists while at the same time exploiting dog whistle issues to win support on a xenophobic and racist basis. It even goes so far as to recover an old colonialist policy designating the key role to the European peoples in rebuilding a moribund European continent. In some cities Forza Nuova is allied with Berlusconi or even the Lega Nord, and in others it opposes them.

In terms of symbols, Forza Nuova has tried to reconfigure the traditional sign of the radical right into a more Christian/Catholic one. The Celtic cross, which is originally a pagan symbol (and then a Nazi one) representing the chariot wheel of the sun god, has now been revamped as the cross of Constantine. In the legend, the emperor has a vision of it before the battle of Ponte Milvio. At the same time, they make repeated and explicit references to the myth of Codreanu, an anti-Semite, hero of the European radical right, founder of the Romanian fascist movement in the 1930s and leader of its 'iron guard'. The latter was an organisation of fanatical Catholics whose organisational model Forza Nuova has borrowed, the notorious

---

[6] Neo-fascist clear to resume charity role, David Pallister, 6 August 1999, *The Guardian*, http://www.theguardian.com/uk/1999/aug/06/davidpallister.

Cuiburi or nests – small cells of three to four activists – which was already being used in the Terza Posizione period.

It goes without saying that Fiore and Morsello escaped to London with the funds of Terza Posizione, the proceeds of various armed robberies and lots of other illegal activity. Fiore and Morello used this money to set up various businesses estimated to have a turnover of tens of billions a year. At the centre of this tidy little empire is a business called Meeting Point, which subsequently changed its name to Easy London.[7] It is a travel agency, as well as being a company providing services for musical concerts, and also a recruitment and personnel agency. After renovating buildings due to be demolished, the company turned them into hostels with 1,300 studio apartments. Branches have been opened in other countries such as France and Spain. In Italy it offers special holiday/accommodation/work packages in London using cramped, dirty rooms, starvation wages and employing a skinhead gang to keep everything under control. As well as various restaurants, a record label and language schools in London,[8] it has also opened a chain of charity shops selling second-hand clothes and other goods, including religious items. These are managed by associations called St Michael Archangel Trust or the St George Educational Trust, both with aims at promoting the teachings of the Catholic Church. Fiore himself is a director, along with Colin Todd, one of the most notorious characters in the English Nazi milieu – a supporter of the Third Position. In Italy, this commercial activity is expanding in various directions from agricultural products (vegetables, pasta and rice) produced in Italy and sold on the English market with a label saying 'buy Italian', to the British chain of skinhead clothes shops (already operating in Rome

---

[7] https://www.indymedia.org.uk/en/2009/02/422265.html?c=on.

[8] Language school run by Italian fascist leader, Ian Cobain and Matthew Taylor, *The Guardian*, 29 February 2008, http://www.theguardian.com/politics/2008/feb/29/thefarright.italy.

and the Latina region) under the shop sign 'The cross and the circle point'. Probably it is this money that has allowed Forza Nuova to open offices in at least 30 cities in three years and to attract groups older than the skinhead movement. Another characteristic of Forza Nuova is the weight and importance given to international relations with the Jean Marie Le Pen's Front National and other similar groups. Fiore and Morsello have also bought an old property not far from Valencia, which they aim to transform into stable centre for their international network. This group is the most internationalist current of the far right.

CasaPound is the organisation that is most ambiguous and innovative. Its forty years old leader, Gianluca Iannone, is also a singer with Zetaseroalfa, a Nazi rock band. It occupies houses and community centres and camouflages itself behind mountaineering and boxing clubs or similar associations. Alongside militaristic mythology, their veneration of American films like Fight Club stands out. These films modernise mythology around struggle, values, ardour, courage, heroism and adventure. These key words really get their members going when they are used on Bandiera Nera (Black Banner) their web radio or when uttered by their leader. This group is the one that takes most care over how to communicate. It often tries to use myths and icons from the left – from Che Guevara to Corto Maltese[9] or Peppino Impastato (left activist murdered by mafia), Vittorio Arrigoni and Capitan Harlock[10]. They promote initiatives with titles like 'Il camerata

---

[9] Corto Maltese is a comic book series created by Italian artist Hugo Pratt in 1967. It features a sailor-adventurer, Corto, who instinctively supports the disadvantaged and oppressed and is skeptical of nationalism and religion.

[10] Vittorio Arrigoni was an Italian reporter, writer, pacifist and activist. Arrigoni worked with the pro-Palestinian International Solidarity Movement in the Gaza Strip, from 2008 until his kidnapping and death in 2011 by Palestinians. The latter were condemned in a Hamas military court. Capitan Harlock is a fictional character created by manga artist Leiji Matsumoto and the protagonist of the Space Pirate Captain Harlock manga series.

(fascist term for comrade) Corto Maltese. Corto Maltese is a comic book hero, a libertarian hero of the 1970s. They also use terms like 'Il compagno Duce' – compagno is the word for comrade used on the left in Italy. Nearly always they want to get themselves talked about in ways that are different from fascist gang attacks. They make a lot of noise but their events do not draw that many people.

The name comes from the American intellectual, Ezra Pound, who in the 1930s put forward a critique of money and capitalism coloured with openly racist and anti-Semitic tones. He supported fascism right up to the end and was put on trial and sentenced for it after 1945. From 2003 to now, with its local offices and occupations, it is present in about twenty cities but the centre of its activity remains Rome.

Clearly there is close collaboration between CasaPound (and also with its *Blocco Studentesco* – Student Bloc) and institutional parties, especially with the PdL to which it is often attached, providing support and candidates for various election campaigns throughout Italy.[11] In exchange it gets money and political/media coverage from the PdL. CasaPound is often able to organise its events mainly thanks to the deployment of the police who are put at their disposal against anti-fascist mobilisations who are often subject to repression by the police and the law. There have been around 500 legal and police actions that have restrained the liberty of these protestors – imprisonment, house arrest, obligatory reporting to police stations, all against anti-fascist students, unemployed and workers who have confronted CasaPound and the Blocco Studentesco.

On the other hand, fascist aggression openly carried out by well-known and identified figures using knives and chains, is not seriously prosecuted while the media portrays it as a normal but confused

---

[11] While this book was going to press there are ever more organic, open and close links between Casapound, other far right groups and the Lega Nord, led by its new leader Matteo Salvini.

'fighting between extremists'. For respectable right-wing papers their violence is a sort of 'benevolent' one.

Walls have been plastered with an out and out declaration of war against India demanding the release of the two Italian marines who, in 2012, had killed a poor Indian fisherman. They say they are not racist but they denounce the racism against Italians caused by multiculturalism. They call themselves fascists of the third millennium. Another technique of these media-savvy fascist gangs is to hang up mannequins (just like the fascists did in the past with real partisans) in public places on the pretext of denouncing extortion, the high cost of living and other injustices.

Finally let us examine La Destra (the Right), which is currently working to rebuild Alleanza Nazionale together with various fascistic groups within the PdL diaspora. It can be defined as a bit like the last gasp of the MSI story, partly the orphans of the centre-right (often linked to the PdL), and to some degree an attempt to gather together those forces coming from the neo-fascist tradition. It is the only group within the fascist galaxy that has the profile of a real, proper party, at least until a split from the PdL launched Brothers of Italy (*Fratelli d'Italia*).

The leader of La Destra is Francesco Storace. He was spokesperson for Gianfranco Fini in the middle of the 1990s when he split in order to become the Italian Le Pen with same racist obsessions (priority to the Italians), against the legacy of 1968 and against the EU. He is the same filth as his French model but with many less millions of votes. He is 54 and was a leader of the most violent branches of the Roman MSI in the 70s. He was elected President of the Lazio region (around Rome) between 2000 and 2005 and then became Health minister in the third Berlusconi government between 2005 and 2006. He broke with Fini over the centrist turn and when the latter declared, when visiting Israel, that 'Fascism was the absolute evil'.

The National Social Front (*Fronte Sociale Nazionale*) led by Adriano Tilgher (born 1947) joined La Destra. Tilgher has always been close to Stefano Delle Chiaie, who set up Avanguardia Nazionale at the beginning of the 70s. Delle Chiaie has been one of the front line personalities of the Italian far right and was implicated (but acquitted) in many trials connected with the strategy of tension.[12] Tilgher has praised Hitler's social policy saying that 'he was a man who fought for his people although, according to official history, he committed some deformed or distorted actions'. He is a member of the political bureau of the group led by Francesco Storace alongside other younger neo-fascist leaders emerging from the football terraces and other small groups within the fascist galaxy. These younger activists also organised an occupation. They took over an old cinema in the centre of Rome that was immediately changed into a commercial discotheque but was subsequently closed by the police. Before its closure, it hosted a sort of assembly of all the hooligans and ex-terrorists with worrying links to the European wide skinhead movement and the anti-Semite currents of the Middle East.

This is the context in which the anti-fascist movement is trying to confront the spread and influence of fascist ideas and aggression. Out of necessity it has to maintain a degree of 'military' organisation – securing demonstrations, pickets and meetings. The weakness of the alternative left is also reflected in the present level of anti-fascist action that is often persecuted by the repressive apparatus. In Italy at the moment, what is working is the attempt to transform the vertical conflict between capital and labour into horizontal conflicts, which is a war between poor people. The main horizontal conflict is where ethnicity takes the place of class. In this way, broad sections of

---

[12] The strategy of tension was tactic used by the right and Western governments during the 'Cold War' that aimed to manipulate public opinion using fear, disinformation, agents provocateurs, and even terrorist actions in order to drive people away from the left.

working people think that the enemy to be defeated are the gypsies, the blacks, Muslims and migrants in general.

In recent years the worsening of the economic crisis, whose end is not in sight, has aggravated these contradictions and social disarray generally. Discrimination and the lack of rights are ever more evident and incidences of racism have increased whether at the institutional level or in society generally. Frontiers have become insurmountable walls and even the right to asylum has been subject to heavy restrictions, while the absence of legal channels of entry has increased the number of illegal migrants.

While the fascists are a marginal factor politically, it is the government parties, the PD (*Partito Democratico*, Democratic Party),[13] Forza Italia and their allies the Lega Nord and the NCD (*Nuovo Centro Destra*, New Centre Right) who are adopting more authoritarian methods. They are combining privatisation and liberalisation with changes to the political system through electoral arrangements that set high thresholds for parties wishing to be represented in parliament as a well as bonus seats for the party with a relative majority. At the same time they are trying to criminalise social conflicts and popular movements through the use of old and new laws, including some that have survived intact from the fascist era. It has resulted in 18,000 people who have been charged, are on trial, imprisoned or have legal restrictions for involvement in social conflicts. One of the first measures adopted by the Renzi (PD) government[14] was to allow electricity, gas and water supply to be cut to people occupying buildings illegally as they campaign for better housing. Before Renzi, Berlusconi managed to designate all sites of major public works projects, such as incinerators, as military zones,

---

[13] The PD was founded in 2007 from the remnants of the PCI (Communist Party of Italy) and the 'left' of DC (*Democrazia Cristiana*, Christian Democracy).

[14] Matteo Renzi became Prime Minister in February 2014, heading a PD (*Partito Democratico*) government.

pure and simple. The Italian security apparatus demonstrated what it is capable of with the police violence at the G8 summit in Genova in 2001. In Italy as elsewhere, the armed forces and police apparatus are heavily permeated by a fascistic subculture, with far right groups infiltrating them in order to gain support.

National-populism in the Netherlands

'The Dutch people have no equal'[1]

Alex de Jong

The Netherlands has a reputation for being a tolerant, open society. Part of the explanation for this myth is that the Netherlands, for a long time, lacked a party like the French *Front National* or the Belgian *Vlaams Blok,* that is a party that was commonly recognised to be racist and on the far right, and which also had electoral success. But in recent years, the Dutch far right has evolved into one of the most successful movements on the European continent. In some respects, its leader, Geert Wilders' party, the Party for Freedom (*Partij voor de Vrijheid,* PVV), has overtaken other parties such as the Danish People's Party, and he is looking to form an alliance with the *Front National* and *Vlaams Belang.* The fact that Wilders, after years of trying to take his distance from them, now wants to form a caucus in the European Parliament with these parties is indicative of his political evolution.

Geert Wilders has become a major political figure in the Netherlands. At the elections in 2012, his PVV (*Partij voor de Vrijheid*) gained over 10% of the vote and played a crucial role in the formation

---

[1] Nederlanders zijn een volk dat zijn gelijke niet kent' - Quote from the 2010 election program of the PVV. PVV, *De agenda van hoop en optimisme. Een tijd om te kiezen; PVV 2010 – 2015* (2010) 5.

of the first government of Prime Minister Mark Rutte from October 2010 to November 2012. In many ways Wilders is the political heir of Pim Fortuyn, a Dutch politician who after a meteoric rise was murdered on 6 May 2002 and who played a crucial role in mobilising a new right-wing current in Dutch politics. After his death, a number of would-be heirs came and went until Wilders managed to stabilise his position. In the years since Wilders left his old party, the right-wing liberal People's Party for Freedom and Democrac (*Volkspartij voor Vrijheid en Democratie*, VVD), he has steadily moved further right. As he did so, he has exercised considerable influence on Dutch politics and society.

Pim Fortuyn played a crucial role in shaping a 'national-populist' current in the Netherlands of which Wilders is now the most prominent representative. Populism is defined here as an ideological feature, and not merely as a political style. A populist 'considers society to be ultimately separated into two homogeneous and antagonistic groups, 'the pure people' versus 'the corrupt elite," and argues that politics should be an expression of the will of this 'people'.[2] The people then are not the whole of society, but rather that part of the whole that's considered pure and whose political will is considered legitimate. The people are a partial object that stands in for the whole. Who is part of the 'people' is not objectively given: the borders of this category are contested and the selection of those considered part of it and those who are not is a political act. Selecting and representing this 'people' creates a new agency out of a heterogeneous group.[3]

Different kinds of populism use different criteria to shape this new agency. Populism is often combined with other ideologies to produce the criteria that shape the borders of 'the people'. The criteria can be social-economic as in the contradiction between those from 'below' and those who are 'above' in the rhetoric of left-wing populists

---

[2] Cas Mudde, *Populist radical right parties in Europe* (Cambridge 2007) 23.

[3] Ernesto Laclau, *On populist reason* (London 2005) 204.

like Hugo Chávez. But the criteria can also be cultural, for example when populism is combined with nationalism, which strives for the congruence of the nation and the state, and of the cultural and the political. In this combination, in 'national-populism', the populist 'people' and the nation tend to overlap. The term 'people' has an historical, ethnic connotation, and the partial object that stands in for the whole in national-populism is a nation that isn't equal to the citizenry. Fortuyn's populism was nationalist in that he called for the assimilation of an 'alien' minority culture into 'Dutchnes'.

Nationalist trailblazers

Fortuyn combined this Dutch nationalism with populism and right-wing, anti-left liberalism, laying the ideological groundwork for a new current in Dutch politics. Wilhelmus Simon Petrus Fortuyn was born in 1948 in a catholic, petty-bourgeois family in a small town in the north of Holland (he would later change his name from Fortuijn to 'Fortuyn', believing this looked more fancy). After studying sociology, he taught 'critical sociology' at the University of Groningen in the early seventies. In 1972, he applied for membership to the Dutch Communist Party but he was rejected because of his association with Ger Harmsen, a Marxist who had broken with the party in the fifties. Fortuyn joined the social-democratic Party of Labour (*Party van de Arbeid*, PvdA), of which he remained a member until 1989. In 1990 he moved to Rotterdam, the second largest city in the country. During the eighties and nineties, as his views became more and more right wing, Fortuyn first worked for different government organisations and then created his own political consultancy firm. From 1991 to 1995, he was a professor in 'employment conditions in the public service' at the Erasmus University in Rotterdam. Years later, Fortuyn would still (wrongly) claim the title 'professor'.

During the nineties, Fortuyn became a public figure. He wrote a regular column in Elsevier, a right-wing liberal weekly, and started to appear on a television talk-show, *Business Class*, of businessman Harry Mens. 'Professor Pim' became one of the regular commentators on current affairs, arguing for strict neoliberal economic policies and for cutting back social services. Fortuyn put down his thoughts in several books. A book like *De Verweesde Samenleving* (The Orphaned Society) showed him to be a conservative cultural pessimist, decrying the loss of community in the modern Netherlands, the decline of patriarchal authority figures and the erosion of (vaguely defined) social norms and values. In *Tegen de islamisering van onze cultuur* (Against the Islamisation of Our Culture), he in particular declared 'Islamic culture' to be a threat to Dutch society. According to Fiortuyn, under the influence of individualism and 'cultural relativism', Dutch people risked losing their own identity to this 'backward' culture.[4]

The threat was a monolithic, backward 'Islamic culture', framed as natural, uniform, and a-historical. From Fortuyn's perspective, 'Islam' was not only a religion, it was also a world-view and a political ideology. Fortuyn motivated his anti-immigration policies as a necessary defence of Dutch society against this threat. Fortuyn deemed Islamic culture to be incompatible with being Dutch. In August 2001, Fortuyn called for a new 'cold war', this time against Islam when he said that 'I also favour a cold war against Islam. I see Islam as being an exceptional threat, as a society hostile to ours'.[5]

Fortuyn was not the first to employ such a discourse. An important step in introducing such views into the Dutch political mainstream was a 1991 speech by future European Commissioner for Internal Market and Services, Frits Bolkestein. He was then the

---

[4] Rob Witte, 'Al eeuwen lang een gastvrij volk' Racistisch geweld en overheidsreacties in Nederland 1950 – 2009 (Amsterdam 2010) 133. Pim Fortuyn, *Tegen de islamisering van onze cultuur: Nederlandse identiteit als fundament* (Utrecht 1997). Pim Fortuyn, *De verweesde samenleving. Een religieus-sociologisch traktaat* (Uithoorn 2002).

[5] Aangifte tegen Fortuyn wegens discriminatie, *De Volkskrant*, 2 November 2011 online at [http://www.volkskrant.nl/vk/nl/2844/Archief/archief/article/detail/605866/2001/11/02/Aangifte-tegen-Fortuyn-wegens-discriminatie.dhtml].

political leader of the right-wing liberal VVD, one of the major parties in Dutch politics. In a speech for a meeting of the Liberal International in 1991, Bolkestein argued that there was a contradiction between European and Christian civilisation, and the culture of the Middle-East and Islam.[6] In this discourse, democracy and Human Rights became products of a single European culture, instead of the results of political conflicts inside different cultures. Likewise, Fortuyn assimilated political concepts like the separation of church and state or equal rights for women and homosexuals into the threatened Dutch culture of his book.

Bolkestein was a pioneer of a discourse that declared that the 'integration' into society of Islamic immigrants to the Netherlands, mainly migrant workers and their families who had started to come to the Netherlands in the sixties, had failed. He argued that this failure was related to their 'culture', and that therefore the 'integration' of their children had also failed because their children remained part of the culture of their parents and not that of their homeland, and that it was the responsibility of migrant communities to overcome this supposed failure.[7] Before then, rhetoric about a contradiction between Dutch and European culture had been the domain of marginalised far-right parties, but Bolkestein was a respected member of the political establishment.

Unlike the elitist Bolkestein, who cultivates a patrician image, Fortuyn combined the idea of culturalism, that people's behaviour is determined by closed cultures, with populism. For Fortuyn, Dutch 'culture', including the democratic gains which he claimed were part of it, was in danger because for years the elites of the Netherlands had refused to recognise the 'threat' of Islamic culture because they 'blinded' by progressive and multi-culturalist ideology. Fortuyn appealed to 'the Dutch people' to defend their culture.

---

[6] Witte, Al eeuwen lang, 100.

[7] Willem Schinkel, De gedroomde samenleving (Kampen, 2011).

In Fortuyn's discourse, Dutch people are construed to be tolerant while society's cultural 'others', especially Muslims, are represented as intolerant. An illustration of this is the early 2001 'El Moumni affair'. In May 2001, the Rotterdam Imam El-Moumni, who is of Moroccan descent, made comments on national television arguing that homosexuality was an illness threatening reproduction and society in general. The comments caused upheaval in Dutch society. People especially took offence because these views came from a cultural 'other', from 'the outside'. In public discourse, Islam has become more and more construed as antagonistic to modern, tolerant, Dutch 'values'. Being 'tolerant' of homosexuality is considered one of the markers of Dutch culture and one of the demonstrations of the superiority of this culture in contrast to 'Islamic culture', which is construed as homogeneously and inherently homophobic. This theme has remained an important element in Dutch national-populism. Increasingly restrictive demands regarding immigration and Islamic culture are framed as defence of 'Dutch tolerance'.[8]

From the margins to the centre

Open anti-immigrant sentiments had generally been 'repressed and stigmatised' in the Dutch public sphere, which was characterised by a strong drive towards consensus and thus the avoidance of political conflicts. Fortuyn attacked this culture of seeking consensus and attacked Muslims for their supposedly 'backward' culture, but not for their ethnicity as such or for being immigrants.[9] In this way, Fortuyn could distance himself from the pseudo-scientific biological racism of

---

[8] Paul Mepschen, 'Against Tolerance: Islam, Sexuality, and the Politics of Belonging in the Netherlands' June 13, 2009 *MRZine* online at [http://mrzine.monthlyreview.org/2009/mepschen130709.html].

[9] Merijn Oudenampsen, 'Explaining the swing to the right. The Dutch debate on the rise of right-wing populism' in Ruth Wodak, Majid Khosravinik, Brigitte Mal (ed.) *Right-wing populism in Europe. Politics and discourse* (London 2013) 191 – 209, there 203.

the extreme right which at the time was much too closely associated with the horrors of Nazism to be politically successful. Fortuyn's avoidance of the charge of 'racism' by claiming he wasn't targeting individuals or a 'race' but a 'culture' or 'religion' remains a standard argument on the Dutch right. In practice, the categories constantly overlap and the distinction often becomes meaningless. In the mid-nineties, Fortuyn, for example, wrote that he considered it impossible for people to 'leave their culture behind'.[10]

Extreme-right-wing and anti-immigrant parties remained small in the Netherlands after the end of the Second World War.[11] Small far-right groups in which ageing Nazis played leading roles, like the National European Social Movement (*Nationaal Europese Sociale Beweging*) were banned by the government. During the sixties, the Farmers Party (*Boerenpartij*, BP) had some electoral success, winning three and then seven seats in Parliament. Although not radical and right-wing as such, the BP's 'diffuse national-conservative programme'[12] did attract a part of the far right. The association with the far-right and old Nazis placed a heavy burden on the party which was plagued by splits. By the end of the sixties, it had lost its appeal. During the seventies, the Dutch far right was dominated by the Dutch People's Union (*Nederlandse Volks-Unie*, NVU), a clear neo-Nazi party. It never grew beyond a few hundreds of members and was nearly banned as a criminal association.

In an attempt to escape the legal restrictions that the Netherlands places on propagating racism and the association with historical Nazism, more 'moderate' members of the NVU and other far-right activists organised several far-right parties in eighties. The Centre Party (*Centrumpartij*, CP), and its successors (*Centrum*

---

[10] Pim Fortuyn, De verweesde samenleving. Een religieus-sociologisch traktaat (Uithoorn 2002) 198.

[11] Cas Mudde, *The ideology of the extreme right* (Manchester 2000) 117 – 121.

[12] Mudde ideology 118.

Democraten, CD and *Centrumpartij '86,* Centre Party '86) had more success. This so-called 'Centre-current' tried to keep its distance from historical Nazism and fascism and from openly racist statements, instead focusing on opposing 'immigration'. The Centre-current had some electoral success in the eighties and early nineties. The CP won one seat in the Parliament 1982 and its successor, the CD, won three seats in 1994. Different far-right parties were able to win dozens of council seats in those years.

But these parties were badly organised and lacked competent activists. Their appeal was severely limited by their association with violence, anti-Semitism and historical fascism, they were excluded by the other parties, and were put under pressure from anti-racist activists and media. The Centre-current never stabilised as a factor in Dutch politics, instead it remained a fairly marginal and isolated grouping of outcasts and the querulous.

Fortuyn, however, was very different. Like Bolkstein, he strongly distanced himself from the parties of the extreme-right and from historical references to fascism, and was a supporter of parliamentary democracy. Maybe unexpectedly considering his moral conservatism, Fortuyn flaunted his homosexuality. This too helped him to avoid being marginalised as 'far-right'. Another element that set Fortuyn apart from the existing far right was that he claimed that he was not anti-Semitic, that he was a supporter of Israel and a right-wing Zionist.

By linking his attacks on the Muslim minority to Muslims' supposed views on democracy, women's rights and equal rights for homosexuals, he also appealed to people who considered themselves to be 'progressive'. Fortuyn's political innovations allowed people to support an anti-immigrant politician without breaking the taboo on open (biological) racism. In this way, Fortuyn did more than represent an already existing constituency, he was also very successful in shaping and voicing anti-immigrant and anti-minority views. Instead of just representing an anti-immigrant and anti-Muslim potential in society, Fortuyn also won new support for his ideas, an original mix of moral conservatism and economic liberalism that integrated elements of the Dutch progressive liberal hegemony that had come into being after '68'.[13] In biological racism, 'inheritance determined all the essential characteristics of human beings. And the quality of inheritance rested not only on individuals and families, but on the entire racial group to which they belonged'.[14] In national-populism, being of a different culture has replaced being of a different 'race'. 'Culture' has replaced 'race' as the category of a hierarchical difference between an inferior 'outsider-group' (for Fortuyn and those following in his tracks, the target are especially Muslims) and the superior 'insider-group'. It is 'a racism whose dominant theme is not biological heredity but the insurmountable nature of cultural differences'.[15]

During the nineties, Fortuyn tried to start a political party in right-wing parties but without success. But in the parliamentary elections of 2002, Fortuyn became the front-runner for a new national party, Liveable Netherlands (*Leefbaar Nederland*, LN). LN was built on the success of similar local parties like *Leefbaar Rotterdam* (LR). A few months earlier, Fortuyn was a candidate for LR and won 30% of the vote. *Leefbaar* combined a populist style of claiming to speak on behalf of 'common people' with criticism of various issues that were seen as neglected by the other parties. These issues varied from insecurity in the public domain to the problems caused by

---

[13] Merijn Oudenampsen, 'De politiek van populisme onderzoek. Een kritiek op Diplomademocratie en de verklaring van populisme uit kiezersgedrag' in Justus Uitermark, et al. (ed.) *'Power to the people!' Een anatomie van het populisme* (Den Haag 2012) 17 -49, Merijn Oudenampsen, 'De revolte van nieuwrechts. Neoconservatisme en postprogressieve politiek', *Krisis. Tijdschrift voor actuele filosofie*, 1 (2013) 72 – 88 and Rogier van Reekum, 'It's the performance, stupid!' in Justus Uitermark, et al. (ed.) *'Power to the people!' Een anatomie van het populisme* (Den Haag 2012) 49 – 57, there 53.

[14] Eric D.Weitz, A century of genocide. Utopias of race and nation (Princeton 2003) 49.

[15] Etienne Balibar and Immanuel Wallerstein, *Race, nation, class. Ambigious Identitie* (London 2005 [1991]), 21.

bureaucracy, from trains arriving too late to the long waiting periods for certain kinds of medical treatment. Fortuyn wasn't the ideal candidate for *Leefbaar Nederland*. Some of the people who launched the party had only recently left the PvdA, and especially on social-economic issues were closer to a vague left-centrism than to Fortuyn. Fortuyn's cold war against Islam did not necessarily appeal strongly to them. But *Leefbaar Nederland* lacked suitable candidates and the skilful Fortuyn had already built himself an audience.

The marriage of convenience between LN and Fortuyn did not last long. A few months before the elections, on 9 February 2002, in an interview with the *Volkskrant*, one of the major newspapers, Fortuyn declared that he wanted to abolish Article 1 of the Dutch constitution. This article bans discrimination and is for equal treatment for all. Fortuyn wanted to abolish it because it prevents policies discriminating against Muslims. He also argued against the Geneva treaty on refugees because he wanted to drastically restrict immigration, in particular that of Muslims and people who are from Muslim countries. In the interview, Fortuyn linked crime to ethnicity: 'Moroccan youth never steal from a Moroccan. Did you ever notice that? But we can be robbed.' Characteristically, 'Moroccans' included people who were born and raised in the Netherlands, with Dutch nationality. In the same interview, Fortuyn declared that the Netherlands was 'full', and said that if it was up to him, not a single asylum-seeker would be allowed in the country. The LN leadership, already uneasy with Fortuyn, had earlier forbidden him to make such statements and he was removed from the party.

In April 2002 Fortuyn had already formed his own party, the *Lijst Pim Fortuyn* (LPF). On economic issues, the LPF was clearly more right wing than *Leefbaar Nederland*. In late 2002, Fortuyn declared that the only possible coalition partners for a government with the LPF were the VVD and the Christian-Democratic CDA. Fortuyn wanted to further liberalise the labour market, push down wages and drastically cut social security. Fortuyn had gathered substantial support criticising long waiting lists for certain kinds of medical treatments and shortcomings in the care for the elderly. He maintained a neoliberal response to these issues: no extra government spending but further liberalisation of healthcare, higher fees for patients and care workers to work 'more efficiently'.[16] Fortuyn boasted that the LPF had received millions of euros from his contacts in the real-estate sector. Referring to the elections in May that he hoped to win, he said 'don't be surprised if after May 15 the laws on land ownership change drastically'.[17]

The incumbent government, the 'purple' coalition of the PvdA and liberals, became hugely unpopular around the turn of the century. Fortuyn played an important role in fermenting this dissatisfaction. During the 'Purple' governments in the nineties that combined the main parties of the 'right' and the 'left', Dutch politics had become highly technocratic. Fortuyn presented himself as a newcomer, as somebody who would use his political power to improve Dutch society, and not just manage it. Fortuyn attacked the consensus-oriented model of politics because he saw it as hindering the introduction of the drastic neoliberal structural reforms he wanted. His polemical style and sense of sarcasm appealed to many. Unlike the existing far right at the time, or the national-populists who would come after him, he did not pose as an underdog, instead he showed off his personal wealth and the dandyesque Fortuyn clearly stood out among the colourless technocrats of the major parties.

Many of the frustrations people felt with the neoliberal Purple coalitions were blamed by Fortuyn on the supposed softness and naivety of the social-democrats of the PvdA. Fortuyn provided people with targets that could be made responsible for their problems: the smug 'left-wing elite' that had become alienated from the 'real world',

---

[16] Ewout Irrgang et al., Leest u zijn boeken maar. De pimpelpaarse antwoorden van Pim Fortuyn (Rotterdam 2002) 20 – 22.

[17] Ewout Irrgang et al., Leest u zijn boeken maar, 33.

and Muslims whose alien culture supposedly eroded the values that had kept Dutch society together.

But on 6 May 2002, Pim Fortuyn was killed by an environmental activist, Volkert van der Graaf. At his trial, Van Graaf declared he had killed Fortuyn because hewas 'scapegoating' Muslims and was a threat to disadvantaged groups in society. The murder led to a dramatic uproar. It was commonly (although incorrectly) claimed this was the first political murder in the Netherlands since 1672. Thousands of people gathered to watch the car that brought Fortuyn's body to his funeral, and many overcome by emotion threw flowers in front of it. For many people Fortuyn had already become a hero figure and now he was a martyr.

The elections nine days later were a political earthquake that left many marks on the Dutch political landscape. On 15 May 2002, the LPF received 15.7% of the vote: with 26 seats (out of 150) it came out of nowhere to become the second largest party in Parliament. At over 80%, the turn-out for the elections was exceptionally high. The PvdA was hammered: it lost 22 of its 45 seats. Fortuyn had succeeded in pulling the political debate to the right. In the days after his death, a strongly anti-left sentiment took hold in the country. Right-wing media commentators and Fortuyn's followers blamed his death on his supposed 'demonisation' by progressive critics. 'The bullet came from the Left' was an oft repeated phrase. This, and Fortuyn's 'martyrdom', made criticising his ideas difficult.

Together with the CDA and the VVD, the LPF formed a coalition that would last only 3 months. The inexperienced LPF quickly tore itself apart with fights between individuals and the coalition collapsed mid-October. In the following elections of January 2003, the LPF received only 5.6% of the vote. The new coalition was made up of the VVD, CDA and another liberal party, D66 (formerly known as Democrats 66). The PvdA recovered and won 42 seats, becoming the second largest party. But the potential for an anti-immigrant party to the right of the VVD hadn't disappeared and different political forces tried to appeal to Fortuyn's followers. Of several potential heirs, Geert Wilders has been the most successful. He has also moved the political landscape much more to the right than Fortuyn ever did.

In Fortuyn's footsteps

Geert Wilders was born in 1963 in a catholic family in Venlo, a small city in the periphery of the Netherlands. His father was deputy director of a factory producing printing and copying equipment. After high school, Wilders visited Israel and worked in a kibbutz north of Jericho. Several times, he had to seek shelter in a bunker during attacks. According to him, this period made him fall in love with Israel, a country he considers his second home, and made him realise the risks of 'Islamic terrorism'. After returning to the Netherlands, he did his military service and started a course for a law degree which he never completed. He became a public servant and worked for the *Sociale Verzekeringsbank*, the institute responsible for national social insurance. He would later say that this is where his distaste for bureaucracy comes from, and that he became politically active because of his aversion to left-wing ideas.[18]

Wilders had always voted VVD and in 1990 he decided to apply for a job with its parliamentary group. His inside knowledge of the complicated system of national insurance was an asset and he became an assistant to the parliamentary group. Wilders strongly admired Bolkestein and became a close associate of his.

In 1997, Wilders became a member of the city-council of Utrecht where he had been living since 1985, and after the elections of May 1998 he became a member of the national Parliament. Wilders

---

[18] Hanan Nhass, 'Ik word gek van dat poldergedoe', *Trouw* July 23, 2003 online at [http://www.trouw.nl/tr/nl/4324/nieuws/archief/article/detail/1781138/2003/07/23/Ik-word-gek-van-dat-poldergedoe.dhtml.]

would live in Utrecht until 2004 and claims that his time there was another key-point in his biography. When he moved to Utrecht, his neighbourhood (Kanaleneiland) was a quiet middle-class part of town. In recent years, it had become known as a neighbourhood with high crime-rates, high unemployment and a large Muslim community. Wilders says he witnessed dramatic changes, talking about the times he 'had to run from his car to his front-door to come home safely'. In reality, he lived in the far wealthier south of the neighbourhood and his memories of the time seem to be quite exaggerated.[19]

In the late 1990s and early 2000s, Wilders was known as a hard-working parliamentarian on the right-wing of the VVD. Wilders regularly criticised the PvdA, until 2002 coalition-partner of the VVD and, following the lead of his mentor Bolkstein, he made the supposed threat of Islamic fundamentalism one of his main themes. For Wilders, the 9-11 attacks became a confirmation of his worst fears. But in these years Wilders was also criticising Fortuyn for not distinguishing between ordinary Muslims and fundamentalist terrorists, and for attacking Islamic culture as a whole. Wilders lost his seat in the elections of May 2002, but returned to Parliament when a number of VVD parliamentarians who were appointed by the new government to posts in the civil service had to give up their seats.

In the meantime, Bolkestein had left Dutch politics to become European Commissioner for Internal Market and Services. A few years later Wilders found another source of political inspiration in Ayaan Hirsi Ali. Hirsi Ali's father had been an opponent of Somali dictator Muhammad Siad Barre. The family left the country for the Netherlands in 1992 when Hirsi Ali was six years old. To escape from an arranged marriage and apply for asylum, she changed her name and incorrectly claimed she came directly from a disaster area in Somalia. She became a Dutch citizen in 1995 and started to work for the scientific bureau of the PvdA in 2001. She became known for her

---

[19] Koen Vossen, Rondom Wilders. Portret van de PVV (Amsterdam, 2013) 20.

criticism of the treatment of women in Islamic communities. However, she felt the PvdA did not support her enough, especially after she started to receive threats from right-wing Muslims. Hirsi Ali moved from attacking certain abuses in Muslim communities like female genital mutilation to attacking Islam as such. In the post-Fortuyn Netherlands, there was a large audience for this argument. In 2002, the VVD offered her a high place on its list of candidates and she became a member of Parliament.

A former parliamentary colleague of Wilders said that Hirsi Ali had a 'magical effect' on him.[20] Wilders and Hirsi Ali together developed what they called a 'critique of the Islamic religion' that saw the behaviour of Muslims determined by their religion, and that blamed the social-economic misery and lack of democracy in many Islamic countries as well as sexism and racism inside Muslim communities as the determining factors of their 'backward' culture. Together with Hirsi Ali, Wilders argued that liberal freedoms, like the freedom of religion, should 'under certain circumstances' not apply to Muslims and called for a 'liberal jihad' against radical Islam. A few years later Wilders would declare he had come to fully agree with Fortuyn's views on Muslims.[21]

After the political earthquake of 2002, the VVD was divided on how to proceed. Unlike Bolkestein, who had sought to push the political debate to the right, Hans Dijkstal, its party leader after 1998, had a more centrist profile. Wilders would later criticise him for squandering Bolkestein's heritage. The VVD lost 13 seats in 2002, many of them to the LPF, and Dijkstal was replaced by more right-wing party-leaders. However, a part of the VVD still wanted the party to become broader and move closer to the social-liberalism of a party like the liberal D66.

---

[20] Paul Lucardie and Gerrit Voerman, *Populisten in de polder* (Amersfoort 2012) 153.

[21] Lucardie, Voerman, *Populisten in de polder* 154.

On the other hand, Wilders wanted the party to become more right-wing, to fill the gap left by the implosion of the LPF and to appeal to right-wing Christian-Democrats. He argued for deeper cuts in social services, more restrictions of immigration and tougher law-and-order policies. Wilders was also fundamentally opposed to Turkey becoming a member of the European Union, a minority view in the VVD at the time. After he had been known for years as being on the right-wing of the party, he became more and more isolated in the parliamentary group. It was not only the positions he took that isolated him, but also his blunt and polarising way of voicing them which other party-members felt was damaging the relationships with other parties, but also his open criticisms of the VVD leadership. In June 2004, Wilders drafted a discussion document that argued for a rightward shift in the VVD. The paper was meant for internal discussion but was leaked to the media (a deliberate move by Wilders, according to his biographer Meindert Fennema).[22] For the VVD leadership, this was the last straw. In September 2004, the VVD and Wilders parted ways. Wilders kept his seat in Parliament as a one-man faction and immediately declared that he wanted to organise a new political movement.

Declaration of Independence

It would take Wilders two years before he launched a new party, the Freedom Party (*Partij voor de Vrijheid*, PVV). In the meantime, he refused an invitation to join the remnants of the LPF.

In these years, Wilders is best described as a neoconservative. In words that came close to George W Bush's 'compassionate conservatism', Wilders stated that his new movement would be 'social,

---

[22] Meindert Fennema, *Geert Wilders. Tovenaarsleerling* 82. Meindert Fennema is emeritus professor in Political Theory at the University of Amsterdam. However, his biography of Wilders presents a quite novelised story.

right wing and decent'. Wilders was a strong supporter of George W Bush, a 'president with guts' and of his 'war on terror'. He started collaborating with the Edmund Burke foundation, a new organisation of right-wing intellectuals that was trying to promote neoconservative ideas in the Dutch political debate. Around the same time Wilders started to receive death threats, something that would take on a whole new significance in the autumn of 2004.

In the morning of 2 November 2004, the film-maker and columnist Theo van Gogh was murdered by an Islamic fundamentalist, Mohammed Bouyeri. Van Gogh delighted in making reactionary statements, insulting gays, women, Jews and most of all Muslims whom he consistently referred as in terms like 'goatfuckers' or 'pimps of the prophet'.

Van Gogh was also a supporter of Pim Fortuyn and Rita Verdonk, the right-wing VVD minister of immigration between 2003 and 2006. Verdonk implemented anti-migration policies that led to the deportation of refugees who had been in the country for years and loudly rejected calls for an 'amnesty' for undocumented migrants. In 2006, Verdonk tried to strip her fellow party-member and former ally Hirsi Ali of her Dutch citizenship because of the incorrect statements she had made in her request for asylum. Verdonk broke with the VVD after an unsuccessful attempt to become its political leader and founded her own party, Proud of the Netherlands (*Trots op Nederland*, TON). TON was an attempt to capitalise on the support for national-populism but after a brief period of popularity it floundered, with most of its supporters switching to Wilders's party.

Van Gogh's murderer originally planned to kill Hirsi Ali. Van Gogh had cooperated with her to make the film '*Submission*' in which women tell of the way their oppression was justified by appeals to Islam. Probably because she was too well protected, Bouyeri choose to kill Van Gogh instead. Like Fortuyn's murder earlier, Van Gogh's death sent shock waves through Dutch society. The fact that the murderer was a Dutch Moroccan was taken by national-populists as proof of the correctness of their anti-Muslim views. In their eyes, 'the Left' had murdered Fortuyn, and now its 'ally', Islamic fundamentalism, had killed another one of them, Van Gogh, because he warned against the 'dangers' of Islam. Dozens of mosques and scores of people were attacked. The *Monitor Racisme en Extremisme,* a regular publication by the anti-racist Anne Frank Foundation and the University of Leiden, recorded 106 cases of anti-Muslim violence between 2 and 30 November.[23] In the aftermath of Van Gogh's death, Wilders received extra protection. For a while, he lived at a military base and he is still under constant protection.

In the months after November 2004, Wilders' popularity increased sharply and in March 2005 he started to organise his new party. In the party's manifesto, *Onafhankelijkheidsverklaring* (Declaration of Independence), Wilders declared himself to be an opponent of the 'complacent political elite' that supposedly rules the Netherlands and that doesn't care enough about preserving 'our democratic rule of law, our safety, our prosperity and our independence'. According to Wilders, the European Union is becoming a 'super state', threatening Dutch sovereignty. The supposed submission of the Netherlands to this EU super state is the work of a political elite that is blinded by 'the so-called progressive spirit of the times'. Because of this, Dutch political life is dominated by 'political correctness, a megalomaniac administration, multiculturalism and submission to the bureaucrats in Brussels'.

Wilders wrote his Declaration of Independence in cooperation with Joost Eerdmans, a LPF parliamentarian and Marco Pastors, who at the time was a city councillor for *Leefbaar Rotterdam.*[24] Attempts by Wilders to form a new party with the remnants of Fortuyn's parties failed – Wilders wanted to have complete control over the new party, hoping that in this way he could avoid the fate of the LPF. Pastors and

---

[23] Witte, Al eeuwen lang, 141.

[24] Fennema, Geert Wilders, 100.

Eerdmans would later form their own national-populist party, One Netherlands (*EenNL*), which ceased to function after it just failed to win a seat in the elections of 2006.

A third collaborator in writing the manifesto was Bart Jan Spruyt, chair of the Edmund Burke Foundation. Established in 2000, the Edmund Burke Foundation was a prominent voice of Dutch conservatism. Spruyt took as his inspiration the conservative Heritage Foundation think-tank in the United States. Through publications and lectures, the Edmund Burke Foundation sought to spread the influence of conservative moral and free-market ideas. It received hundreds of thousands of euros for its work from the Baan brothers, Dutch software millionaires, and from corporations like Microsoft and the pharmaceuticals company Pfizer.[25]

True to its neoconservative inspiration, the Declaration of Independence was a mixture of nationalist rhetoric, moral conservatism, nativism (immigrants could only after ten years and without a criminal record be able to apply for Dutch citizenship and only after this have a right to social security) and free-market policies. Wilders supported a flat (low) tax rate, abolishing the minimum wage and attacking workers' rights. The exception to such policies was the proposal to inject more money into care for the elderly. Before Wilders, Fortuyn had already skilfully exploited public indignation at the sometimes deplorable situation of the care-dependent elderly.

Spruyt saw it as one of his tasks to educate Wilders in the 'conservative canon' of thinkers like Thomas Hobbes, Edmund Burke and Leo Strauss.[26] Part of this was a tour around the US in early 2005 where Spruyt introduced Wilders to neo- conservative think-tanks and politicians. Among others, Wilders visited the Heritage

---

[25] Pieter van Os, 'De Amerikaanse lobby. Hoe Pfizer en Microsoft Nederland beïnvloeden', *De Groene Amsterdammer*, October 14, 2005 online at http://www.groene.nl/artikel/de-amerikaanse-lobby.

[26] Vossen, *Rondom, Wilders*, 47.

Foundation and the American Enterprise Institute and spoke with numerous Republican politicians like former Reagan and Bush advisor, Richard Perle.[27] Since then, Wilders has maintained good contacts with the US right.

In May 2005, Wilders used the referendum on the introduction of a European Union constitution to further build the nationalist and anti-EU side of his profile. Wilders campaigned against the constitution with nationalist rhetoric (the slogan was *'Nederland moet blijven'*, 'The Netherlands must remain'). Turnout for this referendum was 63%, with almost 62% voting against the proposal, despite almost the whole political spectrum being in favour of the constitution. According to Martin Bosma, the ideologue of the PVV, the result showed that 'the ideas of the elite are not the opinion of the people'. In reality, the most visible political force in the No-camp was the left-wing Socialist Party (*Socialistische Partij*, SP).[28] Motivation for the no-vote varied from nationalism and anti-immigrant feelings, to the desire to protect what was left of the welfare state against EU-regulations and a rejection of the neoliberal course of the EU.[29]

The cooperation between Fortuyn-influenced populists and neoconservatives was not without contradictions. The populists were less consistent than somebody like Spruyt in their support for unfettered free-market policies and small government, as the example of more government spending for care of the elderly already showed. During the 2006 election campaign, it became clearer how anti-foreign sentiments took precedence over free-market principles. For instance, playing on nativist sentiments, the PVV supported closing

---

[27] Vossen, *Rondom, Wilders*, 49.

[28] The SP (Socialist Party), organised as a maoist party in the seventies, developed into a social-democratic party in the 1990s and after the turn of the century. It won almost 10%of the vote in the parliamentary elections of 2012.

[29] Willem Bos, 'Netherlands: A vote against neoliberalism', *International Viewpoint* June 10, 2005 online at [http://internationalviewpoint.org/spip.php?article815].

the Dutch labour market to Poles. Education, a core issue for a conservative like Spruyt, disappeared into the background.

In Declaration of Independence and the other early PVV programmatic document, *Een Nieuw-Realistische Visie op Samenleving en Politiek* (A new-realist vision on society and politics) the populist discourse of 'the people', who are sensible, good and grounded in reality, in contrast with a corrupt, ideologically blinded and weak political elite, sat uneasily with the conservative insistence on the cultivation of virtue and its disdain for mass-culture.[30] Proposals to make more public posts electable, e.g., mayors, police commissioners and judges, to abolish the Senate and to introduce binding referenda, were in contradiction with this neoconservative elitism.

The cooperation between Spruyt and Wilders couldn't last. When his foundation lost significant support because it had become too closely identified with one specific (and new) political party, Spruyt broke with Wilders in the summer of 2006 shortly before the elections. In January 2007, he would describe the PVV as 'the embodiment of a panicky kind of conservatism that is in between prudent conservatism and fascism, with a natural predisposition to the latter.'[31]

Wilders' popularity did not last long after the vote on EU constitution. Polls in 2006 predicted that the PVV would maybe get one seat in Parliament and that Wilders had to compete with other right-wing newcomers like *EenNL*. But Wilders managed to turn the fortunes of his fledgling party around: by using more and more anti-immigrant and anti-Islamic rhetoric, he surpassed his rivals on the right. In 2006, he declared his fight against the threat of a 'tsunami of Islamisation' to be the most important issue: 'if we don't defend

---

[30] Geert Wilders, 'Een Nieuw-Realistische Visie op Samenleving en Politiek', *Elsevier* March 21, 2006 online at [http://www.elsevier.nl/Algemeen/nieuws/2006/3/Een-Nieuw-Realistische-Visie-op-Samenleving-en-Politiek-ELSEVIER071305W/].

[31] Vossen, Rondom Wilders, 59.

ourselves against this, all the other points in my programme will turn out to be irrelevant'. All Muslims are enemies because 'their behaviour flows from their religion and culture'. Wilders made clear he did not believe that any kind of Islam could be part of Dutch society.[32] Wilders especially singled out Moroccan migrants and their children.

Highly publicised cases of harassment, rape and other violence against women and gays, a supposed new, imported type of crime that was blamed almost completely on Dutch-Moroccan youth (consistently referred to only as 'Moroccan youth', denying that they are Dutch), played an important role in creating support for Wilders' anti-Muslim positions and his law-and-order proposals. This moral panic - in which certain crimes were made into symbols of a supposed general decline - was exploited and fed by Wilders.[33] Exploiting reflexes conditioned by the climate of the 'war on terror', Wilders blamed these crimes on 'street terrorists'. By blaming issues varying from crime to the cost of social security on Muslims, Wilders distinguished himself from other right-wing groups with what in Dutch political jargon is euphemistically called 'criticism of Islam'.

Although since the rise of Fortuyn the placid political debate in the Netherlands had become significantly more turbulent, Wilders stepped it up with personal attacks on political opponents and with a very combative tone and discriminatory rhetoric against Muslims. He therefore constantly stood in the limelight of the media, managing to mobilise and shape the diffuse anger and anxiety of broad groups of (potential) voters.

The elections showed that Wilders had hit his stride. In its first elections, the PVV won 5.9% of the vote: 9 out of 150 seats in the Parliament. The PVV was the only party to the right of the VVD that

---

[32] Sanne ten Hoove, Raoul du Pré, 'Wilders bang voor 'tsunami van islamisering'', *De Volkskrant* October 6, 2006 online at [http://www.volkskrant.nl/binnenland/wilders-bang-voor-tsunami-van-islamisering~a786026/].

[33] Stuart Hall, et al. *Policing the crisis. Mugging, the state and law & order* (Hampshire 2013 [1978]) contains the classic discussion of the use of moral panics by the right.

managed to get into parliament. Wilders successfully rallied a significant part of the right-wing constituency: about three of seats came from ex-LPF voters and almost four seats came from former VVD and CDA voters. People who hadn't voted in 2003 provided Wilders with one seat and one more seat came from people who had previously voted for one of the left parties.[34] After the elections of 2006, in February 2007, the CDA formed a coalition with the PvdA and a smaller protestant party, the *Christen Unie* (CU). This was the fourth coalition led by CDA Prime Minister Jan-Peter Balkenende and the fourth since Fortuyn upset the Dutch political landscape.

The PVV had now taken shape as a party in which Wilders had gathered a number of trusted supporters like Fleur Agema, spokesperson on healthcare, and Martin Bosma, speech writer and ideologue. One of the first acts of the PVV in the new Parliament was to object to the appointment of two state secretaries, Ahmed Aboutaleb and Nebahat Albayrak, because in addition to their Dutch nationality they respectively also held Moroccan and Turkish nationality. People born in the Netherlands to Moroccan or Turkish parents automatically also have the nationality of their parents. It is difficult, or in the case of the Moroccan nationality, even impossible, to renounce it. In August of that year, Wilders also demanded banning the Qur'an, calling it the 'the *Mein Kampf* of a religion that aims to eliminate others'.

When Wilders was accused of inciting hatred and tried in court in 2011 he was acquitted on the basis that his statements were directed against a religion, and not against individuals.[35] In his closing statement, Wilders re-affirmed that in his eyes there is no distinction between what he considers true Islam and the aims of individual

---

[34] Vossen, *Rondom Wilders*, 63.

[35] Rechtbank Amsterdam, *Uitspraak van de rechtbank Amsterdam in de zaak Wilders*, June 26, 2011 online at [http://www.rechtspraak.nl/Organisatie/Rechtbanken/Amsterdam/Nieuws/Pages/Uitspraak-van-de-rechtbank-AmsterdamindezaakWilders,23 juni2011.aspx].

Muslims. In his conspiratorial worldview, he believes that 'throughout Europe, multicultural elites are waging a total war against their populations, with its prize mass-immigration which will eventually result in an Islamic Europe – a Europe without freedom: Eurabia'.[36] In an interview for the Danish television, Wilders called for the deportation of 'tens of millions' of Muslims from Europe for breaking laws and/or the thought crime of having sympathy for 'jihad' and not sharing 'our norms and values'.[37]

Part of the PVV's nationalism is its opposition to the European Union. For the European elections, the PVV presented a concise election program of just 331 words, calling for a Dutch veto to stop 'mass-immigration', never allowing Turkey to join the European Union and limiting international co-operation solely to economic affairs. Opposition to the supposed 'Islamisation' of Europe was prominent: Islam was mentioned four times.[38]

The PVV again drew votes from across the political spectrum, but mainly from the right: over 23% came from former VVD voters, but 16% came from the left-wing SP which is also known as a 'euro-sceptic' party. The SP's opposition to the EU is based mainly on the lack of democracy at the European level and the neoliberal economic policies of the EU, but the party has played on nationalist feelings and used nationalist imagery to gather support.[39] With a turnout of a bit over two-thirds, the PVV came second with almost 17% of the vote (772,746 votes).

---

[36] Geert Wilders, 'Het laatste woord van Geert Wilders bij het proces', online at http://www.pvv.nl/index.php/component/content/article.html?id=3939:het-laatste-woord-van-geert-wilders-bij-het-proces.

[37] NOS *Wilders op de Deense televisie* June 16 video online at http://nos.nl/video/36125-wilders-op-de-deense-televisie.html.

[38] PVV Verkiezingsprogramma Europees parlement 2009.

[39] NOS *Analyse: PvdA verloor amper aan PVV* online at http://europakiest.nos.nl/nieuws/artikel/id/tcm:44-526405/title/analyse-pvda-verloor-amper-aan-pvv.html. For example, the SP campaigned against the EU constitution with a map of Europe from which the Netherlands was missing.

Polls predicted a strong increase in support for the PVV in national elections as well. But after the beginning of the economic crisis in 2008, Wilders' popularity declined, although polls still predicted the PVV gaining 15 seats in mid-2010.[40] Both the VVD and the PvdA tried to make the parliamentary elections of that year about social-economic issues. In response, the PVV tried to connect its anti-Islam and anti-migration positions to economic issues. Gone is the talk from Wilders' Declaration of Independence about cutting back 'the 'gains' of the trade-unions', introducing a flat tax rate, abolishing the minimum wage and liberalising the law on dismissals. Instead the PVV now promised a defence of the welfare state, rejected liberalisation of the law on dismissals, demanded keeping the retirement age at 65 and opposed increasing the Own Risk in the national health insurance.

The 2010 program of the PVV is an example of 'welfare-chauvinism'.[41] Proposals to preserve social rights are combined with proposals to exclude minorities from those rights, by making social security dependent on length of citizenship and language skills, and prohibiting people from wearing a burka or niqab. The PVV also poses as a defender of small entrepreneurs, claiming its proposals to lower taxes and leave the European Union would benefit them. The anti-EU position of the PVV is likely appeal to small entrepreneurs who feel threatened by increasing international competition.

The 2010 program of the PVV claimed that 'only the PVV defends the welfare-state and that is why we plead for a stop to immigration from Islamic countries. It's one or the other: either a welfare-state or an immigration-country'.[42] This link between 'Islam' and social rights is indicative of the evolution in the ideology of the PVV: a few years before, 'Islamisation' was supposedly one of several

---

[40] Lucardie, Voerman, *Populisten in de polder*, 173.

[41] Mudde, The ideology of the extreme right, 181.

[42] PVV, De agenda van hoop en optimisme. Een tijd om te kiezen; PVV 2010–2015 (2010) 21.

problems facing Dutch society. By 2010 it had become the root cause of social problems, crime, the national deficit, and attacks on social rights.

Supporting austerity

The elections of 2010 brought the PVV its biggest success so far: over 15% (1,454,493 votes in total) or 24 out of 150 seats. As in earlier elections, the PVV had its best results in the periphery of the Netherlands and among voters with middle and lower incomes. Moreover, the PVV's new-found attention for social issues and protecting the welfare state (for some) also brought it new voters: around 1 in 5 votes came from people who before had voted SP or PvdA. The PVV scored its highest percentages in the countryside and in smaller cities, with high results in the commuter towns around the big cities such as Amsterdam, Rotterdam and Utrecht. On average, PVV voters have strong right-wing and anti-Muslim views on migration (expelling undocumented workers, forced assimilation of immigrants, a ban on immigration from Islamic countries). On social-economic issues, like inequality of incomes, their views are less pronounced and can be characterised as centre-left.[43] The primary motivation for many PVV voters is Wilder's anti-Muslim and anti-immigration stance, while social-economic issues are secondary.[44]

After the elections of 2010, the PVV did not enter the government, but instead supported it from the outside. The Dutch electoral system of proportional representation of parties on a national basis in Parliament means that to have a majority, parties need to form coalitions. Usually, such government coalitions consist of three or four parties. In 2010, the VVD and CDA formed the government coalition but to have a majority for its proposals in parliament, it needed the

---

[43] Lucardie, Voerman, *Populisten in de polder* 176 – 177.

[44] Chris Aalberts, Achter de PVV. Waarom burgers op de PVV stemmen (Delft 2012) 200.

support of the PVV. The PVV promised to support the new right-wing government, but did not take part in the coalition and nor did it provide any of its members for the cabinet. Since its support was crucial, the PVV was in a strong position to make demands, and by remaining outside of the coalition it could avoid being identified too much with the government. This set-up was inspired by similar governments in Denmark where the right-wing Danish People's Party also gave support to the government from the outside.

As Wilders put it: 'our profile is culturally conservative, but this year we have again shown we can make inroads in the support for the left. They don't own issues like healthcare, unemployment benefits or protection against dismissal.' When explaining his vision for the new government, Wilders said it would make the Netherlands 'a country where criminals are dealt with more strictly, where there's more safety in the streets, where immigration is limited, where we have more pride in our culture, where the left is in disarray and fighting among itself.' In his 2012 book *Marked for Death*, Wilders described the role of the PVV towards this government as support for an austerity plan in return for it to 'restrict immigration, roll back crime, counter cultural relativism, and insist on the integration of immigrants'.[45]

The government of VVD Prime Minister Mark Rutte reflected a number of the priorities of the PVV. It declared that 'a very substantial' lowering of the number of non-western immigrants into the country was one of its top goals. It proposed doing that by further limiting the right to asylum and with greater restrictive immigration policies. Among typical PVV positions the new government proposed were criminalising undocumented migrants and revoking the Dutch nationality of criminals with double nationalities. In return for policies like these, the PVV gave up many of its 'left-wing' social-economic demands, instead supporting 18 billion euros in austerity

---

[45] Geert Wilders, Marked for death. Islam's war against the west and me (Washington 2012) 450.

measures. Contradicting its election promises, it voted against equal rights for precarious workers to sick pay and unemployment benefits, moreover it supported increasing the cost of healthcare and extending market mechanisms in health-care provision. The party also made a U-turn on the hotly debated Joint Strike Fighter and joined the other right-wing parties to increase the retirement age to 67, even though the PVV election programme had stated that its opposition to increasing the retirement age was non-negotiable.

These choices did not seem to hurt the PVV much. In the regional elections of 2011 it scored 12%. This was lower than in the national elections, but this is not surprising considering the appeal of the PVV is largely that of Geert Wilders and that it was the first time the party participated in such elections.

Crisis and radicalisation

Things started to change when it became clear in early 2012 that economic growth was not about to recover. Economic growth, measured in GDP, in 2011 was only 0.9% while during 2012 there was a 1.2% decline. The government agency, the Central Bureau for Statistics predicted a budget deficit of 4.5% in 2013. In order to comply with the EU limit of a 3% deficit, billions more in cuts were needed. After weeks of negotiations, the PVV withdrew from the talks with the VVD and CDA, leading to the dissolution of the government at the end of April 2012. At the subsequent elections, the PVV took a heavy blow losing ten seats. Even so, with 15 seats it is the third largest party in Parliament (the left-wing SP also has 15 seats). The big winner of the 2012 elections, with over 26% of the vote, was the VVD which has moved further right in recent years. The new government coalition consisted of the VVD and the social-democratic PvdA which had come in second in the election. Mark Rutte again became Prime Minister.

The VVD-PvdA government became increasingly unpopular. Until a few weeks before the 2012 elections, polls predicted that the SP could become the biggest party but it lost a lot of potential votes to the PvdA that tacked left during the election period and presented itself as the alternative to a new VVD government. The new government disappointed many PvdA voters who were hoping to prevent a return of the VVD as a government party. Meanwhile, many VVD voters were dissatisfied that it had formed a coalition with the PvdA after waging a campaign with a strong right-wing profile – partly to attract PVV voters. Polls show a decline in support for both government parties but it's especially the PvdA that is losing support. In the municipal elections of March 2014, the PvdA was hammered, losing a third of its votes compared to 2010 and in the major cities, including in strongholds like the capital Amsterdam.

After it pulled the plug on the government in 2012 and lost ground in the elections, many commentators predicted the decline of the PVV. Supposedly, the party had shown it was unable to govern or achieve its proposals. But the PVV seems to have consolidated itself. In the two cities where it participated in the municipal elections, it lost only slightly, still coming second in The Hague (the seat of government) and retaining its position as the largest party of Almere, a commuter city near Amsterdam. Polls in summer 215 predict a strong growth of the PVV in national elections to over 20 seats.

In late 2013, Geert Wilders declared an alliance with the French *Front National* (FN) with the intention of forming a new caucus in the European Parliament. In the summer of 2013, Wilders had invited *Vlaams Belang* leader Filip Dewinter to cooperate in the European Parliament. Like the FN and Vlaams Belang, other potential partners in the alliance are usually considered to be far-right parties, like the Swedish Democrats (*Sverigrdemokraterna*) and the Freedom Party of Austria (*Freiheitliche Partei Österreichs*, FPÖ). This step surprised many since Wilders, like Fortuyn before him, had always been careful to keep his distance from parties like the FN, the VB and the FPÖ, who for decades have been the core of the European far right. Some years earlier, Wilders had declared he wanted 'nothing to do with the Mussolinis and Le Pen and others like them' and until early 2013 he kept his distance from parties like *Vlaams Belang*.[46]

However, in recent years, the core of the European far-right has been converging with the trajectory of Wilders. The FN has been evolving towards positions that are closer to those of Wilders. The FN today claims to reject its anti-Semitic past. In a 2011 interview with Israeli daily *Haaretz*, Marine Le Pen declared that 'the Front National has always been Zionistic and always defended Israel's right to exist.'[47] Her statement that 'radical Islam' has created in France 'entire regions where it's better not to be a Jew, a woman, a homosexual or even an ordinary white Frenchman' illustrates how close Le Pen and Wilders are ideologically. Both pose as the defenders of certain gains of modernity against a supposed Islamic threat. The FN, like the VB and the FPÖ, still has in it remnants of an older European far-right which is anti-modernist and anti-Semitic and has ties to historical fascism, but this side has been marginalised enough for Wilders to feel that he can now ally himself with such parties.

Then there is also Wilder's political trajectory. Starting out as a conservative liberal, he moved, after a brief flirt with neo-conservatism, to populist far-right positions. His hostility towards people he considers 'Muslims' has intensified. In 2007, Philip Dewinter of the VB said that a proposal like banning the Qur'an went too far and that Wilders was 'radicalising'.[48] One symbolically charged

---

[46] Paul Belien, 'Wilders Looks for European Allies, Suggests Reuniting Flanders and Netherlands', *The Brussels Journal* May 12, 2008 online at www.brusselsjournal.com/node/3244.

[47] Adat Primor, 'The daughter as de-demonizer' *Haaretz January* 7, 2011 online at http://www.haaretz.com/weekend/week-s-end/the-daughter-as-de-demonizer-1.335743.

[48] Robin van der Kloor, 'Dewinter: Wilders radicaliseert', *Elsevier* August 9, 2007 online at http://www.elsevier.nl/Politiek/nieuws/2007/8/Dewinter-Wilders-radicaliseert-ELSEVIER132772W/.

moment in this political evolution was a speech Wilders gave a few days before the municipal elections, on 19 March 2014. Wilders invited his audience to respond to three questions 'that define our party': 'do you want more or less European Union?', 'do you want more or less PvdA?' (these questions were answered with chants of 'less, less') and finally 'do you want fewer or more Moroccans in your city and in the Netherlands?' 'Fewer! Fewer!' the crowd chanted, with Wilders answering: 'Then we're going to organise that.'

Like his meetings with the VB and FN, this was another step in Wilders rightward evolution. Where before his racism was cultural, it had now transitioned into ethnic racism. This wasn't completely new for Wilders who uses religious, cultural and ethnic descriptors interchangeably and we have seen how cultural racism segues easily into somatic racism. What was different was the form, how he invited his supporters to join him, projecting a more activist and militant image.

Since 2013, the PVV has slowly extended its field of activity. In 2010, when Wilders was tried for inciting hatred, the PVV organised a small support rally for him but for a long time this was the only extra-parliamentary activity of the party. However, in early 2013 the PVV opened a website to give legal advice to people objecting to the construction of mosques in their neighbourhood and in February Wilders declared a 'resistance tour' throughout the country to collect signatures against the government's austerity policies. On 21 September 2013, on the same day that left-wing organisations organised an anti-austerity protest, the PVV organised its first large demonstration, with a couple of thousand of participants. Wilders's speech at the rally was a mix of nationalist rhetoric, attacks on austerity policies and against his usual targets like the EU, 'corrupt Greeks', 'mass-immigration' and Islamisation. Something that was new about this rally was the presence of activists from a large range of neo-fascist and Nazi grouplets. Wilders doesn't feel the need any more to distance himself from such groups. After media reports of 'princes flags' at the demonstration (orange-blue-white flags that are associated with the pre-war Dutch fascist movement), PVV parliamentarians wore pins with that flag.

The potential of the PVV to mobilise supporters on the 21 September 2013 was remarkable considering its weak organisational structure. The PVV doesn't have members, branches or publications other than a website. In this way, Wilders is not accountable to anybody: he determines who will be candidate in elections for the PVV and who is allowed to talk to the media. Wilders is a prominent figure in the media, regularly drawing attention with statements intended to provoke, but refuses to participate in news-programs and talk shows, saying he distrusts the 'left-wing' media. However, the PVV and Wilders reach a large audience through right-wing blogs and social media.

Power and influence

Fifteen years ago, Wilders still objected to how Fortuyn attacked 'Islam' in its totality but in more recent years he has become even more systematic than him in essentialising and excluding people that he categorises as 'Muslims'. For Wilders, followers of Islam are necessarily fundamentalists, hostile to democracy and human rights. Other kinds Muslims do not exist for Wilders. If a Muslim doesn't agree with the interpretation of Islam by Wilders, this believer is said to practice *takkiya*, a dispensation that Wilders claims allows Muslims to dissimulate their true religio-political intentions.

In this national-populism, culture functions in a manner analogous to how race functions in biological racism: heredity is taken as determining the characteristics of human beings and cultural 'others' serves the same functions as racial 'others', so that rights are denied to the those that are on the outside. For the PVV, Muslims should be subjected to other more oppressive laws and regulations than people in the 'in-group': their holy book should be banned, there should be a special tax for wearing head-scarves, unlike other religious groups they should not be allowed to organise their own schools, etc. This metamorphosis of racism is not a new development, already in the 1950s Frantz Fanon noted how 'old-fashioned positions', 'the 'vulgar, primitive, over-simple racism' that 'purported to find in biology [...] the material basis of the doctrine [...]' tend in any case to disappear. This racism that aspires to be rational, individual, genotypically and phenotypically determined, becomes transformed into cultural racism. The object of racism is no longer the individual man but a certain form of existing. [...] 'Occidental values' oddly blend with the already famous appeal to the fight of the 'cross against the crescent.'[49]

The ideology of the PVV was described by political historian Koen Vossen as a square with four corners: 'Islam alarmism', populism, nationalism and law-and-order thinking.[50] It's important to point out that of these four, what Vossen calls 'Islam alarmism' is the most important one. The other three elements are related to it and Wilders has shown he is willing to compromise on many points while his anti-Muslim view has steadily been intensifying. The cultural racism in Dutch national-populism has an important role in integrating different ideological elements.[51] In the case of Wilders, it makes his social-economic positions coherent to his supporters by blaming the deficit on Islamic mass-immigration and Muslim welfare scroungers. The PVV today is a nationalist party that demands that the state implements a policy of cultural internal homogenisation. It supports a strong state and is welfare-chauvinist.[52]

---

[49] Frantz Fanon, *Toward the African revolution* 32 -33 (New York 1967) 32 -33.

[50] Vossen, *Rondom Wilders*, 65

[51] Paul Mepschen, 'Gewone mensen. Populisme en het discours van verdringing in Amsterdam Nieuw West' in Justus Uitermark, et al. (ed.) *'Power to the people!' Een anatomie van het populisme* (Den Haag 2012) 78 – 96.

[52] Cas Mudde, *The ideology of the extreme right* (Manchester 2000) 181.

Wilder's ideology has undergone repeated changes in the last 15 years but he rarely elaborates on the reasons for these changes. Early PVV documents written during his 'neoconservative phase' are unavailable on the PVV website. During this phase, Wilders published the autobiographical *Kies voor Vrijheid* (Choose Freedom) but this book can be considered out-dated as well.[53]

One source to understand the current PVV ideology is Wilders' *Marked for Death: Islam's War against the West and Me*. In *Marked for Death*, Wilders gives four priorities for his movement: 'defend freedom of speech, reject cultural relativism, counter Islamisation, and cherish our national identity.' The defence of freedom of speech means for Wilders the abolition of laws against hate-speech.[54] The PVV is hardly consistent in defending freedom of speech as is shown by such demands as banning the Qur'an or suggesting closing the offices of Greenpeace because the organisation supposedly damages the national image.[55]

Rejecting cultural relativism means 'our civilised Western culture is far superior to the barbaric culture of Islam' – 'the West owes nothing to Islam'. Wilders wants this version of history made into laws that state 'our societies are based on Judeo-Christian and humanist values.' Countering 'Islamisation' means 'stopping *all* immigration from Islamic countries'. This is an example of how for Wilders 'Islam' functions as an ethnicity. Only through 'national identity' and by rallying around a national flag can 'liberty' be defended according to Wilders. Wilders sees the European Union as a conspiracy of 'multiculturalists': 'they want to dissolve our sovereignty in a giant, Europe-wide bureaucracy that they control.' In this book, written for

---

[53] Geert Wilders, Kies voor vrijheid - een eerlijk antwoord (Den Haag 2005).

[54] Geert Wilders, Marked for death. Islam's war against the west and me (Washington 2012) 448- 479.

[55] Ron Ritzen, Willem-Jan van Gendt, Wilders' Iran aan de Noordzee. Waarom de PVV de democratische rechtsstaat bedreigt (Puurs 2012) 37.

the market of American right, the PVV's welfare-chauvinism and supposed defence of gay-rights are largely absent.

Martin Bosma's *De schijn elite van de valse munters* is the other main source to understand the PVV ideology.[56] Bosma, a member of Parliament for the PVV, is considered to be the ideologue of the party and is speech writer for Wilders. His book deals with the same issues as *Marked for Death*: the supposed danger of Islam, preserving 'national identity' and the treacherous behaviour of the 'left-wing' elite. The influence of the American right is also clear in how Bosma categorises Nazism and fascism as left-wing ideologies, by basing himself on a popular book among the US right, Jonah Goldberg's *Liberal Fascism*.[57] Throughout the book, Bosma argues that 'Islam' is a totalitarian ideology with close affinities with fascism. Dutch nationalists remember Nazism especially as a foreign occupation and this way the PVV associates Muslims with this threat to the 'nation'. Inspired by similar notions, the PVV does the same with the left: national-socialism is supposedly a left-wing ideology, and today's socialists are part of the same political family as the Nazis.

The PVV's conspiratorial view of Islam, which sees Muslims as involved in an immense conspiracy against 'the west', is inspired by Bat Ye'or, a pseudo-historian who claims the ruling elites in Europe during the nineteen seventies secretly acquiesced in an Arab Muslim plot by allowing immigration into Europe in return for access to oil. She claims that European Muslims are involved in a plot to colonise Europe and turn the continent into 'Eurabia'.[58] Wilders takes Bat Ye'or seriously. His *Marked for Death* repeatedly approvingly quotes her writing and Wilders says Bat Ye'or makes 'a strong case' in her theory

---

[56] Martin Bosma, De schijn-élite van de valse munters - Drees, extreem rechts, de sixties, de Groep Wilders en ik (Amsterdam 2010).

[57] Chris Vials, 'The Invisibility of Fascism in the Postwar United States', Against the Current 168 (2014) 7 – 9.

[58] Matt Carr, 'You are now entering Eurabia', Race & Class 48 (2006) 1 - 22.

of the Eurabia plot. He differs from her in that he thinks the betrayal of the elites is not the consequence of a dependence on oil but of succumbing to multicultural ideology - but he subscribes in essence to her conspiratorial world-view.[59]

One distinctive characteristic of Wilders' political current, and of the new right wing in general in the Netherlands, is its ambiguous attitude to the heritage of the post-68 social movements. It vehemently opposes the ecological movement, the reform of the justice and prison system and of course anti-racism. But (verbal) support for women's rights and those of LGBT's as well opposition to anti-Semitism have been made into hallmarks of 'Dutchness' and modernity. This is also a prominent theme in Bosma's book. The left and progressive background of these ideas is ignored.[60] According to this discourse, the process of emancipation in the Netherlands is completed and further emancipation movements are 'out-dated', except among 'backward' minorities like Muslims. The fight against sexism, homophobia and anti-Semitism is redefined as one against 'non-integrated minorities', especially Muslims who are considered to be inherently misogynist, homophobic and anti-Semitic. In the words of PVV parliamentarian Fleur Agema: 'anti-Semitism and homophobia are not Dutch phenomena. They have been imported, for a deplorable part from Morocco.'[61] The PVV's support for gay-rights is largely rhetoric. The single line dedicated to the issue in its program reads 'we are going to defend our gays against the advancing Islam.'[62]

The decline or even the end of the success of Wilders has been predicted several times but so far in vain. Wilder's 'minder Marokkanen' ('fewer Moroccans') speech of 19 March 2014 was seen as another sign of the beginning of the end for the party. From the

---

[59] Wilders, Marked for death, 395.

[60] Oudenampsen, 'De revolte van nieuwrechts' (2013).

[61] Witte, Al eeuwen lang, 165.

[62] PVV, Hún Brussel, óns Nederland. Verkiezingsprogramma 2012-2017, 45.

liberal left, it was heard that such open racism would not be accepted, even by Wilder's supporters, and that this time he 'went too far'. In the days after March, a number of PVV representatives at the local, national and European level did leave the party, but the organisation has not collapsed like the LPF did. Popular support for the PVV has remained largely intact. One reason why the predicted collapse of the PVV did not materialise is that Wilders has succeeded in bringing a large part of his supporters further to the right along with him.

Another reason is that even without the PVV, racism is deeply anchored in Dutch society. A 2010 report showed job applicants with non-western names had less chance to be invited for a meeting with potential employers: on average 9% less chance for men.[63] More than a third of Dutch jobseekers of Turkish and Moroccan origin experience discrimination when looking for work.[64] Unemployment among people with a non-western background is 14.2%, among indigenous Dutch it is 4.3%.[65] Amnesty International criticised ethnic profiling by the Dutch police and the dominant nature of prejudices and stereotypes among police.[66] One 2010 study showed that over a quarter of the 1,020 respondents had a negative view of foreigners, with 10% stating they were racists. Almost three-quarters of Dutch Muslims feel that since the rise of Geert Wilders Muslims are viewed more

---

[63] Iris Andriessen, et al., Liever Mark dan Mohammed? Onderzoek naar arbeidsmarkt-discriminatie van nietwesterse migranten via praktijktests (Den Haag 2010) 13 – 15.

[64] The Netherlands Institute for Social Research, *Perceived discrimination in the Netherlands* (Den Haag 2014) 17.

[65] CBS StatLine online at [http://statline.cbs.nl/StatWeb/publication/?VW=T&DM= SLNL&PA=71738NED&D1=22,26&D2=0&D3=0&D4=a&D5=31,36,41,46,51,60,65,l&HD=1403 04-1009&HDR=T,G4&STB=G2,G1,G3].

[66] Amnesty International, Proactief politieoptreden vormt risico voor mensenrechten in Nederland (Amsterdam 2013).

negatively and almost a quarter of Muslims experience discrimination on a regular basis.[67]

Several attempts have been made to explain the widespread nature of anti-Muslim views in the Netherlands. For example, the sociologist Bas van Stokkom has pointed to the gap in values between the highly secular Dutch majority, with strongly liberal attitudes, and those of orthodox Muslim communities.[68] However, this doesn't explain why the disapproval and hostility targets much broader groups than only orthodox Muslims. One attempt to explain the popularity of anti-Muslim views in the Netherlands looks at the evolution of the Dutch system of compartmentalisation in society: 'verzuiling', or pillarisation. This system broke down in the sixties. Before that it divided Dutch society in different pillars along mutually exclusive religious and ideological lines. Most of these 'pillars' integrated their members across class lines. For example, the Catholic pillar organised both Catholic bourgeois and Catholic workers who were prohibited from voting for socialist parties or joining socialist unions. Lower-class members of the different pillars were to high degree separated from each other, organised in different parties and unions, and oriented towards different newspapers, radio and television stations. The 'pillar system' broke down in the sixties as Dutch society secularised and religious and ideological ties started to weaken, but it left a strong impact on Dutch society.

One legacy of the pillar-system was the consensus-oriented culture in Dutch politics. The elites of the pillars maintained close contact, bridging the divisions between their followers. This allowed different Dutch elites to reach agreements by negotiations among themselves, without involving their supporters. In the nineties, when ideological differences between the major parties faded under the

---

[67] Fatima Zahra Lachhab et al., Monitoring Islamophobia in the Netherlands – an explorative study (Rotterdam 2013) 19.

[68] Ineke van der Valk, *Islamophobia in the Netherlands* (Amsterdam 2012) 12.

strong influence of neoliberalism, this meant Dutch politics was highly technocratic and many people felt excluded from it. By attacking the consensus model, Fortuyn appealed to many such people while at the same time making space for a further rightward shift in society. Another legacy of the pillar-system is a weak working class consciousness. Only the social-democratic pillar organised its members to some degree on the basis of their own class interests. In the Catholic and Protestant pillars, the lived religious differences were more important to their members than class differences. A relatively strong working-class identity that could act as a counterweight to the cross-class and nationalist appeals of nation-populism is lacking.

As the pillar-system broke down in the sixties, a new national hegemony took shape. Liberal and secular values became hegemonic and there grew a national self-image of Dutch society as a beacon of enlightenment and tolerance, and as a society that had a mission to promote such values across the world. The ritualised memory of the Second World War, the Nazi-occupation and the Shoah, became an important part of this new hegemony. As we have seen, political movements that were in some way associated with fascism and Nazism were stigmatised and marginalised. The national-populist current that took shape with Fortuyn avoided this stigma by integrating parts of the liberal hegemony, such as the supposed privileged connection between 'Dutchness' and tolerance, equality between men and women and 'acceptance' of homosexuality.[69]

Wilders has demonstrated that he is a very skilful political operator, constantly moving to the right but never going so far that he loses contact with his supporters. Wilders' persistent success should be seen in the context of a political landscape that has moved strongly to the right since the rise of Fortuyn after the turn of the century. Wilders both profits from this shift and pushes it. Prominent elements of the national-populist discourse, like the idea of the 'failed

---

[69] I owe this point to Merijn Oudenampsen.

integration' of Muslims, the need to restrict immigration, and repressive law-and-order policies, have become political common sense. This influence spans across the political spectrum and it is for example the PvdA who now suggests cutting social security to people who 'dress inappropriately' (read: wear a burka or niqab) or who don't speak Dutch. Measuring the power of the PVV only in terms of its seats or its relationship to the government coalition ignores such developments. The PVV has been in the vanguard of this rightward shift, dragging other parties with it, although it is too early to say if the party will continue to keep playing that role.

The main party to the left of the PvdA, the SP, has focused on attacking Wilder's economic choices but has remained largely silent about the PVV's racism or that found in wider Dutch society. What it doesn't realise is how racism functions to tie voters to Wilders and how it makes neoliberal economic policies plausible by laying the blame on minorities. During the nineties, the SP grew from being a small radical party with Maoist roots into mass social-democratic party. Since the mid-2000s it has been trying to position itself as a future party of government and it has moderated its positions and discourse. Wilders, however, has adopted a tone of angry opposition, of sustained outrage and of sarcasm that connects well with a part of potential SP-supporters and disappointed members of the working-class. This is also indicated by the considerable exchange of votes between the SP and Wilders.

With the parliamentary left either largely ignoring the various forms of racism or even taking over parts of the national-populist discourse, opposition to the deeply rooted Dutch racism needs to come from somewhere else. The liveliest anti-racist activities have come from outside the established left organisations and structures. There's a strong taboo on the existence of everyday and institutionalised racism in Dutch society since it so strongly contradicts the Dutch self-image as 'open and tolerant'. Many anti-racist organisations and organisations of minorities have become institutionalised, dependent on government funding and are hesitant to rock the boat. The - strong anti-racist demonstration of 22 March 2014 with over 5,000, seen as a reply to the 'minder Marokkanen' speech, was a hopeful sign - but really combating the influence of racism in the Netherlands will take much more.

Bibliography

Aalberts, Chris, *Achter de PVV. Waarom burgers op de PVV stemmen* (Delft 2012)

Amnesty International, Proactief politieoptreden vormt risico voor mensenrechten in Nederland (Amsterdam 2013).

Andriessen, Iris, et al., Liever Mark dan Mohammed? Onderzoek naar arbeidsmarktdiscriminatie van nietwesterse migranten via praktijktests (Den Haag 2010).

Balibar, Etienne and Immanuel Wallerstein, *Race, nation, class. Ambigious identities* (London 2005 [1991]).

Belien, Paul, 'Wilders Looks for European Allies, Suggests Reuniting Flanders and Netherlands', *The Brussels Journal* May 12, 2008 online at http://www.brusselsjournal.com/node/3244.

Bos, Willem, 'Netherlands: A vote against neoliberalism', *International Viewpoint* June 10, 2005 online at http://internationalviewpoint.org/spip.php?article815.

Bosma, Martin, De schijn-élite van de valse munters - Drees, extreem rechts, de sixties, de Groep Wilders en ik (Amsterdam 2010).

Carr, Matt, 'You are now entering Eurabia', *Race & Class* 48 (2006) 1 – 22.

Fanon, Frantz, *Toward the African revolution* 32 -33 (New York 1967) 32 -33.

Fennema, Meindert, *Geert Wilders. Tovenaarsleerling* (Amsterdam 2010).

Fortuyn, Pim, De verweesde samenleving. Een religieus-sociologisch traktaat (Uithoorn 2002).

Fortuyn, Pim, Tegen de islamisering van onze cultuur: Nederlandse identiteit als fundament (Utrecht 1997).

Geurtsen, Karen en Boudewijn Geels, Undercover bij de PVV. Achter de schermen bij de politieke partij van Geert Wilders (Amsterdam 2010).

Hall, Stuart, et al., Policing the crisis. Mugging, the state and law & order (Hampshire 2013 [1978]).

Hoove, Sanne ten, Raoul du Pré, 'Wilders bang voor 'tsunami van islamisering'', De Volkskrant October 6, 2006 online at http://www.volkskrant.nl/binnenland/wilders-bang-voor-tsunami-van islamisering~a786026.

Irrgang, Ewout et al., Leest u zijn boeken maar. De pimpelpaarse antwoorden van Pim Fortuyn (Rotterdam 2002).

Kloor, Robin van der, 'Dewinter: Wilders radicaliseert', Elsevier August 9, 2007 online at http://www.elsevier.nl/Politiek/nieuws/2007/8/Dewinter-Wilders-radicaliseert-ELSEVIER132772W/.

Lachhab, Fatima Zahra et al, Monitoring Islamophobia in the Netherlands – an explorative study (Rotterdam 2013).

Laclau, Ernesto, On populist reason (London 2005).

Lucardie, Paul en Gerrit Voerman, Populisten in de polder (Amersfoort 2012).

Mepschen, Paul, 'Against Tolerance: Islam, Sexuality, and the Politics of Belonging in the Netherlands' June 13, 2009 MRZine online at http://mrzine.monthlyreview.org/2009/mepschen130709.html.

Mepschen, Paul, 'Gewone mensen. Populisme en het discours van verdringing in Amsterdam Nieuw West' in in Justus Uitermark, et al. (ed.) 'Power to the people!' Een anatomie van het populisme (Den Haag 2012) 78 – 96.

Mudde, Cas, Populist radical right parties in Europe (Cambridge 2007).

Mudde, Cas, The ideology of the extreme right (Manchester 2000).

Nhass, Hanan, 'Ik word gek van dat poldergedoe', *Trouw* July 23, 2003 online at http://www.trouw.nl/tr/nl/4324/nieuws/archief/article/detail/1 781138/2003/07/23/Ik-word-gek-van-dat-poldergedoe.dhtml.

NOS *Analyse: PvdA verloor amper aan PVV* online at [http://europakiest.nos.nl/nieuws/artikel/id/tcm:44-526405/title/analyse-pvda-verloor-amper-aan-pvv.html.

NOS *Wilders op de Deense televisie* June 16 video online at http://nos.nl/video/36125-wilders-op-de-deense-televisie.html.

Os, Pieter van, 'De Amerikaanse lobby. Hoe Pfizer en Microsoft Nederland beïnvloeden', *De Groene Amsterdammer,* October 14, 2005 online at http://www.groene.nl/artikel/de-amerikaanse-lobby.

Oudenampsen, Merijn, 'De politiek van populisme onderzoek. Een kritiek op Diplomademocratie en de verklaring van populisme uit kiezersgedrag' in Justus Uitermark, et al. (ed.) *'Power to the people!' Een anatomie van het populisme* (Den Haag 2012) 17 – 49.

Oudenampsen, Merijn, 'De revolte van nieuwrechts. Neoconservatisme en postprogressieve politiek', *Krisis. Tijdschrift voor actuele filosofie,* 1 (2013) 72 – 88

Oudenampsen, Merijn, 'Explaining the swing to the right. The Dutch debate on the rise of right-wing populism' in Ruth Wodak, Majid Khosravinik, Brigitte Mal (ed.) *Right-wing populism in Europe. Politics and discourse* (London 2013) 191 – 209

Primor, Adat, 'The daughter as de-demonizer' *Haaretz* January 7, 2011 online at http://www.haaretz.com/weekend/week-s-end/the-daughter-as-de-demonizer-1.335743.

PVV, De agenda van hoop en optimisme. Een tijd om te kiezen; PVV 2010 – 2015 (2010).

PVV, Hún Brussel, óns Nederland. Verkiezingsprogramma 2012-2017.

PVV, Verkiezingsprogramma Europees parlement (2009).

Rechtbank Amsterdam, *Uitspraak van de rechtbank Amsterdam in de zaak Wilders*, June 26, 2011 online at http://www.rechtspraak.nl/Organisatie/Rechtbanken/Amsterda m/Nieuws/Pages/Uitspraak-van-de-rechtbank-AmsterdamindezaakWilders,23juni2011.aspx.

Reekum, Rogier, van 'It's the performance, stupid!' in Justus Uitermark, et al. (ed.) *'Power to the people!' Een anatomie van het populisme* (Den Haag 2012) 49 – 57.

Ritzen, Ron, Willem-Jan van Gendt, Wilders' Iran aan de Noordzee. Waarom de PVV de democratische rechtsstaat bedreigt (Puurs 2012).

Schinkel, Willem, *De gedroomde samenleving* (Kampen, 2011).

The Netherlands Institute for Social Research, *Perceived discrimination in the Netherlands* (Den Haag 2014).

Valk, Ineke van der, *Islamophobia in the Netherlands* (Amsterdam 2012) 12.

Vials, Chris, 'The Invisibility of Fascism in the Postwar United States', *Against the Current* 168 (2014) 7 – 9.

Vossen, Koen, Rondom Wilders. Portret van de PVV (Amsterdam 2013).

Volkskrant, Aangifte tegen Fortuyn wegens discriminatie, *De Volkskrant*, 2 November 2011 online at http://www.volkskrant.nl/vk/nl/2844/Archief/archief/article/de tail/605866/2001/11/02/Aangifte-tegen-Fortuyn-wegens-discriminatie.dhtml

Weitz, Eric D., A century of genocide. Utopias of race and nation (Princeton 2003).

Wilders, Geert, 'Het laatste woord van Geert Wilders bij het proces', online at http://www.pvv.nl/index.php/component/content/article.html?id=3939:het-laatste-woord-van-geert-wilders-bij-het-proces.

Wilders, Geert, Kies voor vrijheid - een eerlijk antwoord (Den Haag 2005).

Wilders, Geert, Marked for death. Islam's war against the west and me (Washington 2012)

Witte, Rob, 'Al eeuwen lang een gastvrij volk' Racistisch geweld en overheidsreacties in Nederland 1950 – 2009 (Amsterdam 2010)

Swedish fascism – an unbroken tradition

Anders Svensson

The thirties

Between the two world wars, a multitude of fascist parties were created in Sweden. These fascist groups were ridden with personal vendettas, infighting and as a result they fractured, resulting in an immense number of smaller groups. Some were influenced by the Nazis in Germany and some by the fascists in Italy. In 1933 there were five bigger groups and many smaller ones. Between 1919 and 1950, Sweden saw more than 100 different active fascist and Nazi groups.[1] The same people moved from one group to another, different groups merged and some people were even organised in more than one group at the same time.[2] This was the case with Per Engdahl,[3] an important intellectual figure whose writings are still circulated around Swedish

---

[1] Helene Lööw, Hakkorset och wasakärven, en studie i nationalsocialismen i Sverige 1924-1950 (Swastika and Fascism, a Study of Swedish National Socialism 1924-1950), Historiska Institutionen, Göteborg, 1990. Helene Lööw is a historian and works for the Swedish government.

[2] Helene Lööw (1990).

[3] Per Engdahl was born in Jönköping in 1909 to a family with a strong conservative military tradition. He became active in fascist circles in the 1920s and remained so until his death in 1994.

fascist groups.[4] During the war even a former left wing group turned pro-German and Nazi.[5]

Military officers were abundant in the fascist and Nazi groups, often in leading positions. The centres of fascist organisation were the south of Sweden, the west coast and the university city of Uppsala which was a bastion of eugenics and a stronghold of racial profiling. In Uppsala, there was a government run institute for racial biology, the Statens Institut för Rasbiologi. Support for these ideas as well as for anti-Semitism was widespread in Swedish society and in Socialdemokraterna, the Social Democratic Party.[6]

Due to their fragmentation, fascist parties never managed to get any seats in Parliament, but they were more successful at the local level. The Swedish National Socialist Party (*Svenska Nationalsocialistiska Partiet*, SNSP) managed to get 5.7% in Gothenburg[7] and 2.9% in the region of Värmland in 1932, both in the west of Sweden. The west coast of Sweden, Gothenburg and north of the city itself, were areas hit hardest by the depression. They were therefore a good recruiting ground for the Swedish fascist groups, especially from farmers and small-time businessmen, as well as from very poor working-class people.[8]

However, the west coast rural region was also a stronghold for the anarcho-syndicalist trade unions. It was highly socially divided into three groups that seldom interacted, not even at a personal level: working class left-wing stone-quarry workers, evangelical religious

---

[4] Hans Lindquist, Fascism idag, förtrupper eller eftersläntrare (Fascism Today, Vanguard or Latecomers), Federativs förlag, Stockholm, 1979.

[5] Socialistiska Partiet, former member of the London Bureau, from Håkan Blomqvist, *Gåtan Nils Flyg och nazismen*, Carlssons, Stockholm, 1999.

[6] Håkan Blomqvist, *Nation, ras och civilisation (Nation, Race and Civilization)*, Carlssons, Stockholm, 2006. Håkan Blomqvist is an author and historian. He is a member of the leadership of the Swedish section of the Fourth International, the Socialist Party.

[7] Göteborg in Swedish. The english term for this Swedish city will be used in this article.

[8] Helene Lööw (1990).

fishermen, and finally conservative religious farmers and small-time business owners. The city of Gothenburg, on the other hand, was a working-class city with extreme levels of unemployment and poverty. Due to the polarisation in Swedish society, violent clashes and street fights were common, in particular in Gothenburg, between fascist and left-wing groups, including the social-democratic youth. The main fascist groups, the SNSP and the National Socialist Workers Party (*Nationalsocialistiska Arbetarpartiet*, NSAP), organised a militia, the Storm Units (*Storma In the 2006 general elections, Jobbik formed a coalition together with MIÉP delningarna*, SA). The NSAP and the SA sent volunteers to the Finnish army to take part in the war against the Soviet Union. In Sweden, military veterans took the leadership of the SA and reorganised it into a formally independent organisation, the Sveaborg, many of whose members joined the German Waffen-SS.[9]

The survivors

Three main fascist groups survived the end of the Second World War: a Nazi group, the Swedish Socialist Assembly (*Svensk Socialistisk Samling*, SSS, formerly NSAP), a Mussolini-inspired fascist group, New Swedish Movement (*Nysvenska Rörelsen*, NSR) and a pro-German, neo-Nazi nationalist group, the Swedish National League (*Sveriges Nationella Förbund*, SNF) with an extremely conservative agenda.[10] Originally the SNF was a conservative youth organisation without Nazi or fascist affiliations or agenda, but in 1934, it broke away from the Conservative Party with three members of Parliament. During the Second World War, the German government financed its newspaper. Per Engdahl was then periodically a member of both NSR

---

[9] Helene Lööw (1990).

[10] Hans Lindquist (1979).

and SNF.[11] The NSAP dissolved itself in 1950, but the Sveaborg organisation survived and became a vital component in the celebrations for the Swedish King Karl XII on November 30.[12] This tradition later became a main rallying point for Swedish Nazi skinheads.[13]

During the 1950s and 1960s, the SNF was not very active and was careful to hide its anti-Semitic agenda, but in the 1970s it became more active in the 1970s as it joined the King Karl XII commemorations on November 30 together with the Sveaborg. They created new organisations that formally were supposed to be 'apolitical', for example, the November 30 Association, and other groups involved in the celebrations on this date, but they came under pressure to be more outspoken because of the emergence of a violent and intellectual anti-communist movement, the Democratic Alliance (*Demokratisk Allians, DA*). During that time, they tried to eradicate all references to Nazism and anti-Semitism in their programme. In the 1970s, the SNF became the strongest fascist organisation in Sweden, although it had probably less than 100 members. The SNF also widened its agenda to support the apartheid regime in South Africa, the Pinochet dictatorship and similar governments.[14]

The DA became an organisation where several up and coming conservative politicians learned politics together with people who

---

[11] Helene Lööw (1990).

[12] Karl XII has a special place in Swedish nationalist history because of his views on the military, where discipline and refusal to surrender were crucial components, and because of his struggle to constantly expand Sweden's might through war. His death became a major controversy because it was rumored that he was assassinated or betrayed by his own troops, which led to the day of his death being seen as a great tragedy in nationalist circles. His life was glorified in writings by Voltaire and later by national-romantic poets such as Esaijas Tegnér and Erik Gustaf Geijer. The 30th November march to honor his death has been celebrated since 1853.

[13] Helene Lööw (1990).

[14] Hans Lindquist (1979).

later would become fascist leaders. It was a secretive organisation, its membership numbers are not known, and it never took part in elections. Its main activity was disrupting left-wing meetings and events.

The last surviving fascist group into the 1970s was the NSF, led by Per Engdahl. It was a small ideological group with classic corporatist positions in the tradition of Mussolini. Its more activist-oriented members regularly turned to other organisations such as the SNF.

A more openly Nazi-oriented group with very violent supporters and members, the Nordic National Party (*Nordiska Rikspartiet*, NRP) was created in 1956 by former members of the Norwegian Nazi party, the National Assembly (*Nasjonal Samling*, NS). The NRP can be considered as the ideological continuity of the NSAP/SSS but it was not in any way its organisational continuation. Early on it organised a fascist militia, the National Action Group (*Riksaktionsgruppen*, RAG), which attracted a lot of skinheads in the 1970s. The NRP gradually came in contact with the November 30 Association and soon became the dominant force in it. It tried to infiltrate the anti-communist group DA, but it was not successful and instead attacked that organisation's headquarters in Stockholm with a smoke-bomb. It harassed by phone or assaulted in the street journalists, homosexuals, former Norwegian resistance fighters, Jews and immigrants, in particular in Gothenburg. The NRP was mainly present in Gothenburg, the south of Sweden and Stockholm. [15]

Several members of the RAG in Stockholm and Gothenburg and some leaders of the Gothenburg NRP were sentenced to prison in 1986 for murder, aggravated assault, and illegal possession of weapons. In 1990, members in the NRP faced another trial for attempted bombings and yet more murders and violent assaults. Victims of the Nazi-violence in Gothenburg were mainly homosexual men. The trials

---

[15] Hans Lindquist (1979).

severely affected the NRP and it would never again be an organisation of any importance.[16]

Far-right populism

In the middle of the 1970s, the south of Sweden saw the growth of several important regional right-wing populist parties focusing on taxation, racism and Swedish immigration policies. One of these groups was the Scania Party (*Skånepartiet*) founded by Carl P Herslow in 1979. It never became important at a national level, but had a strong local impact in southern Sweden. They had councillors in Malmö between 1985 and 2006.

The Progress Party (*Framstegspartiet*), launched in the early 1970s, was mainly inspired by the Norwegian party (*Fremskrittspartiet*) and the Danish party of the same name (*Fremskridtspartiet*). Despite initial successes, it could not afford to run in elections and soon splits and dissent weakened the party. From around 1979 several groups with the same name existed, but none became important except for an organisation led by Stefan Herrman which turned to fascism in the 1980s.[17]

At the end of the 1980s and the beginning of the 1990s, Sweden saw a strong growth in support for racism and right-wing populism, which was accompanied by a wave of violence against immigrants and refugee camps.[18] This led to the creation of several right-wing populist parties, some of which were parties in favour of more regional independence (especially in the south of Sweden), while others were neoliberal or traditional conservative, but all adopted anti-immigration policies.

---

[16] Anna-Lena Lodenius & Stieg Larsson, *Extremhögern*, 1991 Tidens förlag.,

[17] Lodenius & Larsson (1991).

[18] These were institutions where people applying for asylum were placed while waiting for a decision from the immigration authorities.

In 1990 a national neoliberal right-wing party, New Democracy (*Ny Demokrati*), was founded by two well known public figures, a businessman, Bert Karlsson, and count Wachtmeister. By concentrating on economic issues (e.g., privatisation, deregulation, lower taxes) rather than opposition to immigration, they managed to get seats in Parliament (*Riksdagen*) in 1991. Between 1991 and 1994 they had 25 elected members of Parliament. This was the first time in modern Swedish history that a party on the extreme right had managed achieve such as result, but due to disagreements between the business man and the count, the party fell apart and lost its seats in the 1994 elections, eventually disappearing in 2002. Although New Democracy had very little impact in the evolution of Swedish fascism, the election of its members to Parliament sparked a wave of violent attacks on refugee camps and immigrants.

Fascist reorganisation

In 1979 a new organisation was formed, Keep Sweden Swedish (*Bevara Sverige Svenskt*, BSS), without the formal connections to historical Nazism. However its founders were six men with backgrounds in the Nazi movement: Leif Zeilon, Nils Mandell, Jerker Magnusson, Christopher Jolin, Gösta Bergquist and Sven Davidsson (a former member of the fascist New Swedish Movement, *Nysvenska Rörelsen*) who became its first chairman. The BSS was a creation of forces with a connection back to the original fascist and Nazi parties of the 1930s as well as with the more modern skinhead culture of the RAG.[19] Gradually most skinheads left the NRP and RAG to join the BSS.

The BSS eventually became the main fascist group, with over 1,000 members, organising actions on the streets of Swedish cities, in particular Stockholm, Gothenburg, Malmö, and taking control of the

---

[19] Lodenius & Larsson (1991).

celebrations of November 30. The BSS had close political ties with a Norwegian fascist party, the National People's Party (*Nasjonalt Folkeparti*), the Danish DNSB and the Swedish SNF. Membership of BSS was often combined with membership of the openly Nazi NRP.[20]

In the mid-1980s, the celebrations for the death of King Karl XII on November 30 were met with strong anti-fascist mobilisations both in Stockholm and Lund, a university city in the south of Sweden, where the fascists were forced to cancel their march.[21]

In 1983 a new party was formed, the National Democratic Party (*Nationaldemokratiska Partiet*, NDP). There were close connections between the NDP and the BSS. The NDP was not successful and was dissolved in 1985, but it had gathered a following among skinheads.

In 1986, the Sweden Party (*Sverigepartiet*) was launched by the Progress Party (*Framstegspartiet*) and the BSS, but split in 1987. During 1988 two parties with the name the Sweden Party (*Sverigepartiet*) existed, but soon the former BSS-led party changed its name to the Sweden Democrats (*Sverigedemokraterna*, SD). The SD, led by Anders Klarström, a former member of the NRP with a criminal record, became the biggest Swedish fascist party. The SD adopted a new strategy and tactics: street actions were no longer important, they moved away from the skinheads and their violent culture, distanced themselves from anti-Semitism, concentrated on anti-immigration, and stood in elections. In 1990, they claimed around 4,500 members and 50 local groups around the country.[22]

The transformation of the Sweden Democrats into a more polished and respectable party sparked the creation of new violent groups among skinheads and followers of the NRP. A public meeting in 1991 saw the launch of the White Aryan Resistance (*Vitt Ariskt Motstånd*, VAM) by members in NRP and violent skinheads. The

---

[20] Lodenius & Larsson (1991).

[21] Lodenius & Larsson (1991).

[22] Lodenius & Larsson (1991).

group engaged in thefts of weapons, bank robbery and gang criminality. Several local independent VAM groups had connections to record labels, and publishing companies such as Nordland, Blood & Honour (*Blod och Ära*) and Combat-18.[23]

Out of one of the local VAM groups, the National Socialist Front (*Nationalsocialistisk Front*, NSF) was created in 1994 and by 1998 it had 15 local groups. The NSF had links to the Swedish versions of Combat 18 and Blood & Honour. In different parts of Sweden, many different smaller Nazi groups popped up and existed for a short time as the anti-fascist movement chased them off the streets. Without the possibility of public appearances, and plagued by splits and criminality, they were never able to grow, despite this, there were many attempts at party-building beside the NSF.[24]

A modern fascism with an ideological continuity

The SD grew by moving away from open anti-Semitism and historical Nazism, and merging with local populist parties in the south of Sweden such as the Scania Party (*Skånepartiet*), thereby allowing it its first local electoral success. In 1998, the SD had 8 councillors and by 2002 they had 49, nearly all of them in the Scania region (*Skåne*) of Sweden. This meant an influx of members in the south of Sweden that did not originate from a Nazi and anti-Semitic framework. A group of young members, who had joined on the basis of regional 'patriotism', anti-immigration and islamophobia, organised to take over the party which was then led by faction whose ideology was closer to Nazism. This tension between more traditional anti-Semitic fascism and modern islamophobic fascism has continued to be a major point of

---

[23] Heléne Lööw, Nazismen i Sverige 1980-1999 (Nazism in Sweden 1980-1999), Ordfront Förlag, Stockholm, 1999.

[24] The study of these groups is beyond the scope of this article, but readers who are interested can consult books in Swedish by Heléne Lööw.

contention and splits within the SD, such as in 2001 when a party named the National Democrats (*Nationaldemokraterna*, ND) was created.

Despite trying to become respectable, the SD is still comes across as very racist and islamophobic, and is considered as such by the large majority of Swedes. Nevertheless, in 2006 they got 2.93% of the vote in the general elections, as well as16 regional councillors and 281 local councillors.

The New Swedish Movement (NSR) has a special significance for the SD's ideology. Per Engdahl, who had been the leading figure in several of the major Nazi and fascist organisations since the 1930s developed the ideas that would later become the fundamental principles of the SD. He formulated this in an article written in 1979 in which he argued that immigrants have become the new great threat to Sweden and Swedish unity (previously it had been the world Jewish conspiracy).[25] He argued that racial biology must be abandoned because it was outdated, that Sweden and the Swedish character has to be constructed, and that the nation should have a culture built on Swedish identity and Swedish traditions.

The Sweden Democrats' ideology, formulated from 1989 onwards, is characterised by an old-fashioned conservatism and nationalism. Its first principle is about its vision of society. It rejects the conventional idea of Swedish politics of the state and the legal system as the basis of a democratic agreement, similar to a social contract which is constantly adjusted in political elections and democratic institutions. Instead the Sweden Democrats envision what it terms the organic society: society and the state should be rooted in organic collectives such as the family and the nation. The nation consists of a common identity, and the duty of the government is to protect and preserve this common identity. The nation's interests are the interests of individuals and groups. In this context, the concept of

---

[25] Vägen Framåt, April 1979.

democracy is far down the list, positioned after the family, homeland and fatherland, and after the 'Welfare State'.[26] The second principle, which flows from the first, is nationalism: within the borders of one state, there should preferably only be one nation, a society which should be 'homogeneous in terms of population', and 'uniform in the language, religion, loyalty and origin'.[27]

In its political programme, the SD stresses that it is in the centre ground of Swedish politics and not on the left or the right, just like in the 1930s National Socialism claimed to stand midway between capitalism and communism. The SD's programme of principles expresses this by stating that 'The Sweden Democrats' ideology is a compound of two basic elements, turn of the century national conservatism and parts of social democratic welfare ideology'.[28] The SD is not a neoliberal party with the goal of a small state and a free market economy. It has little in common with racist and neoliberal parties such as the Danish People's Party (DPP, *Dansk Folkeparti*) or the Norwegian Progress Party (*Fremskrittspartiet*, FRP) even though some of its leaders come from a similar political background. Instead the SD represents the logical continuation of the national and fascist movements in Swedish political history.[29] Support for SD is much smaller than for the DPP in Denmark or FRP in Norway, but it is gaining support as a result of the 20 years of neoliberal policies carried out by Swedish governments, both social-democratic and conservative, which has led to relatively high unemployment and poverty.

The Sweden Democrats party is increasingly focussing its propaganda not on immigrants in general, but on the immigrants of a

---

[26] Mats Lindberg, En nytänkt och parlamentarisk nationalsocialism (A New and Parliamentarian Fascism), Nerikes Allehanda, 2010-10-13.

[27] Sverigedemokraternas principprogramme.

[28] Sverigedemokraternas principprogramme.

[29] Mats Lindberg (2013).

particular religion, Islam and its 'perceived' culture, which are considered to be the problem. Northern European immigrants, including those from Poland and the Baltic states, are normally not considered a problem. The party's rhetoric about Islam is similar to the anti-Semitic rhetoric of the 1930s and this demonstrates that it is still essentially a fascist party.[30]

Andreas Malm[31] argues in his book *Hatred of Muslims*[32] that it should be sufficient for a party to be considered fascist if it wants to limit or abolish democracy and the fundamental rights of a particular ethnic group, and bring in authoritarian repression. This is what SD wants in relation to a specific group, Swedish Muslims, whom they argue should not be allowed to have Swedish citizenship, freedom of religion or freedom of expression, forced to have fewer children, and - the ultimate goal - driven out of the country.

At the same time, some people argue, basing themselves on writings of Trotsky from the 1930s, that there is something missing in the situation: for a movement or party to be considered fascist, there should also be violence and storm-troopers. This is not necessary, as Manuel Kellner points out, because Trotsky should be read as a product of his time:

> If we wish to use the heritage of Trotsky in this area for our antifascist struggle today, some caveats should be entered:
>
> • Some aspects of reality have changed significantly. Today the degree of activity and organisation (and armament!) of members of the traditional big left

---

[30] Andreas Malm, *Hatet mot muslimer (Hatred of Muslims)*, Bokförlaget Atlas, Stockholm, 2009.

[31] Andreas Malm is a swedish marxist intellectual and a leading member of the Socialist Party, the swedish section of the Fourth International.

[32] Andreas Malm (2009).

parties, above all social-democracy, is much weaker than in the time of Trotsky.

- Society as a whole has greatly changed. There are new forms of atomisation in the workplace and beyond. The 'traditional' working class no longer has the same weight among wage-earners in the broad sense of the word.

- There is once more great poverty and misery, even in the rich countries. But the poverty of a working class family, unemployed or not, at the time of the Weimar Republic was all the same entirely another thing than what exists today; and the despair of the demobilised sub-officer, ready to fight in the street against the 'reds', is not yet equalled by the sentiments of the majority of those who vote for Le Pen for example.

- Trotsky's slogan 'dictatorship of the proletariat or fascist dictatorship!' which seemed so justified in the 1930s should not lead us to systematically organise our thought and thus our agitation in opposed simple alternatives. Very often, the concrete historic outcome is a third unforeseen variant.[33]

Corporativism and totalitarianism, which are counterposed to democracy, are in the programme of the SD, as well the atomisation of the working class. However, due to the weakness of the working class, the lack of awareness of the threat, and the lack of a radical leadership, the fascists do not need to resort to the violence that was necessary in the 1930s. This is because the bourgeois state has already broadly

---

[33] Manuel Kellner, *Understanding fascism in order to fight it*, International Viewpoint, Oct. 2000, http://www.internationalviewpoint.org/spip.php?article354.

achieved the atomisation of the working class through a succession of defeats with the imposition of neoliberalism since the 1980s. Nevertheless, the SD meets all the characteristics that would be expected from a modern version of fascism. The SD is a fascist party of our time, maintaining a continuity of the skinhead-dominated crude Nazi past. The SD is part of an ideological continuity from the 1930s which also includes an organisational and personal continuity. It is also a fascism based on mobilisation from below as in the 1930s, and which is able to get support from the common people, workers and the petty bourgeoisie.

The change of image and strategy of the Sweden Democrats has paid off. They won 20 members of Parliament and 5.7% share of the vote at the 2010 general election. At the 2014 general election, they doubled their vote to 12.9% and got 49 members of Parliament, becoming the third largest party in Sweden. They also have 16 regional councillors and 612 local councillors, and with 9.7% of the vote at the 2014 European elections, they got two members the European Parliament.

Growth of the violent Nazi groups

Along with the change of their image, the Sweden Democrats is also changing its membership: anti-Semitic members are discouraged or expelled as well as those engaged in violence or crime. This has resulted in the growth of the violent anti-Semitic fascist and Nazi groups over the last few years, while at the same time the SD has still been experiencing a tremendous growth in support.

There were until recently three main anti-Semitic fascist and Nazi groups, the National Democrats (*Nationaldemokraterna*, ND), a split from SD which has now disappeared but which had two local councillors; the Party of the Swedes (*Svenskarnas parti*, SVP), a continuation of NSF which has one councillor; and the Swedish Resistance Movement (*Svenska Motståndsrörelsen*, SMR), a small violent Nazi group which is a continuation of VAM. All of them are continually plagued by infighting and splits as well as violence between each other, and as a result they are no longer able to organise their annual demonstration in a suburb of Stockholm. The Nazi groups are very violent, and are becoming even more so as they are fuelled by the situation in Ukraine. Many fascists from Sweden have taken part in the fascist violence in Ukraine. SVP members have joined the ranks of Svoboda and the Right Sector in Kiev, while members of the SMR fight on the pro-Russian side in Eastern Ukraine. At least one murder a year can be attributed to violent Nazi groups. The victims are mainly homosexual men, people of African origin, anti-fascists and trade-unionists. These Nazi groups are very small and draw their support from the poorer parts of the working class, criminal gangs and surprisingly from immigrants from Finland and Eastern Europe even though the central part of their programme is to get rid of all immigrants, including those from Finland and Eastern Europe.

Anti-fascism in Sweden

Despite the violent Nazi groups and a fascist party in Parliament, the Sweden Democrats, a large section of the Swedish population is opposed to racism and a declining minority (41%) is against the country receiving more refugees.[34] This is noteworthy as Sweden has welcomed more refugees than any other western country as a proportion of its population.

As a result of this, neither the conservative party (*Moderata Samlingspartiet*) nor the social-democratic party (*Socialdemokratiska Arbetarpartiet*) have adopted a racist discourse. The only major political party to do so is the small Liberal People's Party (*Folkpartiet*

---

[34] Gothenburg University, SOM-institute, national suvery about attitudes done every year. http://som.gu.se/undersokningar/den-nationella-som-undersokningen.

liberalerna), along with the liberal dominated media which reports anti-racist and anti-fascist activities with barely hidden hatred or disdain.

Anti-racist and anti-fascist mobilisations have grown significantly after Nazi groups attacked a left wing demonstration in Stockholm, and severely injured a group of anti-racist and feminist activists in Malmö after a feminist demonstration on 8 March 2014.[35] Every fascist meeting is met with a counter-demonstration, whether it is in small cities or big ones. The Nazi groups cannot operate openly in certain parts of Sweden, for example in the Gothenburg area where even the Sweden Democrats have difficulties holding political meetings.

The anti-fascist movements in Sweden are mainly led and organised by the far left, with little involvement of social-democrats and the trade-unions. An important player in the anti-fascist movement is the foundation Expo,[36] which has a newspaper of the same name and which is an organisation founded by the author Stieg Larsson.

---

[35] https://libcom.org/news/fascist-knife-attack-malm%C3%B6-sweden-night-international-womens-day-09032014.

[36] http://expo.se/2010/about-expo_3514.html.

Notes on contributors

TOBIAS ALM

Tobias Alm writes about the politics and activities of the far-right and fascist organisations for a number of Danish publications. He works with Projektantifa in Denmark and Antifaschistische Infoblatt (AIB, Anti-fascist fact sheet) in Germany. He is the joint author of *Rechtspopulismus kann tödlich sein!* (Right-wing Populism can be fatal), 2013, edition assemblage, Münster.

CHECCHINO ANTONINI

Checchino Antonini is a journalist, writer and activist on the anti-capitalist left. He has written detailed enquiries against police misconduct and abuse. He has also reported on the origins of the Anti-Globalisation movement and follows the debate on the radical left. Checchino is one of the founders of the *popoffquotidiano.it* website.

COMMISSION NATIONALE ANTI-FASCISTE, NPA

The *Commission Nationale Anti-Fasciste* (CNAF) of the NPA (*Nouveau Parti Anti-capitaliste*) monitors and analyses the activity and the propaganda of the far right in France and elsewhere. Through the publication of written material and the holding of seminars, the CNAF aims to educate members and sympathisers of the NPA on the dangers of the far right. The CNAF also publishes material at the blog *tantquillefaudra.org*.

PHIL HEARSE

Phil Hearse, a former editor of several left wing journals, is a supporter of Socialist Resistance and Left Unity, and teaches communication and culture at a London college.

ALEX DE JONG

Alex de Jong is co-director of the IIRE in Amsterdam. He is a member of the Socialistische Alternatieve Politiek (SAP), the Dutch section of the Fourth International, and editor of the website grenzeloos.org.

MANUEL KELLNER

Manuel Kellner is a member of the Internationale Sozialistische Linke (isl, international socialist left, one of the two organisations of the Fourth International in Germany), and of the party Die Linke (The Left) and its anti-capitalist current within it. He is an editor of the monthly *Sozialistische Zeitung*.

MICHAEL LÖWY

Michael Löwy is a member of the Fourth International, a Fellow of the IIRE in and a Research Director of Sociology at the Centre National de la Recherche Scientifique (CNRS), Paris. His books include *The Marxism of Che Guevara, Marxism and Liberation Theology*, and *The War of the Gods: Religion and Politics in Latin America*. He is joint author (with Joel Kovel) of the International Ecosocialist Manifesto.

MARTIN MARINOS

Martin Marinos is a PhD candidate in Media and Communication at the University of Pittsburgh, Pennsylvania USA. He is a member of

New Left Perspectives, Sofia, which organises debates and seminars, conducts critical research, and runs a small publishing house.

GEORGI MEDAROV

Georgi Medarov is a PhD candidate in Sociology at the University of Sofia, Bulgaria. He is also a member of New Left Perspectives.

ANDERS SVENSSON

Anders Svensson is a member of the leadership of Socialist Party, the Swedish section of the Fourth International. He has been an anti-fascist activist for 40 years. He writes for *blog.zaramis.se*, of one of the most popular political blogs in Sweden. He also writes editorials for the weekly paper *ETC Göteborg*.

About Resistance Books and the IIRE

Resistance Books

Resistance Books is the publishing arm of Socialist Resistance, a revolutionary Marxist organisation that is the British section of the Fourth International. Resistance Books publishes books jointly with the International Institute for Research and Education in Amsterdam and independently.

Further information about Resistance Books, including a full list of titles currently available and how to purchase them, can be obtained at http://www.resistancebooks.org, or by writing to Resistance Books, PO Box 62732, London, SW2 9GQ.

Socialist Resistance is active in the trade union movement and in campaigns against austerity and in defence of public services. Socialist Resistance believes that the Labour Party and social-democratic parties have become so right-wing that we need to build new broad left parties that support workers struggles and put forward socialist answers to the economic and environmental crisis. We are anti-racist and oppose imperialist interventions. We are ecosocialist – we argue that much of what is produced under capitalism is socially useless and directly harmful. We have been long-standing supporters of women's liberation and the struggles of lesbians, gay people, bisexuals and transgender people.

To find out more about *Socialist Resistance* or to read magazine of the organisation, go to www.socialistresistance.org.

Socialist Resistance can be contacted by email at contact@socialistresistance.org or by post at PO Box 62732, London, SW2 9GQ. *International Viewpoint* is the English language online magazine of the Fourth International, which can be read online at www.internationalviewpoint.org.

The International Institute for Research and Education

The International Institute for Research and Education (IIRE) is an international foundation, recognised in Belgium as an international scientific association by a Royal decree of 11th June 1981. The IIRE provides activists and scholars worldwide with opportunities for research and education in three locations: Amsterdam, Islamabad and Manila.

Since 1982, when the Institute opened in Amsterdam, its main activity has been the organisation of courses in the service of progressive forces around the world. Our seminars and study groups deal with all subjects related to the emancipation of the oppressed and exploited around the world. It has welcomed hundreds of participants from every inhabited continent. Most participants have come from the Third World.

The IIRE has become a prominent centre for the development of critical thought and interaction, and the exchange of experiences, between people who are engaged in daily struggles on the ground. The Institute's sessions give participants a unique opportunity to step aside from the pressure of daily activism. The IIRE gives them time to study, reflect upon their involvement in a changing world and exchange ideas with people from other countries.

Our website is constantly being expanded and updated with freely downloadable publications, in several languages, and audio files. Recordings of several recent lectures given at the institute can be downloaded from www.iire.org – as can talks given by founding Fellows such as Ernest Mandel and Livio Maitan, dating back to the early 1980s.

The IIRE publishes *Notebooks for Study and Research* to focus on themes of contemporary debate or historical or theoretical importance. Lectures and study materials given in sessions in our Institute, located in Amsterdam, Manila and Islamabad, are made available to the public in large part through the Notebooks.

Different issues of the Notebooks have also appeared in languages besides English and French, including German, Dutch, Arabic, Spanish, Japanese, Korean, Portuguese, Turkish, Swedish, Danish and Russian.

For a full list of the *Notebooks for Study and Research,* visit http://bit.ly/IIRENSR or subscribe online at: http://bit.ly/NSRsub. To order the *Notebooks,* email iire@iire.org or write to International Institute for Research and Education, Lombokstraat 40, Amsterdam, NL-1094.